Modern Language Association of America

Approaches to Teaching
World Literature

Joseph Gibaldi, Series Editor

Approaches to Teaching Cather's *My Ántonia*

Edited by

Susan J. Rosowski

The Modern Language Association of America
New York   1989

Copyright © 1989 by The Modern Language Association of America

Library of Congress Cataloging-in-Publication Data

Approaches to teaching Cather's My Ántonia / edited by Susan J. Rosowski.
    p.   cm. — (Approaches to teaching world literature ; 22)
    Bibliography: p.
    Includes index.
    ISBN 0-87352-519-1   ISBN 0-87352-520-5 (pbk.)
    1. Cather, Willa, 1873–1947. My Ántonia. 2. Cather, Willa,
1873–1947—Study and teaching. I. Rosowski, Susan J. II. Modern
Language Association of America. III. Series.
PS3505.A87M8943   1989
813'.52—dc19   88-31154

Portions of Charlotte Goodman's "*My Ántonia* as Double Bildungsroman" are
reprinted from her "The Lost Brother, the Twin: Women Novelists and the Male-
Female Double Bildungsroman," *Novel: A Forum on Fiction* 17.1 (1983).
Copyright Novel Corp., 1984. Reprinted with permission.

Cover illustration of the paperback edition: Photograph of a dugout used as a
home by a pioneer family on the South Loup River, Custer County, Nebraska,
1892. Solomon D. Butcher Collection, Nebraska State Historical Society. Used
with permission of the Nebraska State Historical Society.

Published by the Modern Language Association of America
10 Astor Place, New York, New York 10003-6981

CONTENTS

PREFACE TO THE SERIES

In *The Art of Teaching* Gilbert Highet wrote, "Bad teaching wastes a great deal of effort, and spoils many lives which might have been full of energy and happiness." All too many teachers have failed in their work, Highet argued, simply "because they have not thought about it." We hope that the Approaches to Teaching World Literature series, sponsored by the Modern Language Association's Committee on Teaching and Related Professional Activities, will not only improve the craft—as well as the art—of teaching but also encourage serious and continuing discussion of the aims and methods of teaching literature.

The principal objective of the series is to collect within each volume different points of view on teaching a specific literary work, a literary tradition, or a writer widely taught at the undergraduate level. The preparation of each volume begins with a wide-ranging survey of instructors, thus enabling us to include in the volume the philosophies and approaches, thoughts and methods of scores of experienced teachers. The result is a sourcebook of material, information, and ideas on teaching the subject of the volume to undergraduates.

The series is intended to serve nonspecialists as well as specialists, inexperienced as well as experienced teachers, graduate students who wish to learn effective ways of teaching as well as senior professors who wish to compare their own approaches with the approaches of colleagues in other schools. Of course, no volume in the series can ever substitute for erudition, intelligence, creativity, and sensitivity in teaching. We hope merely that each book will point readers in useful directions; at most each will offer only a first step in the long journey to successful teaching.

Joseph Gibaldi
Series Editor

PREFACE TO THE VOLUME

Unlike some other works represented in this series, such as *The Canterbury Tales* and *The Divine Comedy*, *My Ántonia* is familiar rather than foreign, accessible rather than difficult. Cather's novel is so clear, so apparently effortless, that it hardly seems art at all, and the challenge for instructors is to move their students beyond a surface reading to an understanding of its art and its place in literary history. *My Ántonia* also offers the joy of discovering universality, as students recognize in it voices from the past and themes for all times. In telling of Ántonia's place in American history, for example, Cather drew from Vergilian epic and pastoral. At the same time, the book reveals possibilities of native materials: Cather was the first author to write of the beauty of Nebraska, and *My Ántonia* the major book in which she did so. Particularly exciting for many students today, *My Ántonia* poses profound questions concerning gender conventions. Because it is accessible, because it brings together major literary traditions, and because its plot and narrative strategy pose questions of gender, *My Ántonia* is taught in a wide variety of contexts, including writing courses; introductory courses; and survey courses organized by period, genre (e.g., The American Novel), region (e.g., Plains Literature, Nebraska Writers), theme (e.g., The Immigrant Experience in Literature, Literature of Agriculture), and gender.

Yet while students appreciate and enjoy *My Ántonia*, instructors preparing for sessions on it are likely to feel frustrated. Other than the standard courses in American literature, few have had graduate training in fields related to Cather studies—plains literature, history, or geography—and still fewer have had training specifically in Cather studies. Ironically, a characteristic American college or university literature teacher is more familiar with the social and economic conditions of Chaucer's England than with those of Cather's Nebraska. The aim of this volume is to provide background and ideas others have found most helpful in teaching *My Ántonia*.

This book has two parts: "Materials" and "Approaches." Part 1 describes Cather's role in preparing the text and supervising the physical design of *My Ántonia*, and it reviews other writing by Cather relevant to *My Ántonia*, as well as biographical studies and criticism recommended most often by instructors who teach it. It includes also a selective introduction to materials recommended for instructors' libraries: reference works on Cather, general background, biographical studies, and critical commentary. Finally, it surveys aids to teaching: pedagogical articles and nonprint media.

In Part 2, "Approaches," twenty-five instructors explain ways in which they translate their scholarship, criticism, and other experience into class-room approaches to *My Ántonia*. These essays provide an eloquent testimony to diversity: essays focus on teaching the history of Nebraska, the immigrant experience, and the writing and reception of the novel; the literary and philosophical traditions; specific courses; and, finally, specific aspects. This volume concludes with a list of survey participants, a list of works consulted, and an index.

One pleasure of editing this volume has been in corresponding with various persons about *My Ántonia*, Cather, and teaching in general. I am grateful to colleagues—those who responded to the questionnaire and offered advice in planning the volume as well as those who wrote the essays presented here—for so generously contributing their expertise to the project. I wish also to thank Joseph Gibaldi, general editor of this series, for his sound advice throughout; R. Neil Beshers for copyediting; Bernard Koloski for information about the Chopin volume in this series; and Kathryn A. Bellman and Emily Levine for research assistance.

SJR

Part One

MATERIALS

Susan J. Rosowski

Editions

Because *My Ántonia* remains under copyright, teachers have no realistic alternative among editions: only one edition has been and is available in paperback. Until recently these copyright restrictions have ensured that students have read the novel roughly as Cather intended it, for Houghton Mifflin had honored Cather's wishes by printing its paperbacks from plates of the 1937 Autograph Edition (which incorporated changes Cather made for the second, 1926 edition) and including the Benda illustrations Cather asked for. In 1988, however, Houghton Mifflin reissued *My Ántonia* in reduced type, without illustrations and prefaced by an all-purpose foreword. Critical introductions erect a barrier between reader and fiction, Cather felt, and she adamantly refused them for her writing, wishing readers (and especially students) to enjoy a sense of independent discovery. So Houghton Mifflin's publishing decisions for a student edition are disappointing in themselves, but the resulting foreword by Doris Grumbach is especially so. It consists of facile biography, bland plot synopsis, and sweeping value judgments; it contains the most basic factual errors, such as the title of a Cather volume and the date that the French came to Quebec. Instructors should show students a copy of the book as Cather intended it (a first edition if possible or, at the least, a paperback based on the Autograph plates and including Benda illustrations), and they should advise students to postpone reading the foreword until after completing the novel.

Instructors may wish to provide information revealing how closely Cather supervised the physical design of *My Ántonia*, then to discuss with students how that design contributes to the effect of the novel. In letters to her editor at Houghton Mifflin, Ferris Greenslet (Oct. 1917 to Sept. 1918), Cather specified liberal page margins and heavy type on rough-finish, cream-tinted paper. She wanted her illustrations to have the effect of old woodcuts, explaining that her idea evolved from close study of western photographs. To achieve that effect she selected as its illustrator W. T. Benda, an artist who knew both Bohemia and the West. Moreover, she worked closely with him in planning the illustrations, approving ones he prepared, and instructing her editor on how they should be used: on right-hand pages, facing the text they illustrate, on text paper rather than coated paper, and with blank reverse (the first printing of three thousand included illustrations on coated paper; later printings switched to integral illustrations on text paper). She wanted the illustrations printed small on a liberal page, with the same black ink as for the text. She was particularly careful about the sizing and placement of the illustrations, wanting to provide an effect of a great space of sunlight and air overhead.

When the book appeared Cather was very pleased with its look and the printing of its illustrations, only wishing that the paper were a little more yellow. She was not so pleased, however, with Houghton Mifflin's promotion of it, and following *My Ántonia* she went to the young publisher Alfred Knopf, with whom she remained for the rest of her life.

Other editions of *My Ántonia* generally available to students are the Autograph Edition (1937), corrected and revised by Cather and now in major libraries, and the recent Library of America edition (*Early Novels and Stories*), edited by Sharon O'Brien (1987). The Library of America volume includes with *My Ántonia* other early novels and stories: *The Troll Garden*, *O Pioneers!*, *The Song of the Lark*, and *One of Ours*. It offers the convenience of a compact, standardized format, but that same format undermines the feeling of space and individuality that Cather wished for *My Ántonia*.

Required and Recommended Student Reading

When asked what background and critical works they assign or recommend to students, almost all instructors emphasized that they focus on the primary text. Many assign only the novel, some saying simply that they prefer to stress it, others writing that for students in required, introductory classes who are not habitual readers, the primary objective is to enjoy the text. Many respondents explained that they present background material in lectures or where appropriate in class discussion. Not surprisingly, instructors are most likely to assign background reading to the more advanced students. When assigned or recommended, background reading falls into three categories: other writing by Cather, biographies, and criticism.

Other Writings by Cather

Cather's interviews, essays, and short fiction may well provide the best introduction to *My Ántonia*. For autobiographical background, students will find useful Cather's 1913 interview for the *Special Correspondence of the [Philadelphia] Record* (*Kingdom* 446–49). Recalling her own experience of coming with her family to an open country, feeling "an erasure of personality," suffering homesickness, and then finding comfort in visiting with immigrant neighbor women at their baking or butter making, Cather tells of emotions out of which *My Ántonia* sprang. For more general background about the frontier period, "Nebraska: The End of the First Cycle" provides Cather's views of the geography, economy, history, and culture of the state.

For more extensive introduction to Cather's plains fiction, selected early stories depict harsh frontier conditions, all in a style to which students readily respond. "On the Divide" tells of a homesteader's desperate struggle against an alien land; "The Sculptor's Funeral" and "A Wagner Matinée" present cultural deprivation in small-town life; and "El Dorado: A Kansas Recessional" is a story of westering dreams shattered. All are included in *Willa Cather's Collected Short Fiction: 1892–1912*.

For her views about writing, two of Cather's essays are particularly relevant: "My First Novels [There Were Two]" and "The Novel Démeublé." For a discussion of changes in Cather's themes and techniques, two stories are excellent: "Peter" (1892, in *Willa Cather's Collected Short Fiction*) and "Neighbour Rosicky" (1928, in *Obscure Destinies*). In "Peter" Cather wrote an early version of the suicide of Ántonia's father; in "Neighbour Rosicky," a late version of the contentment in Ántonia Cuzak's family, seen in the final section of *My Ántonia*. Anton Rosicky, the central character of the later story, is based on Leo Pavelka, husband of Annie Pavelka, the prototype for Ántonia; as a result, students enjoy "Neighbour Rosicky" as a sequel to *My Ántonia*.

Biographical Studies

Many teachers summarize and some assign relevant portions of a biography. The most frequently cited was James Woodress's *Willa Cather: Her Life and Art*; Mildred R. Bennett's *The World of Willa Cather* and E. K. Brown's *Willa Cather: A Critical Biography* (completed by Leon Edel) were also mentioned frequently. Two biographies appeared too recently to be included in instructor's questionnaires, but they undoubtedly will be recommended or required reading for appropriate classes: Sharon O'Brien's *Willa Cather: The Emerging Voice* (1987) will be particularly important for classes that focus on women's literary traditions and gender identification; and James Woodress's *Willa Cather: A Literary Life* promises to be the standard full-length biography of Cather. Finally, several instructors recommend Sharon O'Brien's essay " 'The Thing Not Named': Willa Cather as a Lesbian Writer" for a thoughtful argument that Cather was lesbian (defined as having a primary emotional attachment to other women), living in a time when cultural pressures resulted in her masking that lesbianism by various fictional strategies.

Criticism

For specialized and upper-level classes, instructors recommend David Stouck's *Willa Cather's Imagination*, praising its "clear, sensible interpretations that most undergraduates can understand." Teachers continue to recommend Dorothy Van Ghent's pamphlet *Willa Cather* and David Daiches's *Willa Cather: A Critical Introduction*; several mentioned also Philip Gerber's Twayne volume, *Willa Cather*, as well as Edward Bloom and Lillian Bloom's *Willa Cather's Gift of Sympathy*. Among recent books of criticism, Judith Fryer's *Felicitious Space: The Imaginative Structures of Edith Wharton and Willa Cather* interprets *My Ántonia* as the creation of a woman's imagination, telling of knowledge of the earth, retrieved by sensations that trigger memory, and placed by story telling. In *The Voyage Perilous: Willa Cather's Romanticism*, Susan Rosowski interprets *My Ántonia* as a novel structured by feeling, its meaning (which is as personal as its form) revealing how the imagination comes to see the miraculous that resides within the ordinary.

The two essays most frequently recommended are Blanche H. Gelfant's "The Forgotten Reaping-Hook: Sex in *My Ántonia*," for complexities of point of view as affected by gender, and James E. Miller, Jr., "*My Ántonia*: A Frontier Drama of Time," for ways in which Cather structures Jim Burden's growing awareness that human destiny participates in cyclic patterns of the seasons, stages of civilization, and times of human life. Recommended also as particularly effective with undergraduates was Wallace Stegner's "Willa Cather: *My Ántonia*" (*American Novel* 144–53). One instructor wrote that he "frames" his teaching of *My Ántonia* with Stegner's essay, reading the first half to his students before they begin reading Cather's novel, then the second half after they have completed it. In so doing, he reinforces the oral quality of Cather's story telling and introduces the point of view of Stegner, "another Great Plains product."

The Instructor's Library

Instructors indicated that they teach *My Ántonia* in a variety of courses and at all levels, from introductory genre or period surveys to advanced specialized courses. It appears most often in courses on American literature, women's literature, and regional literature (e.g., western, plains, and midwestern literature) but also in general courses (e.g., introductions to fiction, surveys of the novel, and composition classes).

When I compiled this listing of materials, my guiding principle was to include works recommended by at least two instructors in their responses to the questionnaire on teaching Cather's novel: exceptions are books and essays published since 1985, too recent to have been used by those instructors. Thus I have not attempted to provide an inclusive list of materials relevant to *My Ántonia*, or even of first-rate criticism on it. The amount of writing on Cather has reached staggering proportions, and one service provided by this volume is to offer the instructor of undergraduate students a guide through that writing.

In using this section, therefore, instructors should recognize the advantages and shortcomings that accompany such selectivity. The advantage is the selection favors undergraduate teaching, the context in which it will be used; the disadvantage is that much excellent criticism and scholarship, materials of interest to an instructor or student exploring a subject beyond classroom discussion, does not appear here. Fortunately, two inclusive bibliographies of works by and about Willa Cather are now available, a starting place for such exploration.

Reference Works

Willa Cather: A Bibliography, by Joan Crane, provides a complete descriptive listing of all known writing by Cather, in all printings and editions. Moreover, it provides a list of personal letters, statements, and quotations printed or reproduced; translations of novels and stories into foreign languages; foreign editions in English and piracies; large-type books and books for the blind (in Braille and Moon type as well as recorded); and adaptations for film and theater. Crane's list of articles, reviews, and essays in newspapers and periodicals (sec. D) is particularly helpful to teachers who wish to guide students into original research. Because many articles that Crane cites here are available only in their original forms, the bibliography enables students to experience the excitement of working with archival materials, either in their institution's library or through interlibrary loan.

Willa Cather: A Reference Guide, by Marilyn Arnold, provides an excellent annotated bibliography of criticism on Cather from 1895 until 1984, including selected major reviews and a listing of works by Cather. Author and title indexes provide easy access to the bibliography; annotations describe but do not evaluate.

For a discussion of the history of Cather criticism, see Bernice Slote's review essay "Willa Cather"; James Woodress is preparing an update of that essay, to include criticism through 1983. These bibliographies should be further updated and supplemented by *American Literary Scholarship: An Annual*, by the annual bibliography included in the February issue of *Western American Literature*, and by the *MLA International Bibliography*. For information about Cather-related events (conferences, seminars, special sessions, etc.), see *Willa Cather Pioneer Memorial Newsletter*, available in major libraries or from the Willa Cather Pioneer Memorial and Educational Foundation (326 N. Webster St., Red Cloud, NE 68970).

General Background

Instructors overwhelmingly recommended Cather's own writing as essential background for *My Ántonia*. Two volumes present her early essays: *The Kingdom of Art: Willa Cather's First Principles and Critical Statements, 1893–1896*, edited by Bernice Slote, and *The World and the Parish: Willa Cather's Articles and Reviews, 1893–1902*, edited by William M. Curtin. Early stories are available in *Willa Cather's Collected Short Fiction, 1892–1912*, edited by Virginia Faulkner, with an introduction by Mildred R. Bennett; particularly relevant to *My Ántonia* is the section titled "On the Divide." Also relevant to *My Ántonia* are *O Pioneers!* (1913) and *A Lost Lady* (1923), which along with "Neighbour Rosicky" in *Obscure Destinies* tell Cather's more complete story of the frontier and America's westering dream. In "Nebraska: The End of the First Cycle," Cather wrote her version of Nebraska's history. (See section on recommended student reading for details.)

For the classical literary tradition in which Cather placed *My Ántonia*, instructors refer to Vergil's *Georgics* and *Aeneid*; for the popular western American tradition, Owen Wister's *The Virginian*. Several instructors recommended also other plains writing, most frequently Mari Sandoz's *Old Jules* and *Love Song to the Plains*, O. E. Rölvaag's *Giants in the Earth*, and Wallace Stegner's *Wolf Willow*.

Unfortunately, background studies of the frontier period in American history and plains or western literature continue to be gender-specific: almost all general studies on the frontier novel or western literature focus (sometimes exclusively) on a male-dominated tradition, while most studies looking at the female tradition of the same era address solely women's experience and literature.

Frederick Jackson Turner's "The Significance of the Frontier in American History" (1893) remains the starting point for discussion of the historical significance of the frontier. Defining the frontier as the meeting place between civilization and wilderness, Turner argued that this westward-moving line of demarcation shaped American identity and destiny by fostering characteristically American qualities: initiative, individual enterprise, ingenuity, industry, optimism, resourcefulness. In *The Frontier Thesis: Valid Interpretation of American History?* (a collection of essays by various hands, edited by Billington) and *America's Frontier Heritage*, Ray Allen Billington surveys, reappraises, and (finally) defends Turner's frontier hypothesis in the light of subsequent research.

For additional historical background, instructors recommended Gilbert Fite's *The Farmers' Frontier*; for literary-historical context, Roy Meyer's *The Middle Western Farm Novel*; and for political background, Norman Pollack's *The Populist Response to Industrial America*. For Nebraska history, instructors (particularly those in the Midwest) recommended James C. Olson's *A History of Nebraska* and Frederick Luebke's *Ethnicity on the Great Plains*. Robert W. Cherny's *Populism, Progressivism, and the Transformation of Nebraska Politics: 1885–1915* is excellent for political backgrounds specific to Cather's time and state.

For women's experiences on the plains, instructors referred most often to recently published books that provide frontier women's voices, often through journals, letters, and diaries: Glenda Riley, *Frontierswomen: The Iowa Experience*; Joanna Stratton, *Pioneer Women: Voices from the Kansas Frontier*; Elizabeth Hampsten, *Read This Only to Yourself: The Private Writings of Midwestern Women, 1880–1910*; and Lillian Schissel, *Women's Diaries of the Westward Journey*. *Women and Western American Literature*, a collection of essays edited by Helen Winter Stauffer and Susan J. Rosowski, includes John J. Murphy's essay "The Virginian and Ántonia Shimerda: Different Sides of the Western Coin."

Though its text is often simplistic, the Time-Life volume *The Pioneers* (particularly the chapter titled "Sodbusters in the Heartland") contains photographs, advertisements, and paintings contemporary to *My Ántonia*: railroad advertisements; photographs of immigrant families; documents of the Homestead Act; photographs of a Nebraska dugout, sod house, and planted field. In "On the Last Frontier: Women Together, Women Divided," a chapter of *With These Hands: Women Working on the Land*, Joan M. Jensen presents a useful overview of women's settlement on the land from 1865 to

1910, followed by excerpts from *My Ántonia* and from other writing by and about women.

For plains, prairie, and western literature classes, as well as for some American literature courses, instructors most frequently mentioned Henry Nash Smith's *Virgin Land: The American West as Symbol and Myth*, often along with two books by Annette Kolodny: in *The Lay of the Land: Metaphor as Experience and History in American Life and Letters*, Kolodny interprets gender implications of men's writings about the American land, and in *The Land before Her: Fantasy and Experience of the American Frontiers, 1630–1860*, she attempts "to chart women's private responses to the successive American frontiers and to trace a tradition of women's public statements about the West," arguing that "women claimed the frontiers as a potential sanctuary for an idealized domesticity" (xi, xiii).

Among discussions of the frontier in literature, instructors mentioned most often Edwin Fussell's *Frontier: American Literature and the American West* (1965), as useful for interpreting one frontier tradition (that of Cooper, Hawthorne, Poe, Thoreau, Melville, and Whitman), and Richard Slotkin's *Regeneration through Violence: The Mythology of the American Frontier, 1600–1860*, as provocative in extending the frontier hypothesis of Turner to argue that "the myth of regeneration through violence became the structuring metaphor of the American experience" (5). In *Westering Women and the Frontier Experience, 1800–1915*, Sandra L. Myres, beginning also with Turner, provides an important corrective to previous studies of the American frontier experience, which have either ignored or isolated women.

Other background studies on the plains include Everett Dick's *The Sod-House Frontier, 1854–1890: A Social History of the Northern Plains from the Creation of Kansas and Nebraska to the Admission of the Dakotas*. Particularly applicable to Cather, Walter Prescott Webb's classic *The Great Plains* (1931) argues "that the Great Plains environment . . . constitutes a geographic unity whose influences have been so powerful as to put a characteristic mark upon everything that survives within its borders" (vi). For immigrant experience, instructors recommended Oscar Handlin, *The Uprooted*; for the American mythology of innocence versus progress, R. W. B. Lewis, *The American Adam: Innocence, Tragedy, and Tradition in the Nineteenth Century*, and Leo Marx, *The Machine in the Garden: Technology and the Pastoral Ideal in America*, who frequently uses literary texts to interpret the conflict of industrial and pastoral.

For broad interpretations of women's traditions, two studies are especially important. Ellen Moers's *Literary Women* places Cather in a context of women's literary tradition and is particularly suggestive concerning Cather's treatment of motherhood and her creation of female landscapes. In *The*

Feminization of American Culture, Ann Douglas argues that the genesis of modern American mass culture lies in sentimental literature of Victorian women and clerics. While she does not mention Cather, Douglas provides a sound basis for discussing certain elements of *My Ántonia*: Cather's treatment of gender roles, particularly as imposed by Jim Burden and contradicted by both Ántonia and Lena Lingard, and the novel's nostalgia, particularly as a form of protest against modern notions of progress. For feminist theory, *The New Feminist Criticism: Essays on Women, Literature, and Theory*, edited by Elaine Showalter, provides a useful starting place, with an especially helpful bibliography divided into fifteen topics ranging from "Feminist Critical Theory, English and American" to "Bibliographies of Feminist Criticism" and "Current Journals Publishing Feminist Criticism." Finally, several instructors recommend Carol Gilligan's *In a Different Voice* and Nancy Chodorow's *The Reproduction of Mothering: Psychoanalysis and the Sociology of Gender* for theories of female development.

Biographical Studies

Because Cather drew so heavily on her own life in writing *My Ántonia*, most instructors spend some time with autobiography and biography. The instructor may wish to begin with a 1913 interview in which Cather spoke of her feelings on entering Nebraska; the brief description anticipates her fictional depiction of Jim Burden's similar entry (*Kingdom* 446–49).

For a biography of Cather, instructors most frequently recommend James Woodress's *Willa Cather: Her Life and Art*, long the best single introduction to Cather's life and writing. Woodress's much expanded, full-length *Willa Cather: A Literary Life* appeared in 1987. Scholarly, sound, and eminently readable, *Willa Cather: A Literary Life* will be invaluable to instructors and their students. Mildred R. Bennett's *The World of Willa Cather* focuses on Cather's years in Webster County and, particularly, Red Cloud, providing important background to *My Ántonia*. Finally, Sharon O'Brien's *Willa Cather: The Emerging Voice* is richly informative about feminist psychological theories, as well as about Cather's development through *O Pioneers!*, the pioneer novel preceding *My Ántonia*.

Early biographies continue to be valuable, particularly three published in 1953: Edith Lewis's *Willa Cather Living: A Personal Record*, is a respectful account of Cather's personality and working habits provided by the woman with whom Cather lived for almost forty years. Elizabeth Shepley Sergeant's *Willa Cather: A Memoir* draws heavily on letters from Cather, with paraphrases that come close to quotations. Because Cather's will prohibits quoting from those letters, the Sergeant biography is especially interesting for including echoes, at least, of Cather's voice. Finally, E. K. Brown's *Willa*

Cather: A Critical Biography, completed by Leon Edel, combines biography with criticism; Brown's was the semiofficial scholarly biography, written with the full cooperation of Edith Lewis and Cather's publishers.

A recent volume provides additional biographical background that should be particularly useful for teaching: L. Brent Bohlke's *Willa Cather in Person: Interviews, Speeches, and Letters* collects all known published letters, speeches, and interviews; a forthcoming second volume, *Willa Cather Remembered* (also edited by Bohlke), will include reminiscences of Cather by persons who knew her.

Critical Commentary

David Daiches's *Willa Cather: A Critical Introduction* and Dorothy Van Ghent's gracefully written pamphlet *Willa Cather* remain useful for initial reading on Cather's major fiction: both provide clear, sensible critical surveys of her works. Following the Twayne format, Philip Gerber in *Willa Cather* provides an alternative general introduction to Cather's life and writing. David Stouck in *Willa Cather's Imagination* argues that the range of Cather's artistry is reflected in the range of modes, themes, and forms she employed in her fiction.

Two recent books provide additional criticism. Judith Fryer's *Felicitous Space: The Imaginative Structures of Edith Wharton and Willa Cather*, draws on interdisciplinary sources (philosophy, sociology, anthropology, architecture, psychology, literature, and the visual arts) to examine the ways in which Wharton and Cather imagine space; Fryer argues that *My Ántonia* imaginatively structures a landscape from female experiences. Susan J. Rosowski's *The Voyage Perilous: Willa Cather's Romanticism* interprets Cather's fiction in terms of her lifelong commitment to vindicating imaginative thought. A chapter on *My Ántonia* argues that the novel invests traditional Romantic patterns and assumptions with new tension, by infusing them with gender assumptions. A later chapter discusses the gothicism that runs through Cather's works, in *My Ántonia* with such incidents as Wick Cutter's attempted rape and the Peter and Pavel story of throwing the wedding couple to the wolves.

Instructors classify the subject matter and form of *My Ántonia* as variously in their teaching as do critics in their writing. Those approaching it as pastoral recommend John H. Randall III's "Willa Cather and the Pastoral Tradition," Richard C. Harris's "Renaissance Pastoral Conventions and the Ending of *My Ántonia*," and David Stouck's "Pastoral" in *Willa Cather's Imagination* (35–72). Others who consider *My Ántonia* as epic refer to Paul A. Olson's "The Epic and Great Plains Literature."

Narrative method, a central subject for criticism on *My Ántonia*, is also central to teaching the novel. In an early essay on Jim Burden's narration as a structuring device, James E. Miller, Jr. ("*My Ántonia*: A Frontier Drama of Time") argues that the unified effect of the book comes from the cyclic patterns that structure it—the seasons, human life, and civilization—and its drama from Jim Burden's growing awareness that it is human destiny to participate in those cycles. In "The Drama of Memory in *My Ántonia*," Terence Martin relates stages of frontier settlement to *My Ántonia* and argues that the book presents not Ántonia's story but "the drama of memory" in Jim Burden, who retrospectively comes "to see Ántonia as the epitome of all he has valued" (304, 308).

In "The Forgotten Reaping-Hook: Sex in *My Ántonia*," Blanche H. Gelfant addresses questions of gender and sexuality posed by the novel, arguing that Jim Burden's narration reveals an evasion of adult male sexuality characteristic of American literature. In "The Fear of Women in Prairie Fiction: An Erotics of Space," Robert Kroetsch describes the long literary tradition in prairie fiction that presents overwhelming space as antithetical to human communication and, particularly, sexual relationships. More recent critics have viewed Jim Burden's narration as a strategy used by Willa Cather to subvert gender conventions. Susan J. Rosowski's "Willa Cather's Women" and Jennifer Bailey's "The Dangers of Femininity in Willa Cather's Fiction" present two interpretations of the recurrent tension in Cather's fiction between gender conventions restrictive to women and strong female characters capable of defying those conventions. In "The Lost Brother, the Twin: Women Novelists and the Male-Female Double *Bildungsroman*," Charlotte Goodman argues that Cather, like certain other women novelists, dramatized culturally imposed gender roles by splitting experience between two protagonists, one male and the other female.

For plains or frontier experience as depicted in *My Ántonia*, Roy W. Meyer's "The Scandinavian Immigrant in American Farm Fiction" provides general background, focusing particularly on *O Pioneers!* and *My Ántonia*. For background about Peter and Pavel's story of the wedding party and the wolves, Paul Schach's "Russian Wolves in Folktales and Literature of the Plains: A Question of Origins" demonstrates the resemblance of Cather's story to German and Russian folk stories and suggests possible sources for her version.

For political background and Cather's position relevant to it, Robert W. Cherny's "Willa Cather and the Populists" provides information on the populism in Webster County and the antipopulism of Charles Gere, editor of the *Nebraska State Journal* while Cather worked there. For tensions between Old World and New as depicted in *My Ántonia*, Wallace Stegner writes extensively of the novel in one chapter of *The American Novel*.

Aids to Teaching

Surprisingly few publications specifically address the subject of teaching *My Ántonia*. John J. Murphy's introductory pamphlet written for Houghton Mifflin, *A Teacher's Guide to Willa Cather's O Pioneers! and My Ántonia*, is now out of print. In a brief essay, "Discovering Symbolic Meaning: Teaching with Willa Cather," Susan J. Rosowski focuses on *My Ántonia* as a text that teaches students "patterned in habits of radical depthlessness" to read by "an accumulation of meaning, as in poetry" (15–16).

The situation is happier concerning nonprint media to supplement teaching Cather's novel. Instructors often recommend a judicious use of visual materials illustrating the sites and people on whom Cather drew for *My Ántonia*. For a superb photographic history of first-stage settlement on the frontier, see John Carter, *Solomon D. Butcher: Photographing the American Dream*. The volume includes 105 photographs representing the years 1885–1911, all selected from Butcher's nearly four thousand prints and negatives depicting the generation that settled Nebraska. For illustrations specifically keyed to Cather's life and fiction, Bernice Slote's *Willa Cather: A Pictorial Memoir* is very good; it includes photographs by Lucia Woods and others, with text by Slote. For a dramatic photograph of Annie Pavelka (the prototype for Ántonia Shimerda Cuzak), as well as other photographs relevant to Cather, see "Willa Cather Country."

Webster County itself is accessible to many instructors; almost half of those responding to the questionnaire reported that they have visited Red Cloud and its environs, where they took photographs and slides for use in their teaching. Those in the Midwest frequently take their students to Webster County, where they can visit the Pavelka farm, walk on an expanse of unbroken prairie, and see in Red Cloud (the prototype for Black Hawk) various sites Cather included in her novel—most important, her childhood home and the nearby Miner house (the prototypes for the Burden and Harling homes in Black Hawk). All are administered by the Willa Cather Historical Center, Nebraska State Historical Society. Finally, instructors may purchase slides of sites relevant to *My Ántonia* by writing to the Willa Cather Pioneer Memorial and Educational Foundation (326 N. Webster St., Red Cloud, NE 68970).

The film *Willa Cather's America* is a sometimes awkwardly dramatic but generally satisfactory introduction to Cather's life and fiction. Produced for WNET-TV, it is available from Films for the Humanities (PO Box 2053, Princeton, NJ 08450). Several instructors mentioned that when they did use this film, they found it more effective following rather than preceding discussion of Cather and *My Ántonia*.

Of all Cather's novels, only *A Lost Lady* has been adapted for film; after her disappointment in the 1924 version by Warner Brothers and her anger over the same studio's 1934 version, filmed without her knowledge, Cather took legal action to prohibit subsequent adaptations of her work in any form. There is, therefore, no film of *My Ántonia*, and presumably there will be none so long as copyright protection is in effect.

Part Two

APPROACHES

INTRODUCTION

The following essays are arranged in four sections focusing on teaching the life and times, literary and philosophical traditions, specific courses, and, finally, specific aspects of the novel. The authors represent a range of experience: they teach at colleges, universities, and community colleges located throughout the United States and in Canada, and they include *My Ántonia* in courses that range from basic composition to advanced genre and specialized thematic courses.

Approaches represented here illustrate that range. In section 1, "Teaching the Life and Times," Sally Allen McNall combines sociology and literary criticism to discuss immigration to the Great Plains: the history and myth of immigration and its influence on ideas of the family, the church, education, and the economy. In an appendix McNall provides a time line of selected United States immigration laws and programs from 1891 to 1986. Robert W. Cherny discusses background to Nebraska in the 1880s and 1890s, then uses that background to illuminate the historical accuracies and exaggerations of Cather's fictional treatments. James Woodress explains biographical material relevant to the writing of *My Ántonia* and reviews the novel's independent life after its publication as reflected in its sales and reviews. Finally, Philip L. Gerber provides a glossary of terms Cather used, many of which may be completely unfamiliar to students or may have regional and historical connotations lost to students today.

In section 2, "Teaching the Literary and Philosophical Traditions," the first two essays discuss *My Ántonia* in terms of classical traditions: David Stouck describes teaching *My Ántonia* as pastoral, and Paul A. Olson explains how he teaches it as a plains epic. Susan J. Rosowski uses Cather's introduction as a starting place for the novel's romantic poetics of fiction; Josephine Donovan locates *My Ántonia* within the context of early twentieth-century American women's culture, when historic opportunities offered to women meant leaving the traditional domestic world of their mothers; and John J. Murphy describes ways in which he teaches religious allusions that convey the novel's "Nativity dimension." Finally, in "William James, Henri Bergson, and Remembered Time in *My Ántonia*," Loretta Wasserman discusses Cather's themes and ideas "as philosophically of her time, as embracing a worldview concerned with the possibility of human freedom under the weight of biologic determinism, the nature of mind, the power of the unconscious, the interplay of time and memory."

In section 3, "Teaching Specific Courses," Tom Quirk places *My Ántonia* within the historical context of the American novel by surveying Cather's critical attitudes toward both her writing and that of other American novelists—for example, James, Chopin, and Dreiser. Mary Anne Ferguson describes how she used *My Ántonia* as the central text in an interdisciplinary course involving literature, history, and art, intended to introduce "students in both women's studies and American studies to the methods and limitations of the interdisciplinary approach." Barbara Bair explains how she uses Cather's novel "with nineteenth- and early twentieth-century classics . . . to formulate definitions of the 'American' character (based on race, gender, class, and ideology) and to develop ideas about regionalism and . . . American history."

In "*My Ántonia* in the Freshman Writing Class," Jennifer Bradley describes her curricular principles and representative assignments as she uses Cather's novel for clusters of writing assignments. To teach *My Ántonia* in an interdisciplinary course for working adults, Constance Mierendorf draws on themes relevant to adult learners: family, heritage, and community. And in "Teaching *My Ántonia* as a Plains Novel," Robert Thacker writes of teaching Cather's novel about the American westering experience to students who have never been west of the Mississippi. James L. Evans describes teaching the novel to students immediately aware of their immigrant backgrounds, stressing parallels between the lives of Cather's immigrant characters and those of his students.

Section 4 considers specific aspects of the novel that especially interest students. Blanche H. Gelfant explains teaching *My Ántonia* as self-reflexive, so that the text's indeterminacy dispels the naive notion that every story has one "true" meaning, and Charlotte Goodman interprets Cather's narrative strategy of pairing characters, one male and the other female, as emphasizing the limitations of society's gender conventions. Sharon O'Brien discusses the challenge of asking students to question a narrator's authority and considers implications of Cather's possessing a lesbian identity in her "possible use of camouflage, encoding, and metaphor."

Glen A. Love counters the convention that Cather's vision was retrospective by interpreting Cather's narrator as possessing a forward-looking, modern sensibility. Paul Comeau describes his teaching of *My Ántonia* as an American classic, focusing on "the escapist impulse, the questing hero, and the symbolistic style of writing." In response to students' frequent questions about the "point" of the inset stories, Michael Peterman interprets the stories as steps in shaping both the individual imaginations of Jim and Ántonia and also the relationship between them. Jean Schwind explains her use of the illustrations to *My Ántonia* as a visual textual supplement to help correct the "romantic" bias of Jim Burden's account, and Stephen Tatum describes how he focuses on a scene or passage to demonstrate the novel's lyrical power.

Unless otherwise indicated, page references for quotations from *My Ántonia* refer to the text as established for the second printing (trade printing) and used by Houghton Mifflin from 1938 to 1988.

SJR

TEACHING THE LIFE AND TIMES

Immigrant Backgrounds to *My Ántonia*:
"A Curious Social Situation in Black Hawk"

Sally Allen McNall

When teaching Willa Cather, I tell my students that one of her greatest strengths is her ambivalence about the cultural myths of her time—myths that have become a part of our time as well. In the case of *My Ántonia*, this statement can be applied almost indefinitely, but it is nowhere more true than in her depiction of immigrants. In Cather's day it was rare for any member of the dominant culture (and she was that) to see immigrants as subjects, as people acting in their own behalf. Her ability to do so is significant, but it is not the sole significant fact about her vision of them and of their circumstances. At the beginning of section 9 of "The Hired Girls," Jim Burden describes "a curious social situation in Black Hawk." If students are to understand the vital complexity of attitudes involved here and throughout the book, they should be given some information about the historical and cultural context of that situation.

History and Myth

My Ántonia is about the historical period during which the American frontier closed. It is also about the place where that happened, since the Great Plains were settled after the West Coast regions; the people of the Great Plains, more than those of any other region, must be thought of as immigrants (Luebke, "Regionalism" 31). In the nineties, the historian Frederick Jackson Turner began to expound his thesis explaining the American character in terms of the frontier. In shifting emphasis from the East to the "Great West," he also developed an idea of the frontier as a crucible, where European immigrants were "Americanized, liberated, and fused into a mixed race" (James D. Bennett 44–47). The idea of the West as melting pot was appealing in the years before World War I, but it was only one way in which Americans could think about immigrants. Three years before *My Ántonia* was published, the *Nation* printed an influential article presenting another view. According to the philosopher H. M. Kallen, each nationality should express its "emotional and voluntary life in its own language, in its own inevitable aesthetic and intellectual forms" (qtd. in Handlin, *Immigration* 154). This currently popular idea has since been termed cultural pluralism and recently, by Carl Degler, the "salad bowl" (Howard N. Rabinowitz 27). There is no doubt that it appealed to Cather as strongly as Turner's frontier thesis could have done. Her attitude toward the immigrant is partly a matter of deeply personal identification with those who are "different," but it also may reflect Nebraska's relative noninterference with various ethnic life-styles, compared with its Great Plains neighbors (Luebke, "Regionalism" 38).

A first reading of *My Ántonia*, when it was originally published, in 1918, or today, may leave a reader with the impression of either a melting pot or a salad bowl. In "Cuzak's Boys" the respectability of town (the teachings of Mrs. Burden and Mrs. Harling) and the cosmopolitanism of city (Cuzak's background) support Ántonia's role as a "rich mine of life," founding not an old but a new race: Americans, with a living cultural heritage from the Old World. Yet an examination of the book as a whole, in the context of some far less benign theories and myths, will show students that Cather was equally aware of the other side of her cultural coinage.

In its most acceptable form, the earliest theory of "Americanization" can be called assimilation. In Cather's day it deserved the description "doctrine of Anglo-Saxon conformity," and it was a widespread response to the influx of immigration between 1880 and 1914. The years—1883 to 1895—when Cather lived in Nebraska neatly span the middle portion of the two decades during which the national question of immigration become more vexed than ever before in our history. In those decades and the two to follow, the rigid classification of social identities in the United States reached its peak (Higham, *Send These* 246). Nativism, as it was called, had been present from the beginning of the century of immigration (roughly, 1820–1920). In a society always profoundly subject to change, xenophobia was an early and persistent response to insecurity, and in the 1890s Americans were particularly insecure economically. Although immigration to the Great Plains slowed during this decade, immigration on a national level did not; in fact, xenophobia was probably exacerbated by the condition of the numerous urban immigrants. Nativism infected all sections of the country and every class, but it was not new. "If I were to put upon the printed page some of the epithets applied to . . . people from central Europe . . . by their prairie and backwoods neighbors, in the seventies and eighties," observes a Nebraska educator in 1929, "I greatly fear it would not add to the growing cordiality between this group and the rest of us" (Rosický, *History* 16).

The growing movement for regulation of immigration argued that the arrival of cheap foreign labor was not only undesirable competition but a contribution to the widening and hardening gap between rich and poor (Warne 316). Not only labor unrest in cities but the agrarian protest movements Cather knew well were regularly blamed on foreign radicals (Higham, *Strangers* 73). Students should know that between 1895 and the publication of *My Ántonia*, Cather lived in Pittsburgh and (like the "I" of the introduction) in New York City, where the conditions of urban immigrants could hardly be ignored and where—as newspaperwoman and editor for a radical magazine, *McClure's*—Cather was exposed to a variety of facts and opinions on the subject.

During those years, yet another way of viewing immigrants was developing. Immigrants had begun to reach the Great Plains within the decade after the Homestead Act (1862). During that decade and in the seventies, immigrants to America were predominantly from western and northern Europe. Though the promotional activities of the railroads now brought many straight past the cities of the East to the prairies, other immigrants were moving on from earlier settlements in the East. In *My Ántonia*, the Harlings, Mrs. Gardener (née Molly Bawn), and Mr. Jensen, the Danish laundryman, are examples of this group, soon to be called the "old immigrants." These people were more easily integrated into our society than were the "new immigrants" from eastern and southern Europe, whose numbers swelled in the eighties and nineties. The Harlings, in particular, illustrate the proposition that Scandinavian immigrants tended to be upright and cosmopolitan (Commager 6), while Lena Lingard's grandfather was a "clergyman and much respected in Norway" (200). Despite a dubious reputation, Lena does not get in trouble; rather, she is a success American-style, as is Tiny Soderball (299). Though many Czechs arrived in Nebraska at the same time as the western and northern Europeans, the national picture was different, and the Shimerdas reflect this change, arriving late, on the largest wave of Czech immigration (Roucek, "Czechoslovak Americans" and *Czechs*; Laska 29).

By the 1890s, Italians, eastern European Jews, and Slavs (a group that includes Czechs) were arriving in great numbers, and they bore the brunt of the economic insecurity of the period. During the years Cather was writing

My Ántonia, America was making up its mind whether to go to war with Germany and Austria-Hungary. Czechs in America were eager even before our involvement to help free their homelands from the domination of the Dual Empire; early in the book Otto makes an elliptical reference to the background of this situation (21). Yet Czechs like other immigrants felt the force of the Americanization movement in the war years (Rosický, *History* 483), while Germans in America, including Nebraska, were definitely suspect; stories of their victimization can be found in almost any history of a midwestern state. The country's anxiety over the role immigrants were to play in our society did not ease, though the "tide" of immigration was stemmed, briefly, by the war; after the war years, the restrictionists won their battles, in the quota system—based on the preexisting composition of the American population—instituted in 1921 and 1924. The "new" immigrants, then, were regarded with suspicion, which took several forms, each revealing fears about American institutions. Cather misses none of them.

The Family

The most prominent anxiety in "The Hired Girls" is sexual—it concerns marriage. It is no accident that the dancing pavilion that menaces the morals of Black Hawk youth is set up by an Italian couple. Black Hawk attitudes are polarized by the dances along the lines between "old" and "new" immigrant stereotypes—the Danish laundry girls contrasted with the dangerous Bohemian Marys, and Ántonia's success at the tent the first step toward her downfall.

Students may not be aware how xenophobia in America fed, from the beginning, on a set of ideas that can only be termed racist, ideas about "mongrelization" and Anglo-Saxons' being "outbred" by inferior racial groups (see the example of E. A. Ross, a well-known sociologist of the period, and Handlin, *Immigration* 278), ideas of a "dark shadow" or a "black tide." The "new" immigrants were seen as more peasantlike than the "old"; a thread of this sort of distaste on the part of the Burdens runs through "The Shimerdas." Jim reacts with violent self-righteousness to unpleasant facts concerning Ántonia's sexuality: the rape, the first pregnancy. His reactions here ironically prefigure the way he will repeat Sylvester Lovett's pattern, will toy with Lena but marry a wealthy bloodless woman of his own ethnicity and class.

Sexuality, then, threatens both the "racial purity" and the respectability of old Black Hawk residents. It is also a threat to the immigrant, and here Cather takes considerable pains to make her point clear. In Ántonia, she creates a character whose moral isolation is all but total, who must do without the support of extended family and tradition, who must rely on herself alone to make her marital arrangements, and who at first fails disastrously. In the Old World, she would have lived, as virtually all Czech immigrants had, in a village community and would have been courted by someone like Cuzak to begin with (Kutak 10–11; Swehla 474). The absence of community is destructive to her as well as to her father. If they had come to eastern Nebraska, they would have benefited from the colony-based settlement system; Webster County's settlements were never large (Rosický, "Bohemians" 2 and *History* 207). No one is there to understand, much less sympathize with, peasant values; to the Burdens, she seems degraded by her work. Ántonia's status is precarious, then, long before the dance pavilion comes to Black Hawk, and afterward it is clear that she is regarded as "fair game," not only by Wick Cutter but, in his unconscious way, by Jim, who kisses her in a manner that is "not right" (224).

Toward the end of "The Hired Girls," an important passage tells us about the class split in Ántonia's background. Her father "lived in his mother's house," says Ántonia to Jim, "and she [Ántonia's mother] was a poor girl come in to do the work." Ántonia is the daughter of a servant who was no better than she should be, a stereotype of the undesirable immigrant, and temporarily at least Ántonia too fulfills that role.

The Church

Another influence that bound many Bohemians of Ántonia's generation into a community and preserved traditional values for more than one or two generations is all but absent from Cather's picture of the character. Bohemian immigrants, like many others, often settled in communities built around their churches, particularly in the Midwest and West (Baltensperger 77; Roucek, *Czechs* 33). Today's students are generally surprised to learn that a powerful current in American xenophobia, from the days of the Puritans, was a horror of the Roman Catholic church. The Shimerdas (like approximately fifty percent of all Czech immigrants) are Catholic. In the 1890s, American fear of domination or at least subversion by those loyal to a foreign potentate, the pope, and fear of a religious tradition not particularly interested in the cause of temperance were aggravated by conflicts in the East and Midwest over the issue of parochial schools, where classes were often taught in the children's native languages, and which, unlike our public schools, did not "Americanize" (Curran 96–97; Higham, *Strangers* 59–60).

Twice in *My Ántonia*, Cather—most uncharacteristically—emphasizes elements of Catholicism that were, in the eyes of contemporary American Protestants, mere popish superstition. The scenes in question are Mr. Shimerda's spontaneous prayer before the Christmas tree (87)—which Grandfather Burden "Protestantizes"—and Mrs. Shimerda's desire to bury her husband, a suicide and hence a mortal sinner, at a crossroads. This desire is frustrated by later (one assumes Protestant) road makers (113, 119). Cather presents Ántonia and her family as isolates, lacking a stable and coherent religious community and tradition, and therefore the sort of religious ties that could prevent the mistake she makes with Larry Donovan. Yet if the reputable Protestants of Black Hawk participated in the anti-Catholic prejudice of their times, a Catholic girl's fall (and with a Catholic young man) would not have surprised them.

Education

Although Ántonia has no religious training to help her preserve her Czech identity, she is at any rate spared the "Americanization" of the public schools. If our students take the value of public education for granted, they need to be reminded that immigrants did not invariably do so. As another member of Cather's generation in Nebraska observed of his Czech pupils, their families "wanted the children to get an English education, but corn husking took precedence over everything" (Rosický, *History* 15; see Kutak 61–62 for examples of immigrant Czechs' opposition toward schooling). In a 1923 *Nation* article, Cather comments tartly that our lawmakers "have a rooted conviction that a boy can be a better American if he speaks only one language than if he speaks two" ("Nebraska" 237). It is not necessarily Ántonia's loss that she has no time for school, and it is part of her triumph that her children grow up bilingual, speaking Czech at home and preserving Czech ways.

Ántonia's father's plea, "Te-e-ach, te-e-ach my Ántonia!" is that of an educated man helpless to pass his education on to the child who takes after him; it is not a wish that her mind should be molded to that of the New World. Cather points out that "Many of our Czech immigrants were people of a very superior type. The political emigration resulting from the revolutionary disturbances of 1848 was distinctly different from the emigration resulting from economic causes . . . in Nebraska our Czech settlements were large and very prosperous" ("Nebraska" 237). Many such settlements in fact resulted from internal migration from early Czech colonies in Wisconsin and Ohio, but this clustering argues for a considerable degree of difference perceived between the Czechs and the dominant culture (Luebke, "Regionalism" 34 and "Ethnic" 395), and of course the Shimerdas, however superior a type Mr. Shimerda was, do not have the advantage of living in a large settlement.

For Jim, obviously, education—especially higher education—is an important indicator of class and a means of upward mobility. The relative lack of education of the "new" immigrants was one reason nativists gave for fearing them. Ántonia never gets a formal education, nor is she upwardly mobile;

rather, she stays put—a "country girl" (309). Students may need to be told that by the time described in "Cuzak's Boys," farming—however prosperous—had lost the prestige it had had in America since Jefferson's day. Class and immigrant status were intertwined, even in rural Nebraska.

The Economy

In a rapidly industrializing and urbanizing America, economic dislocations between generations were inevitable, particularly for immigrant families who went to cities, but also in rural life. Mr. Shimerda is not the sort of man who can adapt to frontier conditions. As Annie Sadilek Pavelka put it in a 1955 letter, her father, a weaver in the old country, was totally unprepared for the prairies:

> he used to hear how good it was hear as he had letters from her how wonderfull it was out here that there were beautifful houses lot of trees and so on but how disapointed he was when he saw them pretty houses duged in the banks of the deep draws . . . behold our surprise . . . in the old country he was allways joking and happy. . . .

Many Bohemian villagers with crafts found them of little use in the agricultural environment (Kutak 16, 146). In Cather's novel, however, Ántonia and also her brother can and do adapt to the prairie. Cuzak, Ántonia's husband, knew little about farming to begin with, but Ántonia's strength, and the children, have made the difference. "We got plenty boys," he says (chilling any Anglo-Saxon supremacist), "we can work a lot of land" (365). This is traditional farming, and Cather has Jim look back on the stories of the immigrant girls in a way that maintains a distinction between farming and business. "Today," Jim says, "the best that a harassed Black Hawk merchant can hope for is to sell provisions and farm machinery and automobiles to the rich farms where that first crop of stalwart Bohemian and Scandinavian girls are now mistresses" (201).

Cather's vision of immigrants to central Nebraska in the crucial years retains much of the uglier furniture of the American mind at the time. Over Jim's head we see—and, with Cather, may judge—the ethnocentricity permeating every social institution. The harshness of this reality is mitigated by Jim's bemused sporadic attraction to Ántonia's very foreignness. But Ántonia is just that: Jim's romantic heroine. As Frances Harling tells him, "I expect I know the country girls better than you do. You always put a kind of glamour over them. The trouble with you, Jim, is that you're romantic" (229). Because Jim's own life, marriage, and work involve him inextricably in the world of business, as we learn in the introduction, he cannot see the contradictions in the rural lives he idealizes. Cather can, and she even has Ántonia warn Jim as a boy of his blindness: "Things will be easy for you. But they will be hard for us" (140).

Myth and the Present

While she wrote *My Ántonia*, Cather was as aware of the climate of opinion, the emphasis on being one hundred percent American, as was any major writer of her time. She wrote against universal conformity, without polemic and without oversimplification. In a world in which foreignness was the symbol of insecurity and change, she made an immigrant woman stand for permanence and stability. This trick is not the only one she played. In "Nebraska: The End of the First Cycle," she deplored the "machine-made materialism" that industrialization was producing (238). Because she confronts this issue head-on in her 1922 novel *One of Ours*, it is tempting, and certainly easier on our students, to teach *My Ántonia* as a looking back to a time and way of life uncontaminated by materialism, by capitalistic development and its imperatives. For both Jim and the narrator of the introduction, Ántonia means "the country, the conditions, the whole adventure of our childhood." Jim's vision of an immigrant woman triumphing over adversity does indeed look back, but Cather's vision, I try to show my students, examines the social conflicts beneath the mythologies of her day, looks far enough into them to suggest powerfully what our imported labor force was up against in her day.

It is still up against it today. We have not yet made up our minds what we want to do about or with immigrants. Because of this, *My Ántonia* remains a central text in our literature and can heighten our students' awareness of the history of their mythologies and attitudes.

Appendix: Some US Immigration Laws and Programs

1891   The federal government, assuming charge of immigration, opens Ellis Island.

1903   Congress expands the list of excluded aliens (convicts, lunatics, etc.) to include radicals.

1907   Congress raises the head tax on immigrants and excludes those with physical defects and unaccompanied children.

1917   Congress establishes a literacy test.

1921   Congress (having virtually banned Asian immigrants—a ban that endured until 1943) sets a limit on European immigration, according to quotas based on immigrant populations already here.

1924	Johnson-Reed Act: toughens quota system; it is revised downward again in 1927.
1948	Displaced Persons Act: provides for war refugees; its provisions are revised upward in 1950.
1952	McCarran-Walter Immigration and Naturalization Act: eliminates race as a barrier, continues quota system, establishes preference for family reunification.
1953–62	Congress liberalizes provisions for refugees in four successive acts.
1965	Congress abolishes quotas and establishes other limits.
1980	Refugee Act of 1980: further liberalizes policy.
1981	President Reagan proposes an Omnibus Immigration Control Act, addressing issues of illegal immigration, refugee status, and employment, among others.
1983	Senator Simpson and Representative Mazzoli propose a revised Immigration Reform and Control Act; it is adopted by the Senate but not by the House.
1986	Immigration Reform and Control Act: gives legal status to millions of illegal aliens living in the US since 1 January 1982 and establishes penalties for anyone found hiring illegal aliens.

Willa Cather's Nebraska

Robert W. Cherny

Understanding Nebraska in the 1880s and 1890s can be useful background for reading Willa Cather's *My Ántonia*, as well as other of her works. Cather regarded the "years from eight to fifteen" as "the formative period in a writer's life, when he unconsciously gathers basic material" (qtd. in Brown 3). She was ten when her parents brought her to a new home in Nebraska, and she lived in that state for the next dozen years. Jim Burden's experiences in *My Ántonia* have close parallels with those of Cather: coming as a child to Nebraska when it was still in a pioneer stage, living briefly on a farm, residing in town for a longer time, attending the University of Nebraska, and becoming a success in the East. (Mildred R. Bennett in *The World of Willa Cather* presents a detailed treatment of the relations between locations in Nebraska and those in Cather's fiction.)

In 1883, Cather's parents, Charles and Virginia, brought their four children from their native Virginia to Webster County, in south central Nebraska. Charles's father and brother had emigrated there during the previous decade and by 1883 had comfortable and prosperous farms; they enjoyed such prominence that the township was named Catherton. After a brief try at farming, Charles moved his family into Red Cloud, the largest town in Webster county, where he ran a loan agency.

The region to which the emigrants came was new and raw. "There was nothing but land," Cather wrote in *My Ántonia*, "not a country at all, but the material out of which countries are made" (7). Webster County lies toward the eastern side of the Great Plains, that part of the central United States characterized by relatively flat terrain, sloping eastward from the base of the Rocky Mountains toward the Missouri River. Meandering through the central plains from west to east flow rivers that are broad, shallow, and sluggish throughout most of the year. The Republican River, one of these streams, runs across the southern part of Webster County, just south of Red Cloud. When the first people of European descent arrived in the Republican valley, they found a few trees and shrubs growing near the streams and tall prairie grass covering the rolling plains. (Sandoz, *Love Song*, and Webb provide good introductions to the Great Plains.)

The years following the Civil War brought dramatic changes to the Great Plains. Between then and 1880, Nebraska's population quadrupled, and it then doubled during the 1880s. The region that includes Webster County experienced rapid development in the 1870s and early 1880s, when railroad construction prompted large-scale immigration. Census takers in 1870 counted only sixteen people in Webster County; ten years later they found more than seven thousand, so the largest population influx had already occurred before Charles Cather arrived with his family. By 1890, the county had 11,210 residents, with much of the increase in the 1880s coming in towns.

Rapid population growth transformed the plains. Towns sprang up to provide services for the surrounding countryside. Farmers plowed the plains, planted crops, and hoped that the harvest would yield enough to repay their loans, taken to buy new farms and homes. Many came to the plains with little capital, and they had to build everything themselves: house, well, barn, other farm buildings, fences. Charles Cather's parents were fortunate in arriving with enough capital to have a home like that of the Burdens in *My Ántonia.*

Many pioneers could not afford such homes. The high cost of shipping lumber from the East forced some plains pioneers to create a home by digging into the side of a hill or embankment, to make a dugout like that of the Shimerda family in *My Ántonia.* Pioneers cut the tough prairie sod into blocks that could be used for building, and many families resorted to a combination of dugout and sod construction. Sod houses—"soddies"—became common throughout the central plains. A sod house or dugout could be built for three dollars or less, but it seldom made a satisfactory dwelling. The roof almost always leaked during rainstorms and dripped for hours after; nearly every soddie dweller had stories of snakes and insects dropping from the ceiling or crawling out of the walls. (Dick and R. L. Welsch provide information on pioneer farm life in the central plains; Carter features more than a hundred photographs, many of soddies and dugouts.)

Life was often difficult for the early settlers. Everything had to be done at once, from building shelter to planting crops and fencing pastures for livestock. The closest neighbor sometimes lived several miles distant, and many early settlers felt a sharp sense of isolation. Those who, like Mr. Shimerda, could not speak English felt even more isolated. Because of low prices for farm products in the late 1880s and early 1890s, compounded by drought in the mid-1890s, success remained elusive for many until late in the 1890s. By then, many had given up, but for those who remained, wood-frame farmhouses replaced the soddies.

Cather's novels portray the ethnic diversity among the people of the Great Plains, reflecting emigration patterns in the 1870s and 1880s, when the opportunity to start anew brought people to the plains from throughout the eastern parts of the United States and Canada and from western and central Europe. In 1890, only twenty-nine percent of the state's population had been born in Nebraska. Forty-three percent of all Nebraskans were of foreign stock (i.e., either foreign-born themselves or born in the United States of foreign-born parents). Six groups accounted for more than four-fifths of this foreign stock: Germans, 37.6% of all foreign-stock Nebraskans; Swedes, 12.1%; Irish, 10.8%; Czechs (Bohemians), 7.8%; English, 6.6%; Danes, 5.7%.

Immigrants play central roles in several of Cather's novels, and she some-times depicted the differences between their values and behavior and those of old-stock Americans (those whose families had been in this country for several generations). Throughout American history, many immigrants to the United States have sought to adapt to the culture of their adopted land. Except for English immigrants, however, they have often found it difficult to do so, because of differences in language, religion, and custom. Old-stock Americans have frequently discriminated against immigrants whose lan-guage, religion, and customs differed greatly from theirs. Alcohol, especially, provided a subject for conflict; many old-stock Americans considered it sinful, but most Irish, German, and Czech immigrants found no sin in a glass of beer. In *My Ántonia*, Cather notes Grandmother Burden's disapproval of Anton Jelinek's saloon. (Most general treatments of immigrant history con-centrate on urban, industrial areas. Despite their scant attention to immi-grant farmers, for the experience of immigration, see Kraut; Handlin, *Uprooted*. For anti-immigrant attitudes, see Higham, *Strangers*. For prohibition, see Gusfield; Luebke, *Immigrants*, chs. 5, 7.)

In her writing, Cather sometimes depicted rural, foreign-stock commu-nities centered around a church. Throughout American history, immigrants have sought out others of their kind and formed ethnic enclaves where they could speak their language and practice their religion and customs in relative freedom. Ethnic enclaves existed throughout the farming regions of eastern and south central Nebraska, but most immigrants avoided the ranch country and arid areas in the north central and western parts of the state. Germans predominated in the northeastern counties, Danes and Swedes created set-tlements in central Nebraska, and Czech communities tended toward the southeastern part. Members of these and other groups were scattered throughout all the farming regions of the state. Wilber, the largest Czech community in the state, lies about ninety miles east of Red Cloud. Cather has Ántonia's son Rudolph describe Wilber as a place with "a Bohunk [Bo-hemian] crowd for sure" where "we didn't hear a word of English on the street" (357); Cather once wrote that she had herself "walked the streets of Wilber . . . for a whole day without hearing a word of English spoken" ("Nebraska" 237; for Nebraska Germans and the immigrant experience more generally, see Luebke, *Immigrants*. Paul A. Olson's *Broken Hoops* intro-duces a number of Great Plains ethnic groups).

Although Cather wrote extensively of immigrant groups in Webster County, it actually did not have concentrations of immigrants comparable to those in the eastern parts of the state. The largest foreign-born groups in Webster County in 1890, out of a total population of 11,210, were Germans, 550; English, 191; Canadians (French and English), 184; Czechs (Bohemians), 105; Swedes, 84. Young Willa Cather had never encountered European immigrants in Virginia, and she found cultural significance in the immigrants that belied their small proportions in Red Cloud or Webster County. In Red Cloud, young Willa learned piano from a German-born music teacher, studied Greek and Latin with an English-born storekeeper, and had access to the large library of a French-born neighbor woman (Brown 25–27).

One of Cather's essays, "Nebraska: The End of the First Cycle," provides an insight into her understanding of the significance of immigrants. "They brought with them something that this neutral new world needed even more than the immigrants needed land," she wrote, including "sturdy traits of character," "elasticity of mind," "an honest attitude toward the realities of life," and "certain qualities of feeling and imagination" (237–38). For Cather, European immigrants represented a culture older and deeper than that of old-stock Americans, whom she described in the same essay as "seldom open-minded . . . cautious and convinced of their own superiority . . . provincial and utterly without curiosity" (237, 238). For Cather, Europe was a source of culture, but America—or at least Red Cloud—was a parochial backwater.

Perhaps because Cather looked to European immigrants to redeem America from its provincialism, she seems (perhaps unconsciously) to have exaggerated their numbers. She claimed that foreign-stock Nebraskans accounted for 900,571 in a total population of 1,192,214 ("Nebraska" 237). While her figure for the total population is correct, the actual census data shows only 538,218 foreign-stock Nebraskans (United States 590). Apparently her deeply held convictions regarding the cultural significance of European immigrants led Cather to misread the census data.

European immigrants play a major role in several of Cather's works, especially those published between 1913 and 1922. The main characters of her second and third novels were Swedish women, and other characters included French Canadians, Czechs, Germans, Irish, and Norwegians. She created Czech main characters not only in *My Ántonia* but also in "Neighbor Rosicky," one of her best-known short stories, and she gave a significant role to a Czech in *One of Ours*.

The Czechs seemed to hold a special interest for Cather, who sometimes referred to them by the more commonly used term Bohemians. Prague, capital of Bohemia, a part of the Austro-Hungarian Empire, was summer capital of the empire, seat of an ancient university, and home to artists and musicians, including Mozart. Cather believed that "many of our Czech immigrants were people of a very superior type," and she wrote longingly of "the pleasant little theater" in Wilber where she once heard boys and girls recite "the masterpieces of Czech drama in the Czech language" ("Nebraska" 237; for Nebraska Czechs, see Rosický; Kučera; and Kučera and Nováček).

Whether of foreign stock or native stock, most Nebraskans in 1890 lived in rural areas and made their living from the soil. The census takers that year found that forty-six percent of Nebraskans with an identifiable occupation were engaged in agriculture. Immigrants and their children were somewhat more likely than old-stock Americans to live in rural areas and to be farmers. Webster County, in 1890, counted only three incorporated towns or villages within its almost six hundred square miles: Red Cloud, population 1,839; Blue Hill, population 796; Guide Rock, population 336.

Red Cloud, where Charles Cather moved his family in 1885, was typical of the small towns that dotted the plains. Regardless of the names she gave them or the state in which she placed them, the small towns in Cather's works all derived closely from Red Cloud. (Red Cloud was named for a leader of the Sioux; Black Hawk was a leader of the Sac and Fox tribes.) Cather sketched Red Cloud in the opening paragraph of *O Pioneers!*, and she described it at length in *Song of the Lark*. The center of town consisted largely of one- and two-story commercial buildings, several of red brick, stretching for a few blocks along both sides of a main street that ran north and south. On all sides of the commercial district lay residences with large yards, sizable gardens, and chicken pens. The county courthouse sat near the north end of town, and the Burlington railway station was at the south end. The railroad tracks ran east and west, parallel to the Republican River to the south.

Given typical family sizes in the late nineteenth century, a town of fewer than two thousand residents could be expected to contain about a thousand adults and some four hundred households; Red Cloud was no exception to prevailing patterns. As Cather suggests in *My Ántonia*, all the permanent residents in such a small community knew one another, if not as friends, at least as acquaintances. The limited number of offices, stores, shops, churches, and social organizations meant that one constantly encountered the same people in different social or economic roles; one saw the merchant in church on Sunday, the carpenter at the Odd Fellows lodge on Wednesday, and the mayor at the hardware store on Friday. Such a town held few secrets; as Ántonia learned, choice morsels of gossip were savored over dozens of back fences throughout town. Town residents knew which women were pregnant, which lawyers were unscrupulous, which merchants were generous, and which men were womanizers.

The small towns of the Nebraska countryside existed primarily to sell goods to the surrounding farmers and to provide the farmers with a place to market crops. In American agriculture, from colonial times onward, credit was crucial to success, because a farmer's expenses are most heavy at planting time in the spring and income is concentrated at harvest time in the fall. Not surprisingly, the banker or loan agent was an important figure in such a credit-based economy; those who dealt fairly received due respect, but others (like Wick Cutter) had a reputation for treating their clients with all the tenderness of a python. Merchants, too, played an important role in supplying goods on credit, waiting for harvest time for their payment. Red Cloud, like most towns in its region, had a grain elevator, for loading grain into railroad cars; there farmers dealt with grain buyers (like Christian Harling), whom they sometimes accused of cheating them of the full value of their grain. The railroad (Larry Donovan's employer) was seen both as crucial to the economic success of the town and the countryside and as a powerful monopoly, charging whatever it wished to ship grain to market. Those (like Peter Krajiek) who sold land to aspiring farmers usually had their offices in town, and they too were regarded as both boon and bane. (Hicks, chs. 1 and 3, summarizes farmers' complaints about railroads, moneylenders, and land speculators; Cherny, "Willa Cather," presents an analysis of the railroad, moneylender, and land speculator in *My Ántonia*.)

The university plays no role in Ántonia's story, but it is important for Jim as it exposes him to classical culture and leads him (like Cather) away from Nebraska. During the years when Cather lived in Lincoln, the size of the student body nearly tripled, making the university fourteenth in size in the nation. The university's historian has described the 1890s as "the most interesting period" in its history, "for during these years it was transformed from a small frontier college into a major institution" (Manley 111–12). Lincoln, with its 55,154 residents, was a far larger place than Cather had previously known; it had more than quadrupled in size between 1880 and 1890, becoming the fourth-largest city west of the Missouri. There Cather met people with broad cultural interests that stimulated her developing creative impulses, and she explored opportunities for writing that led her first to Pittsburgh in 1896 and later to New York City.

In an essay titled "My First Novels (There Were Two)," Cather noted that when she first began to write about the Scandinavians and Czechs of Nebraska, in 1912 or so, she did so for herself, ignoring prevailing literary conventions regarding setting and characterization. She added that "a New York critic voiced a general opinion when he said: 'I simply don't care a damn what happens in Nebraska, no matter who writes about it' " (94). That critic may have changed his mind after the appearance of Cather's first novel set in Nebraska, and he must certainly have done so after the appearance of *My Ántonia*, her best-known novel and perhaps her best work. Because Cather set her works in Nebraska, people did care what happened there.

The Making and Reception of *My Ántonia*

James Woodress

Willa Cather visited her family in Red Cloud in the summer of 1916. Sometime in September or October she must have driven out into the Bohemian country, as she usually did, to visit her old friend Annie Pavelka. This may have been the trip that Jim Burden takes in the final book of *My Ántonia*, when he sees Ántonia, now middle-aged, married, and surrounded by her large brood of children. The idea of her novel had not yet come to her, however, and she spent the fall working on "The Blue Mesa," which later became "Tom Outland's Story" in *The Professor's House*. Two months after getting to Red Cloud she was still making notes for it, but the materials seemed intractable. Her summer visit to the Southwest, which had inspired the story, was too recent for use and needed to remain a few years in the deep well of her unconscious.

In one sense Cather had been preparing to write *My Ántonia* for a third of a century. She had known the model for its fictional heroine, Annie Sadilek, later Pavelka, ever since she was a child in Red Cloud, and the story of Annie's father's suicide was one of the first stories she had heard on arriving in Nebraska from Virginia. As she looked back in her old age, she felt that the character of Ántonia was the embodiment of all her feelings about the early immigrants in the prairie country, and it seemed then that she must have been destined to write this novel if she ever wrote anything. When Margaret Lawrence's *School of Feminity* appeared in 1936 with a perceptive chapter on Cather, she agreed with its thesis: she could write successfully only when she wrote about people or places she loved (letter to Sherwood, 28 June 1939). The characters she created could be cranky or queer or foolhardy or rash, but they had to have something to them that thrilled her and warmed her heart.

Annie Sadilek Pavelka was such a person. In 1921 Cather told an interviewer, Eleanor Hinman, that one of the people who had interested her most when she was a child was the Bohemian hired girl who worked for one of their neighbors. "She was one of the truest artists I ever knew in the keenness and sensitiveness of her enjoyment, in her love of people and in her willingness to take pains" (Bohlke 44). After Cather left journalism and began writing novels, she visited the Bohemian country during her summer visits to Red Cloud and saw Annie and her family on their farm. The lives of the Pavelkas and their neighbors seemed to her like stories out of a book that went on and on year after year like *War and Peace*. Whenever she went back to Nebraska, her friends filled her in on the details of the narrative that had taken place in her absence.

Once she decided to make Annie the central figure in her novel, she had to work out the narrative technique to present her. She chose a first-person point of view because she believed that novels of feeling, such as *My Ántonia*, were best narrated by a character in the story. Novels of action, she thought, should be told in the third person, using the omniscient author as narrator. But who should the first-person teller of the tale be? She told Hinman that she rejected Annie's lover as narrator because "my Ántonia deserved something better than the *Saturday Evening Post* sort of stuff" (Bohlke 44). But she wanted a male narrator because, as she explained, most of what she knew about Annie came from talks with young men: "She had a fascination for them, and they used to be with her whenever they could. They had to manage it on the sly because she was only a hired girl" (44). Thus Cather created as narrator Jim Burden, whose age, experience, and personal history closely parallel her own. He tells the story as an adult reminiscence. Actually, Cather had been using male narrators in her short fiction for a long time, and there was no novelty for her in this invention.

Once she had decided on her narrative voice and the first-person method, she further planned to avoid any formal structuring of the novel. Jim Burden's memories, which, of course, were her memories, would shape the narrative. She would avoid the opportunities for melodrama that the materials certainly contained and dwell lightly on the incidents that most novelists would ordinarily emphasize. The story would be made up of little, everyday happenings for the most part, for such events made up the bulk of most people's lives. It would be the other side of the rug, the pattern that is supposed not to count. There would be no love affair, no courtship, no marriage, no broken heart, no struggle for success. "I knew I'd ruin my material if I put it in the usual fictional pattern. I just used it the way I thought absolutely true" (Bohlke 77). The result was the creation of a novel that gives the impression of real autobiography rather than fiction. Since the invented narrator is not a professional writer, the apparent artlessness of his memories seems perfectly logical, and readers are willing to suspend their belief that they are in the presence of a perfectly controlled art.

More than most writers, Cather presents readers with the chance to compare biographical data with its transmutation into art. There is a great deal more factual basis in *My Ántonia* than the bare story outline of the title character and the narrator. The town of Black Hawk is Red Cloud, and the Nebraska farmlands where Cather first lived when her family moved to Nebraska provide the locale. Ántonia's farmhouse still stands in the country north of Red Cloud, with the fruit cave a few yards from the back door. Jim's grandparents were drawn from Cather's grandparents; the entire Miner family, neighbors of the Cathers after they moved into Red Cloud, play roles in the story; and Herbert Bates, one of Cather's professors at the University of Nebraska, appears as Gaston Cleric, Jim's college teacher. Minor figures and events are also rooted in actuality. The black pianist Blind d'Arnault, who plays in Black Hawk, was drawn from a real Blind Tom, whom Cather heard in Lincoln, and a Blind Boone, whom she probably heard in Red Cloud. The visitor to the town today can see the home of the original of Wick Cutter, a loan shark named Bentley, who apparently was as evil and unsavory as Cather makes him. The hotel-keeping Mrs. Gardener in the novel was a real Mrs. Holland, and the man who fathered Ántonia's first child out of wedlock was James William Murphy.

After the novel appeared, Cather was pestered by literal-minded readers wanting to know where she got this and where she got that. The people in Red Cloud were continually playing guessing games with her characters and incidents. It exasperated her, but she should have expected her drama of memory to provoke this kind of a response. Sometimes she was patient and discussed her sources with friends—sometimes she even answered letters from students—but usually her reaction was annoyance. Often she did not know where she got things, and after *My Ántonia* was published, her father pointed out half a dozen incidents based on things she had done, seen, or heard of with him, all of which she thought she had invented.

One such episode was the story within a story of the two Russians, Pavel and Peter, and the wolves. It illustrates the way Cather's creative imagination worked, as she fashioned her fictional materials from her memories. The wolf story probably came both from herself and from hearing the tale in her father's presence. It is a tale that folklorists have collected from the oral tradition of Nebraska immigrants in the identical version that Cather uses (see Schach). She no doubt heard the story from the farm people she knew. At the same time, her idea that she made up the story perhaps comes from having seen a well-known painting by Paul Powis depicting wolves attacking a sledge or from a poem by Browning, "Ivan Ivanovitch," which tells a similar tale. Since Cather took a yearlong course in Browning at the University of Nebraska, it seems reasonable to conclude that she remembered the poem.

Cather always insisted that her characters were not drawn from real life but were only suggested by people she knew, or that they were composites. You can never get it through people's heads, she wrote Carrie Sherwood, that a story is made out of an emotion or an excitement and is not made out of the legs and arms and faces of one's friends (27 Jan. 1934). One exception to this assertion, however, was the character of Mrs. Harling. Cather was working on "The Hired Girls" when she read of Mrs. Miner's death in a Red Cloud newspaper. She made a deliberate effort to remember her tricks of voice and gesture, and she made Mrs. Harling a clear little snapshot of Mrs. Miner as she first knew her (see letter to Sherwood, 29 Oct. 1917). All the mothers in her fiction, she admitted, had a little of Mrs. Miner in them, but this fictional portrait was unique, and she hoped the Miner daughters would like it. She dedicated the novel to Carrie and Irene "in memory of affections old and true." The older one grows, she added, the clearer one's early impressions somehow become.

When the novel appeared in late September 1918, the country was preoccupied with the final days of World War I, which ended with the armistice on 11 November. The book did not become a best-seller, though it sold moderately well, passing the five-thousand mark by Christmas and reaching about eight thousand by the time it had been out a year. Cather's royalties for the first twelve months amounted to less than two thousand dollars, however, not enough to support her while she wrote another novel. By the end of 1919 it was only selling five hundred copies a year, and by late 1920 it was briefly unavailable due to a printers' strike. But the reviewers were nearly unanimous in their praise and recognized the novel as a significant contribution to American letters. Ferris Greenslet, Cather's editor at Houghton Mifflin, recorded in his memoirs that when he read the book in manuscript he experienced "the most thrilling shock of recognition of the real thing of any manuscript" he ever received (Greenslet, *Under* 119).

H. L. Mencken led the chorus with two reviews in consecutive issues of the *Smart Set* in 1919. *My Ántonia*, he wrote, was merely one more "step upward in the career of a writer who has labored with the utmost patience and industry, and won every foot of the way by hard work" ("Mainly Fiction" 140). He praised her earlier novels, but *My Ántonia* was a sudden leap forward, "not only the best [novel] done by Miss Cather herself, but also one of the best that any American has ever done." Then he continued with the utmost enthusiasm:

> It is intelligent; it is moving. The means that appear in it are means perfectly adapted to its end. Its people are unquestionably real. Its background is brilliantly vivid. It has form, grace, good literary manners. In a word, it is a capital piece of writing, and it will be heard of long after the baroque balderdash now touted on the "book pages" is forgotten. (140)

Randolph Bourne, whom Cather thought the best reviewer in the business, was equally pleased: "Miss Cather convinces because she knows her story and carries it along with the surest touch. It has all the artistic simplicity of material that has been patiently shaped until everything irrelevant has been scraped away." He concluded his review with the opinion that Cather "has taken herself out of the rank of provincial writers and given us something we can fairly class with the modern literary art the world over that is earnestly and richly interpreting the spirit of youth." The New York *Sun* carried a long, anonymous notice that particularly pleased Cather because the reviewer really understood what she was doing and made all the right comments. "The most extraordinary thing about *My Ántonia* is the author's surrender of the usual methods of fiction in telling her story" (Rev. of *My Ántonia*). It could have been made into an exciting, dramatic novel, but then it would have been just another piece of fiction. Her method left the reader with the conviction of absolute authenticity. "You picked up *My Ántonia* to read a novel (love story, of course; hope it's a good one) and find yourself enthralled by autobiography."

As time went on, however, Cather reorganized her memory of the novel's reception. Four years later she had convinced herself that the critics took two years to discover the book; they didn't like it at first because it had no structure. By 1941 she was writing an old friend that the New York reviewers always lament the fact that her new book (whichever it might be) is a marked decline from the previous one. Logically, she said, she should have reached the vanishing point long ago. She had read practically all the reviews of *My Ántonia* from coast to coast, and only two were favorable. All the others said the book was formless and would be of interest only to the Nebraska State Historical Society (Sergeant 244).

This hostile stance was Cather's characteristic attitude toward critics, but whether or not there was justification for it, Cather always had many enthusiastic readers. Twelve years after the novel appeared, Greenslet sent Justice Oliver Wendell Holmes a copy. The old jurist, then eighty-nine, wrote Greenslet that the book

> lifts me to all my superlatives. I have not had such a sensation for a long time. To begin with I infinitely respect the author's taking her own environment and not finding it necessary to look for her scenes in Paris or London. I think it a prime mark of a real gift to realize that any piece of the universe may be made poetical if seen by a poet. But to be more concrete, the result seems to me a wonderful success. It has unfailing charm, perhaps not to be defined; a beautiful tenderness, a vivifying imagination that transforms but does not distort or exaggerate—order, proportion.   (qtd. in Sergeant 245)

The next year Greenslet sent Holmes *Death Comes for the Archbishop*, and after having his secretary read the novel to him, Holmes wrote Cather directly: "I think you have the gift of transforming touch. What to another would be prose, under your hand becomes poetry without ceasing to be truth. Among the changes of old age one is that novels are apt to bore me, and I owe you a debt for two exceptions, both of which gave me delight" (245).

Few novels are likely to be read longer than *My Ántonia*. It combines character, theme, setting, myth, and incident into a narrative of great emotional power. The prose is limpid and evocative, the product of Cather's nearly three decades of learning to master her instrument. For many readers it is her greatest work. She knew that she had done well with this book and told Carrie Sherwood in 1938 that "the best thing I've done is *My Ántonia*. I feel I've made a contribution to American letters with that book" (qtd. in Mildred R. Bennett, *World* 203). On other occasions she gave this precedence to *Death Comes for the Archbishop*. In May 1943 Greenslet wrote her that *My Ántonia* was a novel to cherish. It had sold twenty-five hundred copies in the previous year, and he didn't think there was another novel published a quarter of a century before that had done so well. These were all copies in the regular hardcover edition, and this was in the middle of the war. Through the years the novel has always sold steadily and never has been out of print.[1]

NOTE

[1]This article is adapted from my book *Willa Cather: A Literary Life*.

The People, the Place, and the Times:
A Lexicon for *My Ántonia*

Philip L. Gerber

advertising cards: small cardboards that carry pictures and other information about products; they were handed out by stores or salespersons and often were collected by children as a hobby.

aigrette: the feathers of the white egret, much used in women's hats in the late nineteenth century.

alcohol lamp: an early form of illumination, using alcohol as a fuel.

anarchist: one who advocates the overthrow of civil government; a political term of derision.

Anderson, Mary: American stage actress (1859–1940) famous for playing Shakespearean roles.

arroyo: Spanish term for gulch or gully; a dry streambed.

asylum: the common name for the public establishment in which persons with mental troubles were locked away from society in the days before psychiatric treatment was available.

badger: a carnivorous burrowing animal with short thick legs and long claws; the hair was used for paintbrushes.

Bad Lands: eroded arid lands in northwestern Nebraska.

batching: to live alone, as a bachelor. Usually pertains to a male settler, but either a man or a woman might "batch it" on the prairie.

bed-ticking: strong linen or cotton fabric woven in white and blue stripes for mattress covers.

Black Hawk: a fictional name for Red Cloud, Nebraska.

blacklisted: to be ostracized from employment on the railroad.

bobs: wooden runners for a sled. In snowy weather certain wagons could be outfitted with bobs.

Bohemia: a central European country, part of Austria-Hungary during the nineteenth century and, after World War I, a part of Czechoslovakia. Many Bohemians settled on the Great Plains of the United States.

Bohunk: a common name for Bohemians, often used derisively.

Bokhara [carpet]: an oriental carpet distinguished by its red, orange, and deep brown colors.

Bouncing Bet: the common soapwort of the Pink family, whose flower resembles a carnation.

Brindisi: a city on the eastern coast of Italy.

brocade: silk or other fine fabric woven with gold and silver threads or ornamented with raised flowers and foliage.

brood-sow: a female pig, kept for breeding new stock.

buffalo: the large bison that ranged over the plains before settlement days.

Buffalo hide was used for leather and the buffalo pelt for lap robes, over-coats, and bed coverings.

buffalo grass: a short, sweet grass two to four inches in height. It covered much of the plains, and the buffalo herds grazed on it in presettler times.

buffalo-pea: the buffalo berry, a shrub with acid edible red berries.

bull-snake: the midwestern name for the most common of United States constrictors. Nonvenomous, it grows to five to seven feet and is yellowish in color, with black blotches on its back. Unlike the rattler, the bull-snake is considered an asset by farmers. Its heavy nose plate aids it in entering the burrows of the small rodents such as rats, mice, squirrels, and gophers on which it feeds.

cabinet work: the making of fine wooden furniture.

calico: cotton fabric on which the colored design is printed rather than woven.

Camille: a popular name applied to Marguerite, heroine of *La Traviata*, because of her love for the camellia flower.

candle-moulds: before liquid fuels were available, candles were made at home, often of tallow, and were cast in a metal mold.

capote: from the Italian for a long cloak with a hood; in *My Ántonia* the term applies to the feathers of a duck.

carded wool: wool brushed with a wire-toothed instrument to disentangle and arrange its fibers; the first step in producing thread for weaving.

catalpa: a tree native to the eastern United States and brought to Nebraska by immigrants. It has very large leaves and showy white blossoms that develop long seed pods.

chaff: waste husks of grain removed by the threshing or winnowing process.

chased [silver]: ornamented by embossing or cutting away parts.

cholera: an often fatal intestinal disease with symptoms of vomiting and diarrhea.

Christmas melon: a melon so called because it will keep through the autumn until the Christmas season.

cigar maker: some immigrants, especially among the Bohemians, were trained in cigar making and set up such businesses in western towns.

Circle City: a settlement on the Yukon River in Alaska, important during the Klondike Gold Rush.

colic: pain due to gaseous distention of the intestines; in sheep, the intestines were pierced to release the gas.

Commedia: The Divine Comedy, a world classic written by Dante Alighieri.

commercial traveler: a sales representative of a large firm, who traveled from town to town taking orders for goods.

conductor: a railroad official in charge of a specific train. Conductors took tickets, called stations, and the like.

corncakes: a kind of corn bread; also called johnnycake.

Coronado, Francisco Vásquez de: a Spanish explorer (c. 1510–54) who explored western America and in 1541 led an expedition northward from Texas into Kansas. He may also have reached the Nebraska area.

corral: Spanish term for an animal pen, especially one for horses.

cottonwood: a form of poplar and one of the few trees native to Nebraska, growing in draws and ravines. A large rough tree with glossy leaves, it provided settlers with firewood and logs for building. Its seeds are covered with abundant cottonlike hairs that the wind carries to new locations.

Count of Monte Cristo: a popular play, based on the novel by Alexandre Dumas. James O'Neill, father of the playwright Eugene O'Neill, toured in this vehicle for many years, a fact that his son exploited in *A Long Day's Journey into Night*.

coyote: a wild, doglike, carnivorous animal that preys on sheep; also called the prairie wolf.

[to] cut bands: before a sheaf of grain could be threshed, the wire bands that bound it had to be cut. See: *shock*.

Daly, John Augustin: an American playwright, critic, and theatrical manager (1839–99).

Dante [Alighieri]: Florentine poet (1265–1321) who wrote *The Divine Comedy*.

Dawson City: a city on the Yukon River in Yukon Territory, Canada. Now called Dawson. The Yukon and Klondike rivers meet here.

day-coach: a comfortable coach for first-class railroad passengers, but lacking facilities for sleeping, dining, and the like.

depot: the train station where passengers alighted or boarded, where tickets were sold, freight loaded, and so on.

drake: a male duck.

draw: the lower portions of rolling land between the rises; the draws provided natural draining channels for water.

drygoods store: a store that sold clothing, hardware, utensils, furniture, fabric, and the like.

dugout: the most primitive form of dwelling on the plains. A cave was dug into the side of a gully and faced with sod or board, providing basic protection from the elements. The Shimerdas live in such a dwelling when they first come to Nebraska.

earth-owl: the burrowing owl of North America (*Speotyto cunicularia*), which lives in holes, often in company with the prairie dog.

Field, Marshall: the owner of Marshall Field's, Chicago's most prestigious department store.

finger-bowl: a saucerlike glass bowl used in polite society for rinsing the fingers after dining; each diner was provided a separate finger bowl.

fire-box: the portion of the railroad locomotive where coal is burned to produce steam under the boiler for power.

fire-break: a strip of land freshly plowed around homes or fields for the purpose of breaking the progress of a prairie fire, always a hazard on the plains of Nebraska.

Fireman's Hall: a prominent structure in any western town; where fire-fighting equipment was kept and where the fire bell was rung to alert volunteers. Also used as a social center for town activities.

flat table land: a description of the western plains; relatively high and flat land, ideally suited to grain farming.

flaxen: the color of flax, source of linen; a creamy off-white.

freshet: a stream of fresh water, particularly one that overflows from a stream after heavy rains.

gaillardia: a perennial plant with daisylike flowers of mixed orange, red, and deep brown.

gelding: a castrated male horse.

General Passenger Agent: a railroad official in charge of a local depot, particularly concerned with facilitating passenger travel, issuing tickets, and the like.

gingham: a cotton fabric woven in stripes or checks. The pattern is not printed; rather, the threads are dyed before weaving.

Gladstone, William Ewart: British statesman (1809–98) who served as prime minister under Queen Victoria on four occasions.

goods box: a box of wood used for shipping food, clothing, equipment, and the like, common before the advent of pasteboard cartons. One would obtain such a box from the dry-goods store.

grain elevator: a tall wooden structure for storing grain; in every plains town the elevator was the dominant structure, standing beside the railroad track, where grain could be emptied into cars for shipment to the East.

ground-cherry: a low herbaceous plant. The seed pod, a well-flavored berry the size of a cherry, is eaten. Also called strawberry tomato.

guinea hen: an African bird, related to the pheasant, whose plumage of dark gray is dotted with small white spots.

gully: an eroded channel worn into the earth by running water of streams and rivers.

gunny-sack: a sack of a strong coarse fabric made of jute fibers, used for sacking rough crops such as potatoes and turnips.

hare: a rabbit; the fur of the prairie hare turns a protective white in winter.

hartshorn: a solution of ammonia in water, with acrid fumes.

Hastings: a city in south central Nebraska, forty miles north of Red Cloud (Black Hawk); an important junction on the Burlington Railroad.

heat lightning: a common weather phenomenon of the Midwest, lightning without rain.

hitching bar: a horizontal wooden pole to which the reins of a horse are tied while the owner conducts business.

horsehair: a strong, glossy fabric woven from the mane and tail hairs of a horse, used in covering chairs and sofas.

horse-sense: strong common sense.

hot bricks: on cold nights, common building bricks were heated and taken into bed as warming devices.

husk: to husk corn is to remove the external covering or envelope from an ear.

immigrant car: a low-fare passenger car provided by a railroad expressly to carry settlers to the West. The cars were roughly furnished with wooden benches and bunks and, at times, crude facilities for cooking meals.

ironweed: a tall weed with purple flowers (*Veronica noveboracensis*).

jack-rabbit: a large, long-eared western rabbit noted for its speed.

Jefferson, Joseph: American actor (1829–1905) famous for the title role in *Rip Van Winkle*, the play in which he toured for many years, beginning in 1865.

Klondike: a river in Yukon Territory, Canada. It joins the Yukon River at Dawson. In 1896 gold was discovered near here at Bonanza Creek, beginning the Klondike Gold Rush.

knocking down fares: an offense that involves taking cash for tickets and not reporting it to the railroad; a form of embezzlement.

kolach [also kolatch and kolace]: a bun of rich, sweet, yeast-leavened dough filled with jam or fruit.

lariat pin: lariat is a Spanish term (*la reata*) for a long, slender rope of hide used to lasso or picket a horse; the pin is a metallic stake driven into the ground, to which the lariat is fastened.

Lincoln: the state capital, in southeastern Nebraska; seat of the University of Nebraska.

lithograph: a color print made by drawing on a stone and pressing paper to the surface, one of the earliest methods for mass production of color pictures.

livery stable: an establishment where horses were boarded for visitors and where horses and buggies could be rented.

livery team: a team of horses rented from a livery stable.

Martha: an opera by Friedrich von Flotow (1812–83), also called *Richmond Fair*; first performed in 1847.

Masonic Hall: the hall of the Masonic lodge where the Masons held meetings, services, and social functions; the Masonic Hall was a prominent feature of most western towns of any size.

mastiff: a breed of large dogs, noted for their strength and courage.

meal mush: a porridge made from corn meal; one of the simplest and least expensive forms of nourishment.

milkweed: a plant abounding in a milky juice. Its seed pods are attached to strands of long, silky down that are carried on the wind.

mimosa: a leguminous plant; the sensitive plants belong to this family.

Mormons: members of Joseph Smith's Mormon faith, also called the Church of Jesus Christ of Latter-Day Saints, founded in 1830. Much persecuted in the East, the Mormons traveled from Nauvoo, Illinois, to Utah in 1846–47, passing through Nebraska on their way and making winter quarters in Florence, Nebraska.

mulatto: of mixed blood, white and black.

Niobrara: the chief river in northern Nebraska, running most of the way across the state.

"Oh, Promise Me!": a popular song of the late nineteenth century, often sung at weddings.

oil cloth: cloth treated with oil and paint to make one of the first types of waterproof plastic, used for garments, floor coverings, tablecloths, suitcases, and the like.

Opera House: an auditorium in which civic meetings and entertainments were held. Traveling theatrical troupes played there. In Red Cloud (Black Hawk), Willa Cather gave her high school valedictory speech in the Opera House.

opium: a narcotic made from the juice of the white poppy and often used in medicine for its pain-relieving qualities.

ox: a full-grown bovine male, castrated.

Paestum: an ancient city in Lucania, Italy, southwest of Palermo, Sicily. Originally founded in 600 BC as the Greek city of Poseidonia, it is noted for its Greek ruins.

peck: a unit of measurement, eight quarts or one-quarter bushel.

pinafore: an apron for a child, to protect the dress.

Plattsmouth: a town in eastern Nebraska where the Platte River meets the Missouri.

Pompeii: a town in southern Italy on the Bay of Naples destroyed in AD 79 by a volcanic eruption of Mount Vesuvius and excavated in the late nineteenth century.

porter: an attendant on a railroad, especially in a Pullman car, who saw to the general needs of passengers.

Prague: a city in central Europe, once the capital of Bohemia and now the capital of Czechoslovakia.

prairie (unbroken): the western land that had never been plowed and that could not be planted until the sod was "broken" with a sod plow.

prairie dog: a small rodent native to the plains. Prairie dogs live in connecting burrows as described in *My Ántonia*.

progressive euchre: a card game in which the jack is high card and the seven is low. In progressive euchre, pairs of players compete, the winning couple at one table moving on to play the winners of an adjoining table, this process continuing until only one couple is left undefeated.

Pussy Wants a Corner: a children's game in which players hold on to trees, except for one who is "it." On a signal, all run to claim other trees. "It" tries to reach a tree and claim it before another player, in which case that player becomes "it."

quail: the American partridge, a game bird native to the prairies.

quarter: a quarter of a section of land, comprising 160 acres. See: *section*.

quinsy: inflammation of the throat affecting the tonsils.

reaping hook: a hand sickle with a hook-shaped blade for cutting grass or grain.

Rigoletto: an opera by Giuseppe Verdi (1831–1901) based on Victor Hugo's novel *Le roi s'amuse*. First performed in 1851.

ringdove: a wild pigeon.

Ringstrasse: a prominent area of Vienna, Austria, established by Emperor Franz Josef I in 1857. The Ringstrasse thoroughfare is a circular road surrounding the central city and lined with important buildings and parks. The Ringstrasse was completed in 1913.

Robin Hood: a comic opera by Reginald De Koven (1859–1920) based on the tales of Robin Hood the outlaw. First performed in 1890.

rose mallow: a form of hollyhock.

roundhouse: a structure in important junction towns where a railroad locomotive could be turned (as at a forty-five-degree angle) to be put on a different track. In the roundhouse at Red Cloud, the engine from the southbound Hastings train could be turned to return to Hastings or to join a west- or eastbound train.

Russian thistle: a thistle growing in a globelike formation; when dry it breaks from its stem and rolls across the prairie on the wind, piling against houses and fences. Also called the tumbleweed.

sachet powder: powder of flowers, packaged as a scent in linen and lingerie drawers.

saddle-bags: a pair of bags, often made of leather, joined by straps so that each hangs on one side of the saddle.

saloon: a drinking establishment, usually with a male-only clientele, where liquor and beer are served; a bar.

scrub oak: a rough, low oak native to the prairie.

section: in the West, land was marked off in townships, each containing thirty-six sections one square mile in size. The section lines refer to the boundary lines of such a unit of land.

sheeting: cotton cloth woven double width for bed sheets.

shelving bank: the bank of a gully, creek, or river, cut through time by running water. The Shimerdas' dugout house is in a shelving bank.

shock: a pile of twelve to sixteen sheaves set up in the field to dry before the grain is threshed. A sheaf is a quantity of cut grain stalks bound together with a wire band.

shoemaker's wax: wax for rubbing threads, strengthening them for use not only in shoes but in leather goods such as saddles.

siding: a side track, or turnout, of a railroad where cars can be stationed for loading and unloading or to wait for attachment to a connecting train.

Skagway: a city in southern Alaska, north of Juneau, important in the Klondike Gold Rush.

smartweed: an acrid plant that produces a smarting sensation when it touches the skin.

sod: the virgin prairie turf, thickly matted with grass roots.

sod corn: usually the first crop grown in newly turned sod; it could be hand sown, and during the growing season the weather would break the sod, separating grass roots from soil in preparation for a second plowing before grain could be planted.

sod house: a house built of sod strips usually twelve inches wide and thirty-six inches long and about four inches thick. The walls were built of these strips laid in alternate directions for solidity; a roof of tree branches was laid over the walls and also covered with sod.

sod plough: a plow with a special plowshare for turning the virgin sod; it cut perhaps four inches deep and laid a strip of sod on its back.

sombrero hat: a man's broad-brimmed hat worn in Mexico and in the American Southwest, especially by ranchers.

sorghum: the Chinese sugar cane, a coarse grass with sweet juice.

sorghum molasses: the juice of sorghum, boiled down to a thick, sweet substance, used by settlers as a sugar substitute.

Squaw Creek: a creek west of Black Hawk (the name may be fictional).

Statius, Publius Papinius: Roman epic poet (AD 45–96).

steam threshing machine: the earliest mechanism for threshing (removing the seeds of wheat, oats, and the like from the chaff). It was powered by a separate steam engine that could be connected to it.

steer: a male ox, raised for beef and often castrated. A steer is from two to four years in age; when full-grown it is called an ox.

Stinking Water: a creek in western Nebraska; it joins the Republican River near Culberson.

sulky plough: a plow with wheels and a seat for the driver.

Sunday-school cards: cards with a religious picture and message handed out to Sunday-school students for their edification. They were often collected as a hobby.

tallow: the fat of sheep or oxen, used in making candles.

telegrapher: a telegraph operator, stationed in the local railroad depot. An important post, as telegrams were the only rapid means of communication on the western frontier.

Tithonus: a Greek mythological character who was beloved by Eos (Aurora), the goddess of the dawn; through her offices he was granted immortality. Hence the expression "bride of Tithonus" refers to the dawn.

topaz: a semiprecious stone light brown in color.

trap: a horse-drawn wagon.

Traviata [*La Traviata*]: an opera by Giuseppe Verdi (1813–1901), based on *La dame aux camélias* by Alexandre Dumas fils. First performed in 1853.

Ukraine: a constituent republic of the Soviet Union located on the far western edge of the USSR. The name derives from *u* (at) and *krai* (edge) to mean "on the edge, or border," and often has been referred to in that sense as "the Ukraine," an area known for its wheat production. During the reign of Catherine the Great, many German farmers were invited to settle in the Ukraine, and during the latter years of the nineteenth century a number of these emigrated to the United States, settling in the great-plains territories where they found farmlands comparable in terrain and fertility to those they had left behind them.

Vienna: the capital of Austria.

violet sachet: the dried blossoms of the violet, kept in a packet for scent.

Virgil [Publius Vergilius Maro]: Roman poet (70 BC–AD 19) who wrote the

Latin epic the *Aeneid,* concerning the adventures of the Greek hero Aeneas following the fall of Troy.

Waymore Junction: now Wymore, in southeastern Nebraska, once an important railroad junction.

west-bound train: soon after 1880 the Burlington tracks were completed from Red Cloud to Denver, and it is on this route that the westbound train would travel.

whiplash: the lash of a whip, braided of cords or leather thongs.

Wilber: a town in southeastern Nebraska north of Beatrice.

windlass well: a well furnished with a mechanism for raising and lowering the bucket by winding the rope on a reel.

windmill: because of the scarcity of water, the windmill was essential to western settlement: the turning blades of the windmill pumped water from wells drilled into underground aquifers.

wire woman: a dress form constructed of wire on which fabric can be draped. Because the form corresponds to the measurements of the garment's eventual wearer, the "wire woman" can be used for preliminary fittings.

work-horse: a sturdy horse used for farm work, as distinguished from a riding horse.

yoke-mate: one of a pair of horses fastened together for pulling a load.

Young, Brigham: a Mormon leader (1801–77) who became the head of the Church of Latter-Day Saints on the death of founder Joseph Smith in 1844. He led the exodus of Mormons from Nauvoo, Illinois, to Utah in 1846–47.

Yukon: a river that runs from southern Alaska into Yukon Territory, Canada. Also, an area of the Northwest surrounding the river, site of the Klondike Gold Rush.

TEACHING THE LITERARY AND PHILOSOPHICAL TRADITIONS

My Ántonia as Pastoral

David Stouck

I have always found *My Ántonia* a difficult novel to teach. How does one generate interest in a seemingly simple, straightforward narrative written in a century when ambiguity and incoherence are prized features of the novel as an art form? Ironically, the difficulty in teaching *My Ántonia* derives precisely from the fact that it is written in a mode that celebrates simplicity—the pastoral. In its archetypal form a pastoral describes a retreat that expresses the human dream of a simplified, harmonious life from which the complexities of society and natural process (age, disease, and death) are eliminated. Pastoral appears when city life becomes too complicated and hurried and the individual, weary at heart, tries to evade its pressures by escaping, in thought at least, to the country. Thus we have a literary tradition that locates innocence and happiness in a rural retreat, a tradition that equates the golden age with the garden of Eden. (See Poggioli on the pastoral mode; Randall, "Willa Cather.")

But pastoral, I argue, is more complex than simply a longing to live in the country. At its heart is a Wordsworthian vision of the good life that derives from childhood, one in which there is no separation of subject and object, no self and other, where the individual is joined to the world in a maternal embrace. Pastoral is the mode of art based on memory and the desire to recover that place and time when life was ideally ordered and secure, when the child was in communion with nature and watched over by loving guardians, frequently grandparents. Consequently, in pastoral art there is a preoccupation with arresting time, for the passage of time moves the adult away from childhood, innocence, and happiness. Similarly, the pastoral imagination attempts to exclude sex, because sexual awakening marks the end of childhood and the entrance into the responsibilities and cares of adult life. (Gelfant is particularly relevant in this light.)

A biographical note at this point helps relate these generalizations to the author. The central idea I draw from the biographical material is that one can view Willa Cather, a sensitive and lonely child, uprooted from her Virginia birthplace at age nine, as engaged in a lifelong search for "home." It is the special measure that she placed on settings in all her works and that made her imaginative return to Nebraska imperative. What makes Cather a classic writer, I argue, is that this quest, which allows her in turn to pronounce judgment on and to celebrate America, is rehearsed in narrative modes and patterns as old as story telling itself. One reads Cather's American stories and is referred back to their venerable lineage in classical epic, romance, satire, and pastoral. One also hears echoed the stories of the great European novelists, for Cather held a cyclical vision of human history's repeating itself. In *My Ántonia* she told the specific and uniquely detailed story of a Bohemian immigrant family pioneering in the American West, but the mood and the larger significance of that story are directed by quotations from Vergil.

Willa Cather began writing *My Ántonia* in 1916. Bereaved by the marriage of her close friend Isabelle McClung and deeply disturbed by the war in Europe, Cather turned to writing a novel about a happier time, about her own growing up in the early pioneer days of the Middle West. In the first edition Cather formally identified her book as a pastoral by illustrating the title page with an Arcadian Pan playing his pipes. And there for an epigraph she quotes from one of Vergil's *Georgics*, *Optima dies . . . prima fugit* ("The best days . . . are the first to flee"). The epigraph is important because it locates happiness and the good life in childhood, but it also states that they soon disappear. Thus we are directed to the central tension in pastoral art —namely, that the good life being celebrated can never be experienced again because its reality is only a memory.

The art of *My Ántonia* resides, I suggest, in a structure informed by that central paradox in pastoral. It is best described as a creative tension between the novel's content and its form. As Jim Burden tells his life story, the tale revolving around Ántonia, he attempts to shape a happy and secure world out of the past, celebrating the world of the pioneers and romanticizing any disturbing and unpleasant memories. Yet the novel's form, its chronology in five parts, each of which represents a significant change in time and place in Jim's life, invalidates the narrator's emotional quest, for the passing of time continually moves the narrator away from the happy point of early childhood and brings the melancholy recognition that he can never recover the past. Having made these generalizations about pastoral, Willa Cather, and the structure of *My Ántonia*, I proceed to examine the parts of the text itself, the introduction and five books, in the light of this tension between the desirability on the one hand and the impossibility on the other of recovering the past.

The brief introduction to *My Ántonia*, in which the "author" meets Jim Burden on a train traveling across the Midwest, is crucial to this reading because it creates a frame around the whole novel that is in tension with the narrator's romantic project (see Schwind). Here we learn that for Jim Burden the best days indeed are the first to flee. Although he is a successful legal counsel for a great western railway and lives comfortably in New York City, his personal life is unsatisfying—his wife is unsympathetic to his quiet tastes, and they have no children. The brief character sketch of Mrs. Burden as a rich patroness of the arts, surrounded by a group of mediocre poets and painters, contrasts strikingly with that scene at the novel's close when Ántonia, surrounded by her children, asks Jim how many he has. Similarly, the image of Jim restlessly crossing the country is juxtaposed with the happiness and fixed security of Ántonia's home in the country. Later, as we read Jim's account of his childhood and of his successful progress toward his professional goals, we are always aware of the eventual futility of that success. As a framework around the whole novel, the introductory sketch sets up the creative pastoral tension between the memory of former happiness and the reality of loss and estrangement in the present.

Looking at certain scenes from the body of the novel will illustrate this tension. In book 1 the pastoral dream of enjoying communion with nature in a timeless realm is most fully realized for Jim in his grandmother's garden on the prairie. There he feels that the world ended and "only the ground and sun and sky were left, and if one went a little farther there would be only sun and sky, and one would float off into them, like the tawny hawks" (16). It is a transcendental experience of living beyond temporal change and outside the boundaries of a specific place. This experience of complete happiness contrasts starkly with the winter suicide of Mr. Shimerda. Although Jim does not yet realize its implications, Mr. Shimerda's experience in America is one of alienation, loss, and grief. In Renaissance paintings of pastoral fields and gardens a persistent motif is the presence of a skull in the grass that says, *Et in Arcadia ego* ("I am in Arcadia too"), reminding the viewer of the mutability of all earthly things. Mr. Shimerda's death has the same powerful function in the first part of the novel.

The pastoral dream of erotic happiness without physical sexuality is experienced by Jim with Ántonia and the hired girls in book 2 as they picnic on the river bank. In this scene Cather has created, in the manner of the Greek and Latin pastorals, a *locus amoenus*, and the hired girls like Lena Lingard, who watch over their fathers' livestock in the fields, are New World shepherdesses. But this pleasure in the country girls turns ugly for Jim when Ántonia's employer, Wick Cutter, mistakes him for Ántonia and tries to rape him in her bed. The experience for Jim is disgusting beyond measure and taints Ántonia as a sexual being.

In book 3 Jim is a university student in Lincoln seeing Lena Lingard, who has set up a dressmaking shop in the city. Already he begins to think back to his childhood in Black Hawk. When he reads the classic authors, his train of thought returns nostalgically to the people he had known, and he reflects on Vergil's statement of artistic purpose, "I shall be the first, if I live, to bring the Muse into my country" (264). To recover the past, Jim is already thinking of transforming it into art. Two years later, in book 4, when he visits Ántonia in Black Hawk, he tries to forget that she is now a mother out of wedlock and thinks of her as an older sister and guardian of precious childhood memories. As he and Ántonia, in their twenties, walk across the field at sunset he wishes he "could be a little boy again, and that [his] way could end there" (322).   D.H. Lawrence

In book 5 Jim attempts to accomplish that dream. He visits Ántonia again after twenty years have passed, and his narrative becomes a pastoral of innocence celebrating family and domestic life. The picture he creates of Ántonia and Anton Cuzak is like that of Baucis and Philemon in pastoral mythology; theirs is a story of married love and hospitality. In Cuzak's relation to Ántonia there is no suggestion of sex: theirs is a friendship in which he is simply "the instrument of Ántonia's special mission" of procreation.

Jim's desire to see Ántonia as an older sister or mother figure is fully and legitimately realized now. Surrounded by her children who come running out of the fruit cave in "a veritable explosion of life," Ántonia assumes mythic dimensions as a maternal figure. Standing in the orchard with her hand on one of the trees she has carefully nurtured, she suggests both earth mother and fertility goddess. In her presence Jim feels like a boy again, and Ántonia says to him appropriately: "You've kept so young." He in turn delights in Ántonia's young sons and chooses to sleep with them in the haymow rather than in the house. He says, "I felt like a boy in their company, and all manner of forgotten interests revived in me" (345). Sitting under the grape arbor in Ántonia's orchard with its triple enclosure of wire, locust, and mulberry hedges, Jim finds a perfect pastoral retreat and "deepest peace."

When Jim goes into town his mood is temporarily broken, for he finds so many things changed—friends dead or moved away, old trees cut down, strange children playing in the street. But in Ántonia's family he has found a connection with his own childhood again: "There were enough Cuzaks to play with a long while yet. Even after the boys grew up, there would always be Cuzak himself!" (370). As he looks at the old road he first traveled with Ántonia he philosophically complements his feelings of having come home again by envisioning life as a circle that invariably returns us to our beginnings.

When teaching *My Ántonia*, one is tempted to yield to the general opinion that the novel's nostalgic conclusion is unsatisfactory—that the book's vision is escapist, its protagonist pathetic and self-deluding. Such qualities were not the author's intention, though, nor does this view accord with the intent of pastoral art. Instead, we as readers should recognize the validity of a more ambiguous feeling at the end, one that sustains the tensions we have experienced throughout. For if we read the novel sympathetically we are drawn, like Jim Burden, to Ántonia and her farm; at the same time, however, we are aware that we have gone beyond, that we can't go home again, and that Ántonia and her family must remain in the precious but irrecoverable past.

we go back in order to say goodbye

My Ántonia as Plains Epic

Paul A. Olson

When I assign *My Ántonia*, I teach it to the sons and daughters or more distant relatives, in blood or spirit, of the people it treats. I have had relatives of Mrs. Pavelka in my classes, citizens of Red Cloud and Wilber, Czechs who still retain their Czech culture, and classicists at the University of Nebraska who study what Cather studied here. It is thus impossible entirely to make the work of art defamiliarize the experience, as Shklovsky would have it do, nor would I want it to remove the students from their pasts and knowledge of family or milieu (Shklovsky). Indeed, I try first to place them firmly in their own history and ask them to act on that history. But I also seek to introduce them to literary meanings that Cather asks us to see from afar; I use *My Ántonia*'s references to the classics, to Vergil's *Aeneid* and *Georgics*, to distance them from the parochialism of Nebraska and help them see their history as part of a pattern experienced by travelers and immigrants before, one often repeated on the long corridor of time and discovered there by Homer and Vergil.

To situate the students in their history, I remind them that *My Ántonia* was published during World War I, with its insistent chauvinism, repression of linguistic and cultural minorities, and elevation of the gun. Some students will have tales of when their families were forced by the Councils of Defense to quit speaking German or Czech, of house porches painted yellow in accusation of cowardice, and of forced purchases of war bonds. I may read sections from *One of Ours* that deal with the repression of German minorities and pacifists in Nebraska during the period. I ask students to pay particular attention to the uneasy situations of Bayliss, the pacifist (bk. 3, ch. 8), and of Oberlies and Yoeder, German-Americans put on trial for supposedly making disloyal comments about America and the Kaiser (bk. 3, ch. 9). Sometimes I ask students to read Cather's "Nebraska: The End of the First Cycle," written shortly after *My Ántonia* and World War I, to give them a sense of Cather's personal respect for the immigrant European ethnic cultures and her perspective on the period's cult of material progress and the materially prosperous nation (see esp. 4–8).

I then ask the students to look back at Jim Burden's view of Czech and German culture, his early response to the Shimerdas' Czech rye bread and dried mushrooms, his prejudices about central European Catholic belief, and his contempt for the settler's barren struggle for survival. The point is to make the student examine Jim's rejection of the tougher aspects of Ántonia's and Mrs. Shimerda's immigrant culture and the realism of his sympathy for the delicate, depressed, and, ultimately, maladaptive Mr. Shimerda. Once the students have learned to doubt Jim Burden's perspective, they may question not only his early negative response to the immigrants but

58

also the some of his later, lyrical response to them. Though I set the novel first against World War I, I generally question its relation to World War I's specific forms of chauvinism and militarism only when we reach the last book and see Ántonia, surrounded by her fertile Eden, telling Jim that she can't ever shoot a gun anymore. The passage makes its own statement.

My Ántonia opens in the 1870s, that is, in the period after the Civil War and during or immediately after the Franco-Prussian War. Since this period forms the fundamental political background to World War I, I ask students to recapture in their minds the cultural and historical events that account for the milieu of the Burden household and the European immigrant households. In the Burdens' case, we look at the Civil War, the Virginia background (11), the southern tradition of courtesy and distance, the simultaneous respect for and condescension toward other cultures (particularly black culture), the Virginia Baptist tradition to which the Burdens belong, and traditional southern classicism. Though compulsory education was not part of the post–Civil War South, families of even modest means employed tutors to educate boys and, sometimes, girls in Greek and Latin literature. The tradition goes from Jefferson through the southern plantation house to recent writers such as William Faulkner, Allen Tate, Caroline Gordon, and Robert Penn Warren, who testify to its liveliness in their youths. A standard study such as Reinhold's *Classica Americana* may be helpful here. Using one informal source of information or another, my students generally form a picture of the milieu from which the Burdens have come. They often have some understanding of how the values of that Virginia milieu support the keeping of hired men who live out the cowboy mythos formulated in *The Virginian* not too many years before Cather wrote.

But if my students are relatively clear about what happened in this country during the World War I and Civil War periods, they are much less certain in their knowledge of the conflict between the new liberal order and the ancien régime of the nineteenth century: Europe from Napoleon I's rise around 1800 to Napoleon III's fall in 1870. To encourage students to examine this dimension of the novel, I call attention to a number of details: (1) Otto Fuchs's background in Austria and Bismarck, North Dakota, and his (or his mother's) sentimental middle European Catholicism, represented in his Christmas-tree ornaments and his contempt for Czechs (131); (2) Mr. Shimerda's affection for his fellow Slavs, Pavel and Peter, his life as a weaver in Bohemia (20), his reliance on aesthetic experience for solace in contrast to his family's reliance on the Catholic Church, and his musical service on a semifeudal estate; (3) Jelinek's service in an Austro-Prussian war (probably the Seven Weeks' War of 1866); (4) Cuzak's life as a Czech journeyman, pushed out of his family's guild into a Viennese guild that prepares him for his service as a scab in New York; (5) Lena Lingard's double root in the

Norwegian clergy and in pagan or secular Lapp people; and (6) Mrs. Harling's origin in Christiania, Norway, where pietism flourished during Hauge's lifetime and long after his death.

To give the students tools for interpreting these references, I ask them to find accounts in encyclopedias or popular history books of the post-Napoleonic efforts to revive the liberal movement and eliminate central Europe's semifeudal system of landed estates. I also ask them to examine the reaction to the liberal movement in the period 1830–70, particularly in Prussia, Austria, and the Scandinavian countries. Because Ántonia is Czech, I usually concentrate on the Bohemian liberal independence movement and Austrian Hapsburg conservative repression, the interaction between the conservative Catholic Bohemian and the Bohemian freethinker aesthetic movements in the movement for Czech freedom, and the conflicts between Prussia and Austria that were to determine whether conservative central Europe would be predominantly Catholic or Protestant. These topics assist the students in understanding the Shimerdas and Otto Fuchs in particular. To understand Mr. Shimerda's attraction to Peter and Pavel, I examine the Pan-Slavic movement binding Bohemia to Russia, and to account for the Shimerdas' immigrating, I look both at the uprisings in the textile industry in Prague, which destabilized that industry (see Peck), and at the difficulty of acquiring land in the old Austro-Hungarian Empire. Finally, to account for Lena Lingard and Mrs. Harling, I briefly examine the conflicts between Puritanical pietism and "pagan" Romanticism in the Scandinavian countries by looking at the Hauge movement in Norway with its emphasis on grace, personal piety, conversion, and abstention from drinking, dancing, and other "worldly" sins, and at the saga- and myth-based romanticism of Atterbom, Wergeland, Bjornson, and Hans Christian Andersen in some moods. Often in Scandinavian literature, the Lapps (Lena Lingard's ancestors) are used as metaphors for this more Dionysiac tradition. In short, 1870 is a mirror of 1918.

The students may then, in discussion, see the characters of the novel as carrying the culture and the conflicts of the Old World with them to the frontier, but they also see the frontier rendered by Cather as potentially a more fluid place than Europe. It is governed more by a cultural than by a political conservatism; the ancien régime's political reaction and imperialism exist only in the Wick Cutters and the Krajieks, never in the whole system. Some students see the repetition of Old World conflicts on the frontier as entirely accidental, as not related to the 1870s or to World War I, and I do not try to persuade them otherwise. Furthermore, my students usually do not agree—cannot agree—as to whether this European background implies any systematic political statement by Cather about World War I or the political movements of the nineteenth century. They see clearly that the children of the imperial powers, who would have killed one another had they stayed in Europe, are forced to construct an uneasy sense of community in the presence of frontier hardship and that this phenomenon, in turn, comments on the inevitability or lack thereof of what George Kennan has described as one of history's most unnecessary wars.

The defamiliarization of the familiar comes in Cather's reliance on epic and georgic and on the second, ancient perspective through which Jim Burden sees the events of the novel. Most of my students have never read the *Aeneid* or the *Georgics*. They are products of the education Cather deplores in "Nebraska: The End of the First Cycle." A few have read the *Odyssey* because it was commonly included in a ninth-grade curriculum once popularly taught in Nebraska. I provide summaries and excerpts to give the students something to go on. As I have argued elsewhere, Cather invents in *My Ántonia* a "georgic epic," as Fielding had invented a "comic epic in prose," an epic that has a woman as hero and fields for monster-filled waters (Paul A. Olson, "Epic").

The students need some sense of what the *Aeneid* is and what the *Georgics* say to understand what Cather is doing with ancient literature. I introduce sea-travel passages from *Aeneid*, book 3, to place beside Cather's description of the wavy plains in book 1; Dido's suicide (bk. 4) to place beside Shimerda's; Aeneas's shield predicting the future of Rome (bk. 8) beside the plow silhouetted on the horizon predicting the future of the plains; some of the monster passages in *Aeneid*, book 3, beside the passages describing plains monsters such as the serpent. I place Vergil's "tears in the nature of things" beside Shimerda's response to the captured green insect to whom he listens "full of sadness, of pity for things" (42). Turning to the *Georgics*, I give the students excerpts from book 1 on the tilling of fields and the life of the farmer, from book 2 on trees and vineyards and the satisfaction of the farmer, and from book 4 on vegetables. I supply the passage from *Georgics*, book 3, that includes the motto of *My Ántonia* (*Optima dies . . . prima fugit*) and allow the students to discuss Vergil's point about the lives of herds and of people. I do the same for the passages about bringing the muse to the *patria* that begin book 3, and finally I turn to the section where Cleric compares the *Aeneid* and the *Georgics*, much to the advantage of the latter (bk. 3, ch. 2), and ask what Burden's choice of the *Georgics* means for his epic.

I cannot teach students everything at once, and I do not try. I use Vergil to give a perspective. I try to get the students to look carefully at what use Cather makes of Gaston Cleric, a classicist at the University of Nebraska for whom the texts of antique poetry are never mere texts but are meant to make Jim Burden and his other students imagine ancient life. I usually read and discuss the description of Cleric as teacher, one who "could bring the drama of antique life before one out of the shadows" (261).

Clearly, the defamiliarized has a function in Cleric's life. But I also read and discuss the passage where Jim Burden meditates on the meaning of the classical world and of the *Aeneid* as "mother to me and nurse in poetry," and I ask the students to consider why a second set of pictures (the reverse of the second *Aeneid* picture that appears in Tom Outland's imagination) arises behind the text of the *Aeneid* (262). The heroic forms that fill Jim Burden's imagination are a "strengthened and amplified" Jake and Otto and Russian Peter, the avatars of a new epoch in a new world, unlike the dead Trojan races. Some students are simply puzzled as to why Black Hawk intrudes on Jim Burden's recollection of the epic; some attribute his vision of his childhood to homesickness; and some see that Jim and Ántonia are reliving a heroic pattern.

I ask students to consider why, later in the book, Ántonia is described as "a rich mine of life, like the founders of early races" (353)—that is, like the epic heroes—and why she is apotheosized in Jim Burden's memory in "immemorial human attitudes" that one recognizes as "universal and true." The students then work out in what sense she is like the founders of early races, what is the essence of her heroic character, and how her heroism differs from that popularly held up to admiration during World War I. Generally, they speak of her strength, persistence, bravery, and individual fight; of her creation of a new-old culture; and of her physical stamina and wisdom. Students may remark how these heroic qualities take peculiarly female forms in Ántonia.

In the *Aeneid*, as in most major epics, the other major actor aside from the hero is destiny. I am not certain exactly how to deal with destiny in *My Ántonia*, but I try. I point out that Jim Burden seems to have the perception that he is dealing imaginatively with material that somehow deserves to stand by Vergil, or at least by the epics that posit a controlling destiny: "For Ántonia and for me this had been the road of Destiny; had taken us to those early accidents of fortune which predetermined for us all that we can ever be. Now I understood that the same road was to bring us together again. Whatever we had missed we possessed together the precious, the incommunicable past" (372). Burden constructs this meditation on destiny as he looks at the road over which he and Ántonia have come since as children they first arrived on the frontier, as his memory recapitulates it with such vividness that he can touch its feelings, can by contemplating it "come home to himself" and know "what a little circle man's experience is" (371–72). It is not clear, however, what Jim Burden means by the word *destiny*—the popular conception ("We were destined to meet"), the Vergilian stoic idea, or what. I do not have an answer to this question; I do try to go through the book looking for passages where a future pattern is adumbrated.

Another way I approach the question of destiny is by asking students to wrestle with Burden's conception of art as setting the form for civilization.

In the introduction, Jim Burden is represented as a disappointed legal counsel for one of the "great western railways"; the legal portfolio he presents to Willa Cather tells the life not of a failed lawyer, however, but of a poet of the *patria*—of the patriotic in its original meaning: "Primus ego in patriam mecum . . . deducam Musas" ("for I shall be the first, if I live, to bring the Muse into my country [*patria*]"):

> Cleric had explained to us that "patria" here meant, not a nation or even a province, but the little rural neighbourhood on the Mincio where the poet was born. This was not a boast, but a hope, at once bold and devoutly humble, that he might bring the Muse (but lately come to Italy from the cloudy Grecian mountains), not to the capital, the palatia Romana, but to his own little "country"; to his father's field. . . . (264)

Cleric goes on to speculate that Vergil in dying remembered this passage and "decreed that the great canvas [of the *Aeneid*], crowded with figures of gods and men, should be burned rather than survive him unperfected" (264). I point out that Cleric and, probably, Jim Burden see the militaristic canvas of the *Aeneid* as imperfect, when put beside the *Georgics'* perfection. The dying poet turned his mind to his "perfect utterance," the *Georgics*, "where the pen was fitted to the matter as the plough is to the furrow" (264). As he gave up his life, he is said to "have said to himself, with the thankfulness of a good man, 'I was the first to bring the Muse into my country,' " that is, his *patria* (264).

Later, as he sees Lena Lingard in the lamplight, Burden understands his muse. He thinks of her as in a dream, "coming across the harvest-field in her short skirt"; with her comes an echo of the Vergilian motto, *Optima dies . . . prima fugit*. With her comes also the memory of the Danish laundry girls and the three Bohemian Marys. Suddenly he understands what the muse is: "It came over me, as it had never done before, the relationship between girls like those and the poetry of Virgil. If there were no girls like them in the world, there would be no poetry" (270). Poetry and art emerge from concrete experience of a certain order—the Danes, the Marys—and return to concrete experience in poetry telling one how to plow. I try to get my classes to wrestle with Burden's conceptions of poetry and art: what the *patria* means against the background of World War I, what bringing the muse into Black Hawk society means, what the quotation from the *Georgics* means—whether each of these ideas is a sentimental bit of nostalgia or a profound statement on art—and what sexual and/or aesthetic motive is behind Jim Burden's casting Lena and the other frontier women in the role of the muses.

Whatever aesthetic theory students construct from these meditations on the art of civilizing and the muses that inspire it, they see pretty clearly that Jim Burden's experience of Ántonia is a heroic reliving of the *Aeneid* or *Odyssey*. Yet the novel has a different ending from the old epics. What *My Ántonia* finally values is not heroic military enterprise, as found in World War I, in 1870, or in the founding of Rome—not the work of Thanatos, but that of Eros. The novel's heroic work requires planting grains and gardens and raising livestock—the stuff of the *Georgics*. I then ask the students to go back to Vergil to observe how far the *Georgics* and *Aeneid* analogies go: whether the prairie sea's "wine red" is part of it; whether the suicide and funeral of Shimerda work into the pattern; how Larry Donovan's seduction works; how the visit to Black Hawk, the plow image, the visions of Ántonia in the fields and later of Ántonia in her fruitful orchard relate to epic or heroic perspectives. Some students see all these elements as fitting into a pattern as clear as Joyce's in Stuart Gilbert's account of *Ulysses*. Others say that the analogies are purely fortuitous. What is important is that they have had to deal with how persons construct meaning for their lives by playing between art and history. They have had to look at the process of development in the 1870s on the frontier. And they have had to look at Cather's mirror of the civilizing process set before the barbarous world of World War I, even as Vergil's mirror is set before the rough world of the 1870s in Jim's life.

I end my discussion with an effort to have my students evaluate Cather's reasons for her double perspective, classical and nineteenth-century European, on the events of a novel written in World War I and set at their back doors. I consider the structure of the book, looking particularly at what books 1, 3, and 5 have to do with one another structurally. What can I get across to my students of this? They can see that Cather, in the context of the imperialism of World War I, creates a hero in Ántonia who is like the founder of early races but looks forward to no empire and loves no fight save the fight for survival.

The Romanticism of *My Ántonia*:
Every Reader's Story

Susan J. Rosowski

Romanticism is fundamental to *My Ántonia*, shaping the attitudes that control its structure, style, and narration, as well as its expectations of a reader. I immediately face a dilemma in teaching this romanticism, however, for most of my students haven't even the most rudimentary understanding of what romanticism is. They have negative associations of something emotional, irrelevant, and backward-looking; asked for details, they describe surface features that vaguely concern poets brooding about nature. Almost none understands romanticism as a way of knowing, by which individuals use their imaginations to create value in an otherwise meaningless world (Rosowski, *Voyage*).

Happily, Cather provided in her introduction a romantic poetics of fiction, a starting place for her readers—and our students. After explaining that the introduction exists in two forms (the original, 1918 version and the condensed but otherwise unaltered 1926 version that students have in their paperback editions), I distribute copies of the 1918 version, in which Cather makes an agreement with Jim Burden: "I would set down on paper all that I remembered of Ántonia, if he would do the same." Cather emphasizes again the distinction between her story and Jim's in two sentences at the end of the original introduction. After Jim brought to Cather his manuscript, he said it hadn't any form or any title either: he wrote "Ántonia," then "frowned at this a moment, then prefixed another word, making it 'My Ántonia.' That seemed to satisfy him." Thus ends the 1926 version, but in 1918 Cather had included two additional sentences: " 'Read it as soon as you can,' he said rising, 'But don't let it influence your own story.' My own story was never written, but the following narrative is Jim's manuscript, substantially as he brought it to me."

After we have read the original introduction, we may note that it includes incidental features of romanticism: it announces its subject as childhood close to nature; it establishes its narrator's "romantic personality"; it specifies that "romantic" means Jim's imaginative capacity to love the country and to lose himself in an idea. We quickly move, however, to the more important stress Cather places on method. Indeed, the introduction resembles a contract, filled with stipulations about how the story was written and how it should be read, in both cases as the creation of an imagination, true to experience that is individual, unique, and ongoing.

In discussing method, we note that before Jim began to write of Ántonia, he stated his condition that he would do so from his unique experience of her: "Of course I should have to do it in a direct way, and say a great deal about myself. It's through myself that I knew and felt her." I ask what he is doing here, and we talk about the assumption that knowledge is individual and unique. (I may compare Jim's statement to Wordsworth's terms for *The Prelude*, "to describe what I had felt and thought.") We note that before giving his story to his reader, Jim warned her that it is accurate according to the way his memory worked, however fragmentary and incomplete by conventional notions of plot: he didn't "arrange or rearrange" but "simply wrote down what of herself and myself and other people Ántonia's name recalls to me." Again, I ask students to consider what the stipulation means in terms of the novel, and we talk about romantic concepts of form as true to individual experience rather than to theories of unity or expectations of genre.

We talk also about the relation of Jim Burden to Willa Cather, and here I resist the temptation to insist on critical distinctions between the "real" Cather and the invented one (the authorial pose) of the introduction. My students know that in her introduction Cather provided details from her "real" life sufficient for them to recognize her as a writer, and that's where we begin—with the flagrantly fictitious device of the character's giving to his creator a manuscript and calling it *his* story, then of Cather's reinforcing that idea with her last words of the original introduction: "My own story was never written, but the following narrative is Jim's manuscript, substantially as he brought it to me." It is as if Cather is playing a game with us, my students say with considerable irritation, and as we discuss the effect of this game it becomes clear that Cather has done something most unsettling: she has renounced the authority of text (by reminding us it is an artifact), author (by distancing herself from it), and narrator (by having a fictitious character tell the tale).

If we cannot trust the text, the author, or the narrator, what can we trust? To consider what is authentic here, we return to Jim Burden's charge to his reader (i.e., to Willa Cather, and by extension to each of us) when he gives to her the manuscript: "read it as soon as you can . . . but don't let it influence your own story." As we consider implications of the introduction and, particularly, of the title, someone will often say something such as, "I get it! *My Ántonia* becomes *our* Ántonia, as we read it here together," and another student might respond, "but your reading is different from mine," and we go on from there, until we are talking about each reader's making the story his or hers with each reading. Again without resorting to secondary definitions, what students are discussing is Cather's extension to the reader of the romantic premise that meaning in an epistemological sense is an individual creation. By renouncing conventional authority in the narrator/writer, she has validated it in each reader.

To discuss how Cather engages the reader in creating a story, we turn to the body of *My Ántonia* and read one episode closely. Because I wish to discuss what is characteristic, I avoid the overtly dramatic scenes—Jim's first morning in his grandmother's garden, ending with his feeling "that is happiness, to be dissolved into something complete and great"; Jim's picnic with the hired girls, ending with their seeing the plow magnified against the sun; and Jim's return to Ántonia, seeing her children emerge from the fruit cellar and recognizing her as "a rich mine of life." Instead, I select a less obvious episode—Jim Burden's first visit with his grandmother to the Shimerdas' dugout, for example (19–27).

I ask where Cather begins with us, then read the paragraph that starts, "One Sunday morning Otto Fuchs was to drive us over to make the acquaintance of our new Bohemian neighbours," and includes details about provisions: they take with them "a sack of potatoes and a piece of cured pork from the cellar, . . . some loaves of Saturday's bread, a jar of butter, and several pumpkin pies." We discuss how Cather opens the episode as a factual account, placing it in historical time and geographical space, then recounting specifics.

Next we read the second paragraph, which begins with Jim's anticipation of "what lay beyond that cornfield," includes his disappointment on seeing "there was only red grass like ours, and nothing else," and builds to his description:

> The road ran about like a wild thing, avoiding the deep draws, crossing them where they were wide and shallow. And all along it, wherever it looped or ran, the sunflowers grew; some of them were as big as little trees, with great rough leaves and many branches which bore dozens of blossoms. They made a gold ribbon across the prairie. Occasionally one of the horses would tear off with his teeth a plant full of blossoms, and walk along munching it, the flowers nodding in time to his bites as he ate down toward them.

I ask where we are by the end of this second paragraph, and students respond with Eden, a fairy tale, a magical world, paradise. Whatever their term, they recognize that the narrative has extended the world of ordinary life to romance. We may note the change in sentence structure, from simple sentences to cumulative ones, and the repetition of Jim's straining to see, of the refrain "I could see nothing" and "I could still see nothing," followed by sequences of "I saw" and "I felt" as his imagination takes over.

As we move to the core of this episode and read the paragraph describing Jim's approach to the Shimerdas' dugout, we note again the recurring pattern: first the reason presents particulars as facts, then the imagination works on those facts, transforming them by feeling. Initially Jim describes things as they are. He sees "nothing but rough red hillocks, and draws with shelving banks and long roots hanging out," then sees an object (a shattered windmill frame), which he calls a "skeleton" (no longer simply an object, but an object infused by feeling into a symbol of death). Finally, he describes a door and sunken window. What is Jim writing about? I ask. A dugout, yes, but also about a feeling of death and desolation. Some students note that the image of the windmill as a "skeleton" is strong enough to color the entire setting, and others say the dugout with its door and sunken window seems like a skull.

Next we read the description of the Shimerdas, as each emerges from the earth. First there appears a woman of indeterminate age wearing a shawl, "her face . . . alert and lively, with a sharp chin and shrewd little eyes." I ask who she is, and in every class I have taught students immediately identify her as a witch. Next, the oldest son, foxlike with little, shrewd hazel eyes that were "sly and suspicious" and "fairly snapped at the food"; then as if princesses, Ántonia, with eyes "big and warm and full of light, like the sun shining on brown pools in the wood," and brown skin, her cheeks glowing with "rich, dark colour" and curly, wild-looking brown hair, followed by her younger sister, who was "fair . . . mild and obedient."

Just as we begin to predict other recognizable transformations of a fairy tale, the scene exceeds formulation when Marek appears, showing his webbed fingers, like a duck's foot, and crowing like a rooster. Finally, most unexpectedly of all, the father emerges, wearing a grey vest and "a silk scarf of a dark bronze-green, carefully crossed and held together by a red coral pin," and bending over Mrs. Burden's hand, as if he were in the most formal of drawing rooms rather than on an unbroken Nebraska prairie.

Once we have read the episode closely, we need only the briefest comment about how it works. Cather never leaves the prairie; throughout, we believe in the particular reality of a specific time and place. Yet the imagination transforms this most ordinary of scenes into something extraordinary. Anything at all might emerge next from the Shimerdas' dugout, for a desolate Nebraska country has become a place of miracles, created by the informing power of Jim's and our imaginations (see also Rosowski, "Fatality").

We turn next to ways in which Cather invokes the reader's imagination to join scenes that are apparently disparate. For example, Jim's battle with the snake is complete in itself, a childhood episode that the middle-aged narrator recalls as a mock adventure (43–50). In it Jim follows the familiar pattern: First, he describes the object as it is, a snake "lying with long loose waves, like a letter 'W.' " He then tells of feeling revulsion, implicitly associating the snake with threatening sexuality when he describes "his abominable muscularity, his loathsome, fluid movement, [that] somehow made me sick," compares it to "the ancient, eldest Evil," and extends the reference to "his kind [that] have left horrible unconscious memories in all warm-blooded life." As the incident unfolds we focus on the action of Jim's killing the snake and returning triumphantly home with it, and we consider the episode closed when Jim reflects, "I had killed a big snake—I was now a big fellow."

One chapter ends and another begins with a quite different subject, that of Peter and Pavel. Yet as an aside in the third sentence of this new episode, Jim mentions "Wick Cutter, the merciless Black Hawk money-lender, a man of evil name throughout the country, of whom I shall have more to say later" (50). With the repetition of the letter W (now as "Wick") associated with the idea of Evil ("a man of evil name"), it is as if the snake had reappeared, reincarnated in human form. The aside points ahead also, for Jim's promise to say more of him anticipates Cutter's attempted rape of Ántonia, when dark sexuality threatens to disrupt Black Hawk Eden.

Individual scenes are structured by movement of the mind as it transforms the ordinary into the extraordinary, and apparently disparate scenes are joined by movement of the mind as it recognizes echoes; the overall novel is structured by the way the mind formulates meaning. We recognize the circular movement of a romantic lyric when a middle-aged Jim returns to Ántonia, recognizing her as a rich mine of life. The physical return of Jim mirrors the circular imaginative process: in the end the speaker returns to the object he described at the beginning, an object now informed with memories.

While we talk about how each section relates to the whole, I may sketch their circularity on the chalkboard. In "The Shimerdas," the child Jim describes direct experience of the physical world, his sensory descriptions reminiscent of Wordsworth's "fair seedtime of the soul." In "The Hired Girls" Jim's youthful energy has become intensified by adolescent sexuality, presenting possibilities that culminate in one experience of ennobling creativity (awe at the plow magnified against the sun) and another of disillusioning excess (revulsion at Cutter's attempted rape of Ántonia). In "Lena Lingard" Jim leaves physicality behind him to revel in a newly discovered world of ideas. With "The Pioneer Woman's Story" he begins his return to that physical, natural world, though by imposing his ideas on it rather than recognizing ideals residing within it. Finally, in "Cuzak's Boys" Jim closes the circle, fusing the idea with the particular. Jim's revelation in the fruit-cellar scene is quintessentially romantic: he sees Ántonia in all her particularity, an aging woman with missing teeth and grizzled hair, and he recognizes the universal idea of an earth mother residing within that particularity.

Just as we earlier looked closely at the opening of *My Ántonia*, we now look closely at its ending. I read the last paragraph aloud, and students often reply by saying it is "perfect," with everything resolved: Jim has returned home to Ántonia and to himself. (My students here sometimes charge Cather with escapism, saying that such resolution is *too* perfect.) Then we look again at the last sentence. "Incommunicable," a word students initially overlooked, stops them short on rereading, for they suddenly realize that with it Jim has excluded us from his resolution. If the past Jim possesses is "incommunicable," what are we left with? Apparently we don't get at Ántonia's truth, or Jim Burden's, or Willa Cather's.

We explore this idea further in discussing other questions students have about the novel. Why didn't Jim "get together" with Ántonia? The discussion ranges, but what is relevant for this essay is that it includes our role as readers. "What does 'get together' mean?" someone asks; someone else says, "But they do 'get together,' just not in the sense I meant," and we begin to talk about our stories, fictions that we are creating about these characters. Students mean that Jim should marry Ántonia, an action that can only be described as wildly improbable when we consider characterization, theme, and plot as Cather gives them to us. Why do we expect him to do so? What are our conventions for characters (I cannot remember a student's asking why Ántonia didn't marry Jim; it's always the reverse), and what are our expectations of a novel?

Such questions return us to the introduction, in which Cather laid down her poetics. I remind students that they had said the novel would have been better without it, and we talk about how that might be so. We could have rested easy in the illusion of receiving truth, in having entered into Jim's skin, retraced his past, and discovered his self, as if it were our own. Instead, Cather framed her novel with reminders that Jim cannot give to us "his Ántonia." In forcing us to create our own Ántonia and thus extending responsibility for her story to her reader, Cather reveals the forward-reaching tendencies of her romanticism. She has made her narrator an instrument of perception and a maker of meaning, but she has withheld from him the power of making the novel's validity. Instead, she extends to the reader the romanticist's premise that meaning is in an epistemological sense an individual, personal creation. Cather created a narrator through whom she imagined one story, which she in her introduction distinguishes from *her* story. In the novel's conclusion, she reminds us that one person's meaning is "incommunicable" to another, thereby charging each reader to create his or her own story.

The Place of *My Ántonia*
in Women's Literary Traditions

Josephine Donovan

A feminist or women's studies approach to the teaching of *My Ántonia* locates the novel within the tradition of American women's literature and the author within the historical context of American women's culture—in this case, white and middle-class—of the early twentieth century. While a history of American women's literature has yet to be written, its contours are apparent. Cather's immediate foremothers include the realists of the New England local-color school, in particular Sarah Orne Jewett (1849–1909), who became Willa's personal and artistic mentor, probably the most important influence in her life.

Cather belongs to the generation of women realists of the early twentieth century that included Edith Wharton and Ellen Glasgow. Her gravitation to Jewett was anomalous in this generation of "new women" writers who were in strident rebellion against what they saw as the false sentimentalism of their literary foremothers. Wharton, for example, once stated that she had written her stark novel *Ethan Frome* (1911) in order to belie the "rose-coloured" vision of New England presented by "her predecessors in the field," Mary E. Wilkins Freeman (1852–1930) and Jewett (Wharton 293). Cather also rejected the sentimentalist feminine tradition. Her critique of Kate Chopin's novel *The Awakening* (1899) is characteristic (*World and Parish* 2: 697–99). Cather also comments negatively on women's literature in "The Literary Situation in 1895" (*World and Parish* 1: 277; see also 2: 694, n. 3, and 2: 961–64).

This wholesale rejection of their "predecessors" in the women's literary tradition engendered a complex of problems for the women writers—as indeed for all the "new women" in rebellion against their mothers—of Cather's generation. The most serious was a profound ambiguity about gender identity. The temptation to adopt a masculine self-identification while rejecting the feminine, to assume that "serious" authors were masculine, and to see themselves as such, in contrast to the silly "scribbling" women of the nineteenth century, proved compelling for the women writers of Cather's generation. Wharton, for example, nearly always used a Jamesian male persona in her fiction, and, in a problematic gesture, Cather used male personae more often than not as narrators and sometimes as protagonists—an issue that numerous Cather biographers and critics have addressed (see especially Brown; Woodress, *Life and Art*; O'Brien, " 'Thing Not Named' ").

An understanding of the social and intellectual climate in which middle-class American women came to maturity in the early twentieth century will enable the student better to understand the gender-identity problem seen in Cather's fiction, in particular her continuing use of male personae. The early 1900s was a period of extraordinary opportunity for such women. It offered them for probably the first time in history the possibility of entering professional fields hitherto barred them, of entering the "man's world" of public life. At the same time, however, such opportunities required leaving the traditional women's world of "love and ritual," of domesticity—the world of the mothers. The new woman-daughter thus found herself with ambivalent feelings. On the one hand, she longed for the autonomy and excitement afforded by the careerist-assimilationist course; on the other, she felt cut off from the emotional strength and inspiration that had bonded nineteenth-century women. Yet she also feared being reenveloped in the negative aspects of the domestic feminine world, its stasis and repetition. (Numerous articles treat the nineteenth-century "female world of love and ritual" that was being abandoned by turn-of-the-century "new women." Teachers may wish to assign some of the following to help students understand the social and emotional context in which Cather came of age: Smith-Rosenberg; Sahli; Freedman; and Donovan, "Silence or Capitulation.")

Cather was seriously affected by these ambivalences, and her work—particularly *My Ántonia*—may be seen as an attempt to resolve the dilemma of the "new woman," to reunite the wayward daughter with the rooted mother, to reconnect the autonomy of the logos with the emotional sources of the collective. The myth that best allegorizes this reconnection is that of Demeter and Persephone; this myth of feminine resurrection—understood in the historical context of early-twentieth-century American women's culture—is central to *My Ántonia*, as Evelyn Helmick remarked over a decade ago. It was, ironically, through the influence of her feminine "predecessor" Sarah Orne Jewett that Cather was able to achieve the mythic vision of feminine resurrection that is central to her great early novels: *O Pioneers!* (1913), *The Song of the Lark* (1915), and *My Ántonia* (1918).

Cather met Jewett in the fall of 1908 in the Back Bay Boston home of Jewett's intimate companion Annie Adams Fields. Cather records these meetings in "Miss Jewett" and "148 Charles Street" in her 1936 collection of essays *Not under Forty*. Cather claims to have first learned of Jewett from her picture on the "Authors" card deck she played with as a child. She had read with enthusiasm Jewett's masterpiece *The Country of the Pointed Firs* (1896) soon after it appeared and had found an earlier novel of Jewett's, *A Country Doctor* (1884), admirably "austere and unsentimental," according to George Seibel (qtd. in Robinson 153). In her 1925 preface, Cather estimated *The Country of the Pointed Firs* as one of three American works guaranteed literary immortality, the others being *The Scarlet Letter* and *Huckleberry Finn*.

A series of remarkable letters exchanged between Jewett and Cather in 1908 gives primary testimony to the Jewett influence. In Cather's unpublished letters to Jewett she wrote that she always carried a copy of Jewett's stories "A White Heron" (1886) and "The Dulham Ladies" (1886) with her when she traveled and that she had brought them, along with "The Flight of Betsey Lane" (1893), with her on a trip to Italy (10 May 1908).

In a later letter, a tightly spaced eight-page epistle dated 18 November, Cather voices doubts that she will ever be able to write competent fiction and wonders whether she is being stifled by her newspaper environment (she was then on the staff of *McClure's* magazine in New York) and should perhaps take time off to devote herself wholly to her fiction. She concludes by praising Jewett's "Martha's Lady" (1899), which she finds humbling yet inspiring, making her willing to start all over again.

In October, Cather sent Jewett a copy of her story "On the Gulls' Road" (later published in *McClure's*, Dec. 1908). Cather feared, however, that Jewett would find it artificial, with the air of the tube-rose still hanging about it (24 Oct. [1908]). She was right.

Jewett's most trenchant criticism of Cather's work came in her response to this story, a letter dated 27 November. While she prefaces it by remarking Cather's "unerring touches and wonderful tenderness," Jewett questions Cather's use of a male persona.

> The lover is as well done as he could be when a woman writes in the man's character—it must always, I believe, be something of a masquerade. I think it is safer to write about him as you did about the others, and not try to be he! And you could almost have done it as yourself—a woman could love her in that same protecting way—a woman could even care enough to wish to take her away from such a life, by some means or other. (*Letters* 246–47)

The difficult issue of Cather's continuing use of male personae, despite Jewett's advice, will be treated further below; clearly, however, Jewett's principal message here is that it is unnecessary to disguise or "masquerade" a romantic friendship between two women as a heterosexual affair. That Cather felt the need to do so is another aspect of the complex psychological transitions women were undergoing at the time. As O'Brien points out in her review of the problematic relation of Cather's lesbianism to her fiction, intense "feminine friendship" was considered "unnatural" in Cather's formative years, whereas it was a norm in Jewett's day (O'Brien, " 'Thing Not Named' " 582; see also Faderman; Chauncey; Donovan, "Nan Prince" and "Silence or Capitulation"; Smith-Rosenberg; Sahli; and Freedman).

Jewett's next letter, dated 13 December, has been characterized by E. K. Brown as "the most important letter, beyond question, that Willa Cather ever received" (140). An apparent response to Cather's 18 November letter, it cautions Willa that her talents were not maturing "as they should" and suggests that she remove herself from the hubbub of New York's publishing scene to devote full time and concentration to her fiction. Jewett also suggested that Cather use her "Nebraska life" as well as her "child's Virginia" and bohemian New York as her fictional milieus (*Letters* 247–50). But more than specific advice, it was the earnest and loving tone of Jewett's letter that must have impressed the young author. Her obvious concern—"I have been full of thought about you," Jewett wrote Cather (250)—must surely have removed any lingering doubts Cather had about her own artistic worth.

Later Cather commented that she had despaired in her early years as a writer of ever effectively capturing her Nebraska material.

> Then I had the good fortune to meet Sarah Orne Jewett, who had read all of my early stories and had very clear and definite opinions about them and about where my work fell short. She said, "Write it as it is, don't try to make it like this or that. You can't do it in anybody else's way—you'll have to make a way of your own." (*Kingdom* 449)

The "anybody else" that Jewett undoubtedly had in mind was Henry James. Several of Cather's stories in the early 1900s had a decidedly Jamesian, and thus inauthentic, air. E. K. Brown suggests that "The Namesake" (1907) and "Eleanor's House" (1907) may have particularly displeased Jewett (141–45).

Jewett herself was, however, a countervailing influence. Even before their meeting and before Cather received Jewett's specific advice, Jewett influences are evident in Cather's fiction. "A Resurrection" (1897), published shortly after *Pointed Firs*, uses the characteristic local-color narrative format of two women gossiping. The story includes a lament on the "waste" of the talent of intelligent women that is reminiscent of Jewett's similar elegy in *Pointed Firs*, which states: "It was not the first time that I was full of wonder at the waste of human ability in this world, as a botanist wonders at the wastefulness of nature, the thousand seeds that die, the unused provision of every sort" (174). "Eric Hermannson's Soul," published in 1900, the year after "Martha's Lady," similarly concerns the visit of a lively, exciting young woman to a rural area where she inspires and animates a deadened soul. In Jewett's story the passion awakened is between two women; in Cather's, however, the relationship is heterosexual, possibly another "masquerade."

"The Treasure of Far Island" (1902), one of Cather's first Nebraska stories, uses a format she may have derived from Jewett's *Pointed Firs*: the return of the native, a persona for the author. In Jewett's case the urbane and sophisticated visitor is a woman; in Cather's—for example, Jim Burden in *My Ántonia*—it is nearly always a man.

The two stories that are probably immediate responses to Jewett's 1908 written advice are "The Enchanted Bluff" (1909) and "The Joy of Nelly Deane" (1911). Cather sent the former, her first great Nebraska story, to Jewett in January 1909. One can only hope that Jewett had a chance to read it, for she had an incapacitating stroke in the spring of that year and died in June. "Nelly Deane" is one of Cather's few stories that deal overtly with a passionate friendship between women and that have a female narrator. It seems likely that in this story Cather was directly responding to Jewett's challenge of "Gulls' Road."

Cather once said that she was inspired to write her first novel, *Alexander's Bridge* (1912), while on a visit to Jewett's home in South Berwick, Maine, in the summer of 1911. Sitting at Jewett's desk, she felt Jewett's "spirit" "warned her that time was flying"; it "goaded" her to begin the novel, which she in fact began to write in South Berwick (O'Brien, "Mothers" 278). Significantly, the novel was originally published as *Alexander's Masquerade* (Slote, Introd. 98), surely a verbal echo of Jewett's use of the term in her critique of "Gulls' Road." In her 1922 preface to the novel Cather cited advice Jewett had given her—that one must see the world before one can describe the parish (Woodress, *Life and Art* 143).

It was in *O Pioneers!*, however, that Cather finally hit her stride and that Jewett's counsel and influence became most apparent. Appropriately, Cather dedicated her first great novel to her mentor, saying she had done so "because I had talked over some of the characters in it with her . . . and in this book I tried to tell the story of the people as truthfully and simply as if I were telling it to her by word of mouth" (*Kingdom* 448). This statement suggests that Cather had been wrestling with the problem of how a woman writer may tell a story authentically—the issue raised by Jewett in her "Gulls' Road" comments. Here Cather proposes to "tell" *O Pioneers!* as if she were relating it directly to another woman author, thus inscribing herself in the traditions of American women's literary history.

My Ántonia belongs in the tradition that evolved out of women's local-color literature developed in nineteenth-century New England by Harriet Beecher Stowe (1811–96) and Rose Terry Cooke (1827–92). A topos central to this literature is that of a redemptive rural matriarchy (Donovan, *New England*). Grandmother Badger in Stowe's great but neglected novel *Oldtown Folks* (1869) is indeed a literary grandmother of Ántonia in that she similarly presides over a female-centered Edenic realm on the margins of capitalist patriarchal society. In between are numerous other rural female powers, most notably Jewett's herbalist-witch Almira Todd in *The Country of the Pointed Firs*.

Almira is a Demeter figure like Ántonia, and as in Cather's novel the

Persephone-Demeter myth is central to *Pointed Firs*, which critics Ammons and Sherman have recently recognized. In Jewett's work the traveling daughter is a woman writer who returns, jaded, from the city, which is emblematic of patriarchal captivity, to the rural fount where she reconnects with the sources of artistic inspiration in the matriarchal figure of Mrs. Todd. The rural world, that of Demeter, is one of fecund vegetation, of ancient feminine rituals, the green-world sanctuary found in so much of women's literature (Pratt).

In a 1976 article Helmick identified as the underlying ritual pattern in *My Ántonia* that of the Eleusinian mysteries—the ancient religious rite based on the Persephone-Demeter myth (176). Helmick traces in detail the parallels between the phases of the Eleusinian rituals and the passages of Ántonia—particularly in the final section, "Cuzak's Boys," where she has achieved full status as Demeter.

But it is also evident that the Persephone-Demeter pattern underlies the connection between Jim Burden and Ántonia, if we interpret Burden as a Cather persona, representative of the daughter-artist who has assimilated into the realm of patriarchal discourse—the realm of the logos—but who finds herself cut off, her sources dried up. Just as Cather, deadened in her urban newspaper world, turned to Jewett, as to a matriarchal muse, for reinspiration, and as the writer returns to rural Maine in Jewett's *Pointed Firs*, so Burden returns to Nebraska and reconnects with the matriarchal mysteries of Demeter/Ántonia. Jim represents the autonomous daughter whose return signifies a reunion with the feminine side of life, the matriarchal mysteries, the repetitive cycle of birth and rebirth that characterizes the nonoedipal feminine condition. Perhaps, therefore, Cather felt the need to use a male figure to emphasize its autonomy, its character as logos.

A feminist or women's studies approach to a work of literature thus requires an interdisciplinary knowledge of historical, sociological, and psychological sources that help to identify the author's ontological orientation. It proposes that literature is not simple mimesis but an expression of a desired ontic reorientation; it reveals the modes of being allowed women in a given historical period and the conflicts such modes may have entailed. The mythic structure of women's works can be fully described only in terms of this reality.

Biblical and Religious Dimensions of *My Ántonia*

John J. Murphy

Although not as overtly religious as, say, *Death Comes for the Archbishop*, Cather's *My Ántonia* nevertheless has rich religious implications. As we are continually discovering, Cather's intriguing method of allusions and juxtapositions, while apparently natural and sometimes even invisible to the casual reader, can be as provocative as Melville's and T. S. Eliot's. Cather designed "The Pioneer Woman's Story," book 4 in *My Ántonia*, to recall the Christian mystery of the Nativity, both for what that story has in common with the one she is telling and for what is radically different in it. Through juxtaposition, imagery, biblical implications and rhetoric, and religious perspectives (both Protestant and Catholic), the first and last books of the novel, "The Shimerdas" and "Cuzak's Boys," prepare for and develop, respectively, this Nativity dimension and contribute to underlying themes of birth, death, resurrection, and the founding of a new race in a new land.

A good place to begin exploring how Cather links the Nebraska scenes to Christ's birth and resurrection is to have students look at the way the chapters are clustered in book 1, where Jim recounts his first Christmas in Nebraska and Mr. Shimerda commits suicide. Cather's use of the blizzard as a framing device for the Christmas picture should be pointed out, as should the traditional images associated with Christmas: farmhand Otto Fuchs's cardboard crèche cutouts from Austria and the cedar tree his partner Jake Marpole brings in from the fields. Cather lists first among the cardboard cutouts the "bleeding heart, in tufts of paper lace," a symbol of Christ's love (Hardon 479). The sacred heart is followed by other conventional and a few exotic figures: "there were the three kings, gorgeously apparelled, and the ox and the ass and the shepherds; there was the Baby in the manger, and a group of angels, singing; there were camels and leopards, held by the black slaves of the three kings" (83). Jim refers to the decorated tree as "the talking tree of the fairy tale," and it reminds Grandmother Burden of the tree of knowledge.

At this point I refer students to a scene in Cather's 1931 novel, *Shadows on the Rock*, where Cécile Auclair and her waif friend Jacques Gaux set up a Christmas crèche from France, arranging the figures of Jesus, Mary, Joseph, the ass, and the ox under a booth of fir branches on a window shelf. This Mary and Joseph recollect Ántonia Shimerda and her husband, Anton Cuzak, in the last books of *My Ántonia*: "The Blessed Virgin . . . looked like a country girl, very naive, seated on a stool, with her knees well apart under her full skirt, and very large feet. Saint Joseph, a grave old man in brown, with a bald head and wrinkled brow, was placed opposite her . . ." (*Shadows* 108). Noting the peasant characteristics of Mary in this passage, we discuss how they associate her with Ántonia.

Now I discuss the role of different religious perspectives and orientations in *My Ántonia* and how they contribute to its biblical dimensions. Note the undercurrent of religious tension when Ántonia's brokenhearted homesick father, whose violin is stilled in the alien New World, visits the Burdens on Christmas Day. Jim lights the candles on the tree, and the old man crosses himself and kneels before it. The Protestant perspective of Cather's novel is obvious, as narrator and consequently reader view a Catholic world as alien. Grandfather Burden immediately becomes uncomfortable: "There had been nothing strange about the tree before, but now, with some one kneeling before it—images, candles. . . . Grandfather merely put his finger-tips to his brow and bowed his venerable head, thus Protestantizing the atmosphere" (87). Later, of course, in *Death Comes for the Archbishop* and *Shadows on the Rock*, Cather would adopt the Catholic perspective, viewing as an insider a world replete with candles, holy images, ritual, and miracles.

After this scene the frame around the prairie Christmas closes; snow becomes slush and black water: "The soft black earth stood out in patches along the roadsides" (88). There follows a brief altercation between Jim and Ántonia when she and her mother visit the Burdens and complain about their need compared to their neighbors' plenty. On the twentieth of January, as the winter's biggest snow begins to fall, a new frame opens, to enclose a picture of death that bears on the Christmas chapters. News arrives that old Shimerda has killed himself in his barn, in surroundings recalling the Nativity story. "He must have gone right down to the barn and done it then," relates Otto Fuchs. "He layed down on that bunk-bed, close to the ox stalls, where he always slept" (96).

Scriptural echoes and conflicting religious perspectives continue to dominate the text after the suicide: Grandmother Burden exclaims, "Oh, dear Saviour! Lord, Thou knowest!" (95); Ántonia's brother Ambrosch devoutly prays the rosary; and the elder Burdens look "very Biblical as they set off" to help the bereaved family (100). As Jake describes it, the situation at the Shimerdas is pathetic: a lighted lantern is kept over the corpse, still housed in the barn with horses and oxen, and Ántonia, her mother, and her brother kneel beneath the lantern and pray for the suicide's soul. Jim then questions the Catholic doctrine of purgatory: "this idea of punishment and Purgatory came back to me crushingly. I remembered the account of Dives in torment, and shuddered" (103). There is a disagreement between the sympathetically drawn Bohemian Anton Jelinek and Grandfather Burden about the need for a priest for the dead. Jelinek relates his boyhood experience of helping a priest distribute the Sacrament to dying soldiers during a cholera epidemic: "But we have no sickness, we have no fear, because we carry that blood and that body of Christ, and it preserves us" (106).

Jelinek's story reflects Catholic literalism toward Christ's discourse at Capernaum: "As I, who am sent by the living Father, myself draw life from the Father, so whoever eats me will draw life from me. This is the bread come down from heaven; not like the bread [manna] our ancestors ate: they are dead, but anyone who eats this bread will live for ever" (John 6.57–58). This biblical passage relates directly to the Jelinek episode. From his religious perspective, and that of the Shimerdas, the Sacrament proclaims redemption through crucifixion and resurrection through suffering and death. The discussions of Christian burial, the last rites of the Church, and "the propitiatory intent" (119) to bury old Shimerda at the crossroads after his rejection by various Christian groups should be considered as prefatory to Cather's most dramatic resurrection image, the explosion of life from the fruit cave in book 5.

I now ask students to consider Shimerda's death and burial, especially the image of his frozen, contorted corpse, lying on its side, the knees drawn up, the head bandaged like a mummy's. This is Cather's primary image of death, set as it is against the image of Otto Fuchs's stiff cardboard cutout of the baby in the manger, which Jim hangs on the Christmas tree. I introduce here St. Paul's proclamation that through the Christ child "all men will be brought to life; Death came through one man and in the same way the resurrection of the dead has come through one man" (1 Cor. 15.21–23). Students may observe that Cather's cardboard Christ anticipates the living girl baby of Christmas, Ántonia's illegitimate daughter, whose birth is recorded in "The Pioneer Woman's Story." They should begin to notice the chain of related images embroidering this novel: the stiff holy child, the frozen corpse, the primitive prairie birth—each set in winter.

We discuss also the gospel quality of retelling in the story of Ántonia's triumph over disgrace. Jim, as evangelist, records what he hears about her from other sources, including Frances Harling, her mother, the Black Hawk photographer, and Widow Steavens. Significantly revealing regarding "The Pioneer Woman's Story" and, indeed, the entire novel is the prologue to Luke's Gospel (1.1–4), with its promise of an "ordered account." Ordering the accounts of others in his own is exactly what Jim Burden does, despite the disclaimer in the introduction that he "didn't take time to arrange it. . . . I suppose it hasn't any form." And gospel style is evident throughout Jim's narrative. Near the beginning of book 4, for example, Jim introduces Tiny Soderball's story of material success, obviously a foil for Ántonia's story of spiritual riches; his declaration, "This is what actually happened to Tiny . . ." (299), recalls Matthew's introduction to the Nativity: "This is how Jesus Christ came to be born" (1.18).

Jim gives Mrs. Steavens's account verbatim, including in it her asides and complaints of ailments. She tells of Ántonia's excitement at the prospect of marrying Larry Donovan, adding details about her sewing and assembling of a modest dowry; then of her abandonment by Donovan, who left her penniless, pregnant, and unmarried; and of her return in shame to Black Hawk. When she tells of Ántonia's confession to her, the widow's response, "I sat right down on that bank beside her and made lament" (313), echoes the beginning of Psalm 137 ("Ballad of the Exiles"): "Beside the streams of Babylon we sat and wept at the memory of Zion. . . ." The widow marvels at the girl's calm, her perseverance, her humility: "She was quiet and steady. Folks respected her industry and tried to treat her as if nothing had happened. They talked, to be sure; but not like they would if she'd put on airs. She was so crushed and quiet that nobody seemed to want to humble her" (314). There follows a dark period of suffering, of ulcerated teeth and hard work in the fields, before the snowy December day when Ántonia turned her cattle into the corral and "went into the house, into her room behind the kitchen, and without calling to anybody, without a groan . . . lay down on the bed and bore her child" (312).

Thus Cather's story of the birth of an illegitimate girl parallels the birth in faraway Bethlehem celebrated by Jim during his first Nebraska winter. I have students read in Matthew and Luke to detect echoes in Ántonia's story of Mary's shame in being discovered with child by her fiancé, of Joseph's attempt to put her away (Matt. 1.18–20), of Mary's humility ("My soul proclaims the greatness of the Lord . . . because he has looked upon his lowly handmaid" [Luke 1.46–48]), of the humble stable birth when another mother, "natural-born" like Ántonia (318), "wrapped [her child] in swaddling clothes, and laid him in a manger" (Luke 2.17). The link between Mary and Ántonia is confirmed when Jim finds Ántonia alone in the fields after his visit with the widow. Jim's paean makes her the epitome of womanhood, all - that woman can be to man—sweetheart, wife, mother, sister. As he and Ántonia cross the fields, the "golden" sun sets and the moon rises, "pale silver" and "streaked with rose colour." Both heavenly bodies appear in Marian iconography based on Revelation 12.1: "Now a great sign appeared in heaven: a woman, adorned with the sun, standing on the moon, and with twelve stars on her head for a crown."

Having prepared students thus far in examining biblical echoes, I turn them loose to discuss the culmination of this theme in the final book, "Cuzak's Boys," in which Jim associates Ántonia with imagery of maternity and nur- - turing that reaches divine proportions. Ántonia sits in her orchard within a triple enclosure of wire fence and locust and mulberry hedges, surrounded by her adoring children and life's good things: hollyhocks and French pinks, grapevines and cherry trees, gooseberry and currant bushes, and even barnyard fowl. There is "the deepest peace in that orchard. . . . It seemed full of sun, like a cup, and one could smell the ripe apples on the trees" (341). This Della Robbia image of maternity clothed in light amid blossoms recalls Dante's dawn-bright vision of Mary in paradise surrounded by festive angels and enthroned in the mystical rose among the saints, who from a distance resemble banks of flowers. If not exactly Mary, we have in Ántonia the complementary female nature, the earthly if not the heavenly mother; on her own level, she is a nurturer, coredeemer, instrument of resurrection.

The climactic image—the completion of the embroidered pattern of birth, death, resurrection/rebirth—is the celebrated fruit-cave scene. After cataloging the nourishing foods Ántonia had prepared for her family, Jim leaves the cave and looks back at her brood: "they all came running up the steps together; big and little, tow heads and gold heads and brown, and flashing little naked legs; a veritable explosion of life out of the dark cave into the sunlight" (338–39). The structure of the pastoral sections of the novel is now illuminated: first, a mystical birth long ago in a foreign land is commemorated; then death is confronted in the rigid corpse of a suicide; finally, a peasant girl's story is traced from degradation and loss to restoration of life. Ántonia's fruit cave reminds me of the resurrection image in Whitman's "Song of Myself": "The grave of rock multiplies what has been confided to it, or to any graves, / Corpses rise, gashes heal, fastenings roll from me" (*Leaves of Grass*, lines 968–69). Toward the end of the novel old Shimerda's violin, until now stifled in the New World, is played by his faunlike grandson Leo. But this explosion of life is more than resurrection, for superimposed on it is the birth of a new generation, a new people, a new race in a new country.

Integral to Cather's resurrection theme are Ántonia's terrestrial qualities. From the novel's beginning, she is associated with the earth: her eyes are "like the sun shining on brown pools in the wood. Her skin was brown, too. . . . Her brown hair was curly and wild-looking" (23), and she rescues a freezing insect in that hair. "Her arms and throat were burned brown as a sailor's. Her neck came up strongly out of her shoulders, like the bole of a tree out of the turf" (122). Her affair with Donovan is distanced for a purpose. Figuratively, her children are not of men; they are of the spirit of the land. The key to their conception is in Cather's earlier prairie novel, *O Pioneers!*, when Alexandra returns to the high land after visiting the river farms and experiences a plains-inspired ecstasy: "Then the Genius of the Divide, the great free spirit which breathes across it, must have bent lower than it ever bent to a human will before" (65). This passage recalls the annunciation to the Virgin Mary: " 'The Holy Spirit will come upon you,' the angel answered, 'and the power of the Most High will cover you with its shadow' " (Luke 1.35). This genius fathers the race Ántonia founds. Her husband, Anton Cuzak, is, like the biblical Joseph, a foster parent. Like Joseph, Cuzak is older than his wife (although not as much older as the Joseph crèche figure in *Shadows*) and is more helpmate than husband: "Clearly, she was the impulse, and he the corrective" (358), comments Jim, adding, "It did rather seem to me that Cuzak had been made the instrument of Ántonia's special mission" (367).

My final suggestion regarding these biblical and religious dimensions of *My Ántonia* involves the episode in book 1 where Jim and Ántonia discover the rattlesnake in the prairie-dog town. Ántonia first sees and warns Jim of the snake, which Jim brands "the ancient, eldest Evil" (47). Note the implications in the following lines: "Ántonia, barefooted as she was, ran up behind me. Even after I had pounded his ugly head flat, his body kept on coiling and winding, doubling and falling back on itself" (46). Recall God's words to the tempting serpent in Genesis: "I will make you enemies of each other: you and the woman, your offspring and her offspring. It will crush your head and you will strike its heel" (3.15). The woman referred to is Eve; the woman anticipated is Mary.

Certainly we should read and teach *My Ántonia* from biblical and religious perspectives. Even its most famous image—that of the plow against the setting sun, which appears to Jim and the foreign girls after they talk about the buried swords of the conquistadores—echoes a familiar biblical passage hopeful of the prosperity of new countries: "He will wield authority over the peoples; these will hammer their swords into plowshares, their spears into sickles. Nation will not lift sword against nation, there will be no more training for war" (Isa. 2.4). The novel's birth, death, and resurrection themes are as definitely present as those involving the phases of American civilization, the psychology of sex, fertility myths, and feminism. This religious perspective, while essentially Protestant, anticipates in its focus the Catholic novels Cather would write in the twenties and thirties.

William James, Henri Bergson, and Remembered Time in *My Ántonia*

Loretta Wasserman

As Katherine Anne Porter recounts in her appreciation of Cather, the early modernists, equating surface obscurity with depth, found Cather's limpid prose insufficiently challenging. Cather's simplicity, Porter writes, ". . . finally alienated me from her, from her very fine books, from any feeling that she was a living working artist in our time" (31). Now, as modernism recedes from us, replaced by postmodernism, even post-postmodernism, its roots and skeletal forms are becoming clearer, the breaks with the past less sharp. At the same time, critics are noting the structural underpinnings of Cather's art in myth, in forms borrowed from music and painting, in storytelling and folktale—the repertory, in short, of modernist techniques. The English major who used to feel let down turning from "Sunday Morning" or *Absalom! Absalom!* to *My Ántonia* now finds at hand a wealth of critical and biographical readings revealing Cather as very much a twentieth-century writer. Yet "The Case of Willa Cather," as Phyllis Rose has called her search for the modern in Cather, is still being made. I contend here that viewing Cather's themes and ideas against the theories of two thinkers seen as central to the modernist sensibility—William James and Henri Bergson—reveals her as philosophically of her time, as embracing a worldview concerned with the possibility of human freedom under the weight of biologic determinism, the nature of mind, the power of the unconscious, the interplay of time and memory. Once alerted, students with an interest in psychological and philosophical ideas (not always English students) find the transmutation of these ideas into fictional form an intriguing study.

Cather's affinity for William James has been noted in both biographical and critical writing (Seibel 202; Curtin). Bergson has received little mention, although Cather's friend Elizabeth Sergeant, herself a writer and Francophile, says firmly of Cather, "Though she rejected Freud, she was a reader of Henri Bergson" (203). Sergeant's characterization is borne out by a letter Cather wrote to her in 1912, in which Cather agrees that *Creative Evolution*, recently translated, is glorious (letter to Sergeant). In 1922, writing a preface to *Alexander's Bridge*, then being republished after ten years, Cather turns to Bergson for authority. A writer, she says, must depend on "the thing by which our feet find the road home on a dark night, accounting to themselves for roots and stones which we had never noticed by day." She adds, "this thing" corresponds to "what Mr. Bergson calls the wisdom of intuition as opposed to intellect" (vii).

From this distance it is not easy to comprehend the excitement that greeted the works of James and Bergson—James writing first, beginning with his *Principles of Psychology* in 1890; then Bergson, working along parallel and complementary lines, as both quickly and generously recognized. No longer viewed by the dominant academic trends in psychology and philosophy as voices to be reckoned with, each remains a luminous figure in the history of ideas, honored for opening new lines of thinking for a generation, as well as for bravura eloquence (Bergson won the Nobel Prize for literature in 1927, and James remains honored in part for his masterful plain style). James's centrality for American studies continues to be examined; Bergson's influence on American writers around the time of World War I, notably on Eliot and Faulkner, is fully acknowledged.

Some statistics and anecdotes may indicate the early reputations of James and Bergson (Bergson's approached celebrity). By 1902, 8,115 sets of *The Principles of Psychology* had sold, and 47,531 copies of *Psychology: Briefer Course*, the abridged and somewhat altered version James had prepared for college use (*Briefer Course* xii). A generation thus introduced to this "new" scientific approach to mind was an audience for James's later, more philosophical works, *The Varieties of Religious Experience*, *The Will to Believe*, and *Pragmatism* (the last published shortly before his death in 1910). Bergson, some thirty years younger, rose to popularity through his speaking as well as his writings. In the early years of the century his lectures at the Collège de France attracted not only students of literature, philosophy, and science (Bergson was trained as a biologist, as James in medicine) but people from the fashionable world. It is said that ladies sent their grooms into the crowded hall to hold seats. The young T. S. Eliot came to Paris to hear him in 1910. Gertrude Stein was another American who attended. Artists and writers were especially responsive to Bergson's ideas, and in the early years of the century Cather was a part of this mildly bohemian world, traveling to England in search of manuscripts for *McClure's*, meeting William Archer, Wells, Ford, Yeats, Gosse. It is my belief that as she turned from journalism to serious writing in 1912 her mind was furnished with the speculations of James and Bergson—particularly those of Bergson—and that these ideas blended with her native romanticism to form her particular cast of mind.

Here we can only gesture in the direction of the theories James and Bergson were developing, noting common areas. Central to their popularity was their welcoming stance toward evolution. Both *Principles* and *Briefer Course* were commissioned by Henry Holt for a science series designed to popularize evolution for an American audience. But the picture of evolution that emerges in James—and more explicitly in Bergson's *Creative Evolution* of 1907—is not of imponderable material forces, of chance and mortal struggle, but of vital, dynamic change driven by mind, or spirit. What James and Bergson postulated, in differing ways and with different terminology, is a purposive, energized—indeed, spiritualized—process: matter altering in response to, or accompanying, a vital pulse, an élan vital, to use Bergson's famous phrase. The universe was no longer closed, bound by iron determinacies, but open and free, still being made. From these presuppositions stem a number of related notions. An important one for Cather is the connection between consciousness and the flow of evolutionary change. James writes, "If evolution is to work smoothly, consciousness in some shape must have been present at the very origin of things" (*Principles* 149). Further, the individual consciousness is connected to this evolving consciousness, and thus connected it feels not overwhelmed, or isolated, or a victim of unseen forces, as in a novel of Thomas Hardy, but enhanced and made whole. Henry Grenfell, the central consciousness in the late Cather story "Before Breakfast," regains his spiritual equilibrium by watching a young swimmer face the challenge of an icy ocean. Grenfell meditates, "Anyhow, when that first amphibious frog-toad found his water-hole dried up, and jumped out to hop along till he could find another—well, he started on a long trip" (156). Evolutionary time is both distant and present: often in her novels and stories Cather presents a contact with remote time as restorative—an Indian cliff dwelling, a bit of decorated pottery, the trace of early explorers.

Thus linked to the vitality of the universe, mind, for James and Bergson, expands in power, becomes mysterious. James writes, "It is . . . the reinstatement of the vague and inarticulate to its proper place in our mental life which I am so anxious to press on the attention" (*Briefer Course* 150). No longer "I think, therefore I am," but rather, "I sense, I feel, I perceive, I am an *I* that knows a *me*, the accumulation of all my past experiences" (see the chapter "Self" in *Principles*). Instead of a searchlight, mind is a dissolving fluid, a stream of consciousness flowing seamlessly, carrying what is past into a future, creating as it moves: "Every image in the mind is steeped and dyed in the free water that flows round it. With it goes the sense of its relations, near and remote, the dying echo of whence it came to us, the dawning sense of whither it is to lead" (James, *Briefer Course* 151). Similarly, Bergson sees consciousness, stored as memory, as a force in the present: "Memory . . . is not a faculty of putting away recollections in a drawer. . . . In reality all that we have felt, thought, and willed from our earliest infancy is there, leaning over the present which is about to join it, pressing against the portals of consciousness" (4–5). Through intuition and openness to involuntary memory, we have the power to use, to bring into the present, our individual pasts. When spatialized and intellectualized, past time lies in inert units; when allowed to interpenetrate the present, however, it becomes renewing and invigorating. The logical and abstracting power of mind must be complemented by this intuitive power.

As noted, Cather's one published reference to Bergson alludes to this power of intuition, this "thing by which our feet find the road home on a dark night." Significantly Cather had already used this imagery in her fiction. Ántonia, talking about her memories of Bohemia, tells Jim,

> . . . if I was put down there in the middle of the night, I could find my way all over that little town; and along the river to the next town, where my grandmother lived. My feet remember the little paths through the woods, and where the big roots stick out to trip you. I ain't never forgot my own country. (237–38)

The act of remembering "my own country" is the structural principle of *My Ántonia*. In the closing pages Jim revisits Black Hawk; the town is altered and disappointing, the Lombardy poplar now a stump and strange children in the Harlings' big yard. But on a walk out of town Jim has "the good luck to stumble upon a bit of the first road that went from Black Hawk out to the north country." Like the big roots that trip Ántonia (also like Proust's madeleine), the ruts in this old road lead Jim into the past that will be his book. "I had only to close my eyes to hear the rumbling of the wagons in the dark" (371). In structure *My Ántonia* takes the form of what M. H. Abrams calls " 'creative autobiography'—the more or less fictional work of art about the development of the artist himself, which is preoccupied with memory, time, and the relations of what is passing to what is eternal" (180).

But let us look more particularly at the novel itself against a grid of these ideas. The land that young Jim finds an empty, erasing prairie is in reality replete with life, as Jim gradually sees. The land appears to be responding to a life current ("I felt motion in the landscape . . ." [16]). With winter, "The snow reveals . . . a great circle where the Indians used to ride . . ." (62). In the autumn Jim follows roads edged by sunflowers growing from seeds that Mormons, passing from persecution through the wilderness, had scattered—a legend the adult Jim still likes to believe, so that "sunflower-bordered roads always seem to me the roads to freedom" (29). Cather is building for us the sense of an underlying vitality, an élan vital, flowing from past to present and beyond.

Then too there are the myriad pasts brought by the immigrants—the smell of the Shimerdas' dried mushrooms, Peter's melons, and on and on. The Burdens' Christmas tree, decorated with Otto's colored-paper figures from Austria, appears an emblem of all these pasts. It becomes "the talking tree of the fairy tale; legends and stories nestled like birds in its branches. Grandmother said it reminded her of the Tree of Knowledge" (83). At times Cather allows herself an extravagant figurative expression to expand our sense of what Bergson calls "lived time" (*durée*): the hour of late afternoon on the prairie was "like a hero's death" (40); the clouds of a summer storm (the scene ending book 1) were "like the quay of some splendid seacoast city, doomed to destruction" (139). In all these ways she makes us see the long vista of evolving human time as a backdrop to the "people and places" of Jim's "infinitesimal past" (262).

The persistent pulse of energy we sense in the land is also evident in the lives of the characters who most engage us, Ántonia and Jim. The immediate source, or conduit, is Mr. Shimerda, even though for much of the novel he is a ghost, a tutelary spirit, hovering over their lives. He, as much as Jim, gives the novel its title: "I used to think of the tone in which poor Mr. Shimerda, who could say so little, yet managed to say so much when he exclaimed, 'My Án-tonia' " (126). Perhaps Jim had Mr. Shimerda in mind as he wrote his memoir, as long before he had him in mind as he penned his high school valedictory talk. "I dedicated it to him," he tells Ántonia, when she says, ". . . there was something in your speech that made me think so about my papa" (230). Earlier, forced to give up her own classes, she pleads, "Sometime you will tell me all those nice things you learn at the school, won't you, Jimmy? . . . My father, he went much to school. . . . You won't forget my father, Jim?" (124). Jim promises. But even earlier the young Jim had absorbed Mr. Shimerda's yearnings. Left alone on the farm just after the suicide, he senses Mr. Shimerda's spirit in the comfortable room. "Such vivid pictures came to me that they might have been Mr. Shimerda's memories, not yet faded" (102). It is their common consciousness of Mr. Shimerda's striving for beauty and harmony that binds Jim and Ántonia. Readers who feel disappointed that Jim does not marry Ántonia and rescue her from disgrace (and that includes most of us on first reading) come to see that Ántonia sends him forth, rather as a lady of old sent her knight, to realize her father's hopes. To this end, she protects Jim from Lena in Black Hawk, and even from herself, when his kiss threatens to become passionate. When she sends Jim off to study in the East, she likens the coming separation from him to the separation she feels from her father—or rather, to the closeness she feels: "Of course it means you are going away from us for good. . . . But that don't mean I'll lose you. Look at my papa here; he's been dead all these years, and yet he is more real to me than almost anybody else. He never goes out of my life. I talk to him and consult him all the time" (320). The "incommunicable past" that Jim and Ántonia possess together is not of childhood memories only, however sweet, but of the intuitive purposes that have guided their lives. At their last meeting they hear Mr. Shimerda's violin played again by his grandson, little Leo. Beneath apparent loss and change, there is continuity.

One scene in particular can dramatize for us how a sense of the past, both personal and communal, can penetrate and vitalize the present. As the hired girls of Black Hawk gather on the bluff to pick elderberry blossoms for wine, they begin to remember the old country in their families' pasts—Lena Lingard and the Marshalls' Anna talk of Norway, Ántonia of Bohemia, Tiny Soderball of Sweden. As they look about they can see the newly created country—the town, the farms. "It seems like my mother ain't been so homesick, ever since father's raised rye flour for her" (239). The past, in being allowed to emerge into the present, brings a moment of tranquil happiness. Then the past enlarges. They speak of the explorations of Coronado, and of how a farmer has found a sword with a Spanish inscription on the blade, and of how, according to school books, Coronado died "in the wilderness with a broken heart" (244). "More than him has done that," Ántonia says, linking the legendary figure to her father—and we see for a second *two* lonely graves. As the sun goes down the memorable image of the plow, enlarged to heroic size, appears. We juxtapose the plow to the sword of the hero Coronado—a sword beaten into a plowshare—and sense the continuity and unity behind changing forms (Wasserman 230).

Much later, as Jim sits in his student rooms in Lincoln studying the *Aeneid* (a poem of continuities and of fidelity to a "divine flame"), he thinks of ". . . my own naked land and the figures scattered upon it. . . . They stood out strengthened and simplified now, like the image of the plough against the sun" (262).

The glimpses we are given of Ántonia in her many transformations—the vibrant girl, the farm drudge, the small-town flirt, then "poor Ántonia" (297), seduced and abandoned, and finally the aging wife and mother—bring to the fore the principle we have been stressing, the continuity beneath apparent discontinuity. The last scene of the novel turns back to the earth itself, and the marks it bears of effort and consciousness. The traces of the old road out of Black Hawk that Jim finds on his last visit are now no more visible than are the circles left by Indian ponies, yet they are not eradicated: they are "shadings in the grass" and ruts that "the sod had never healed" (371). Cather's concern for the past, so often mistaken for mere self-indulgent nostalgia, is a thoughtful one, grounded in the philosophical ideas current in early modernism.

TEACHING SPECIFIC COURSES

My Ántonia in a Survey of the American Novel

Tom Quirk

Because a survey of the American novel is perforce exclusionary (a student can read only so many novels a term, after all) and because one tries to render the American literary tradition by assembling a constellation of exceptional and diverse novels, a single book must serve as adequate representative of several cultural, historical, or aesthetic tendencies at once. There is a double difficulty with such an arrangement. Pushed too far in one direction, a course in the American novel can become no more than an exercise in the history of ideas; too far in the other direction, it becomes a literary-appreciation course, in which, to all appearances, the novels merely happen to be by American writers and happen to be arranged chronologically on the syllabus. I sometimes wonder whether one can make interesting or convincing generalizations about the American novel or the American tradition for a class required to read a dozen or so novels, including, say, *Moby-Dick, Adventures of Huckleberry Finn, The Awakening, As I Lay Dying,* and *Death Comes for the Archbishop.* Surely, one can establish some sort of continuity by noting mythic or thematic resemblances—the peculiar treatment of love and/or death in the American novel; the ritual of innocence and initiation, or of escape and return; the edenic experience attained, lost, regained, or glimpsed by a new Adam or a new Eve. Those methods whereby such continuity and conventions are established and conveyed (that is, "taught") are no doubt necessary and fruitful, but is not something of the individual artist's ambition and original achievement lost in the process? And is not a writer such as Willa Cather, whose devotion to form and craft was paramount, unjustly served by such an arrangement?

Those of us who consider Cather a writer of the first rank may sometimes feel that her unique talents and circumstance make her difficult to include in such a course. Cather has to some extent always been hard to classify. When she advised those perplexed reviewers of *Death Comes for the Archbishop* not to trouble themselves about trying to classify the book, she recommended instead that they think of it as merely a "narrative." What is a novel finally, she wondered, if not "merely a work of imagination in which a writer tries to present the experiences and emotions of a group of people by the light of his own" (*On Writing* 12–13). However eloquent the author may be on the point, the teacher can't very well find the solution to the pedagogical problem by simply dismissing the question. In some way, if she is to be taught at all, Willa Cather must be classified and located within the context of the American novel and its tradition.

One way to accomplish this task is to let her speak for herself. By surveying her critical attitudes toward other American novelists, we may begin to establish a network of relations that allow for generalizations about her place in the American tradition at the same time that we identify her special contribution. A way to classify her as a writer, a way that does not too severely limit an appreciation of her unique artistic gifts, is to think of her as something of a cosmopolitan regionalist. The term is ambiguous enough and broad enough to allow for her self-evident literary sophistication and for her equally self-evident attachment to place, to local color and local custom. But the term is more than an empty convenience, for it identifies in her a literary mode and an aesthetic ambition. These two ways of treating Cather in a historical survey of the American novel are closely related to one another, but for the sake of clarity it is necessary to speak of them separately.

When the student takes it up, *My Ántonia* will no doubt appear in some sort of historical context anyway. In a course on the twentieth-century novel, she may be the first or second novelist discussed. In a class such as the one I teach, which examines the American novel from its beginnings to 1914, I may begin with Charles Brockden Brown's *Wieland* (1798) and conclude the course with *O Pioneers!* (1913) or *My Ántonia* (1918), though obviously I must fudge a bit in order to include the last. Over the course of the term, we shall have read and discussed novels by Cooper, Hawthorne, Melville, Twain, Howells, James, Crane, Chopin, Dreiser, and several others. There are innumerable associations one may make here: For those students disturbed by the fact that Cather adopted a male narrator for her book, one only need remind them that Brockden Brown told his story with a female narrator. (This kind of response doesn't answer the question, of course, but it does force the students to make generalizations and allowances on the basis of their reading in American novels.) No doubt some time might be fruitfully spent comparing Cooper's pioneers with Cather's. The scorn Ántonia receives from the community when her illegitimate child is born may bring to mind the circumstance of Hester Prynne. In a word, the students, even if their reading in American literature does not exceed the dozen or so novels assigned for the course, are nevertheless equipped to make some sorts of statements about the tradition of the American novel and, in the same stroke, to establish and appreciate Cather's contribution to it.

Perhaps the students' reading of *My Ántonia* follows the reading, in succession, of *Portrait of a Lady*, *The Awakening*, and *Sister Carrie*. The obvious similarity in this grouping—all four are concerned with rendering a portrait of a rare, or at least unconventional, woman—may or may not yield more significant comparisons. But to locate more precisely Cather's novel in this context, it may be helpful to rely on Cather's guidance as it is provided, from time to time, by her critical statements.

We may note, for example, that by her own account, delivered in a rather dramatic fashion, Cather wanted not to render an interior view of the life of Ántonia Shimerda so much as to provide multiple perspectives of her character's effect on others, principally but not exclusively on Jim Burden. She wanted, she told Elizabeth Shepley Sergeant as she placed an apothecary jar in the center of an antique table, her title character to be "like a rare object in the middle of a table," something that might stand out, command attention, and be viewed from all sides (Sergeant 139). In that simple gesture Cather signaled her originality of purpose in a way that distinguishes her ambition from that of James or Chopin or Dreiser. She did not (to borrow the language of Melville) wish to lift the "soul's lid." Instead, she wished to preserve the mystery of, and thereby what was essential in, her title character at the same time that she made her stand out.

In 1899, Cather had complained in a review of *The Awakening* that Kate Chopin had written a second *Madame Bovary*, and in so doing had sacrificed an exquisite style to a "trite" and "sordid" theme, that there was nothing new in Chopin's story, neither "matter nor treatment" (*World* 2: 697). However unjustly harsh we may find Cather's judgment in this instance, we may nevertheless discern the high premium she placed on originality of conception. The pedagogical advantage of communicating this familiar notion through a discussion of Cather's criticisms of *The Awakening* is that the student can participate fully in developing the point.

The teacher may convey Cather's departure from Dreiserian naturalism by noting those artistic principles announced most familiarly in the essay

"The Novel Démeublé." Her disdain for the minute and journalistic enu-
merations of naturalist writers in favor of an attempt to simplify rather than
complicate, to suggest rather than identify, is easily enough suggested by a
comparison of passages from *Sister Carrie* and *My Ántonia*.

> The first snowfall came early in December. I remember how the world
> looked from our sitting-room window as I dressed behind the stove
> that morning: the low sky was like a sheet of metal; the blond cornfields
> had faded out into ghostliness at last; the little pond was frozen under
> its stiff willow bushes. Big white flakes were whirling over everything
> and disappearing in the red grass.   (*My Ántonia* 62)

How clotted the following passage from *Sister Carrie* appears beside Burden's spare recollection.

> It was truly a wintry evening, a few days later, when his one distinct
> mental decision was reached. Already, at four o'clock, the somber hue
> of night was thickening the air. A heavy snow was falling—a fine
> picking, whipping snow, borne forward by a swift wind in long, thin
> lines. The streets were bedded with it—six inches of cold, soft carpet,
> churned to a dirty brown by the crush of teams and the feet of men.   (430)

Cather strove for the evocations of a Hawthorne in her art; as she remarked
about *The Scarlet Letter*, the "material investiture of the story is presented
as if unconsciously" (*On Writing* 41) through the memories of her narrator in
a way that emulates the equally remote though duskier tones of Hawthorne.

Of Cather's response to James one must be more careful, for she was,
without doubt, admiring, particularly of the refinements of his style. But
her admiration was something that had to be outgrown. She had tried to fit
the Jamesian mold in her first novel, *Alexander's Bridge*, but soon after its
publication rejected the Jamesian fashion as ill suited to her talents. In that
first novel, she had tried to explore her version of a Jamesian international
theme. Her hero, Bartley Alexander, a successful bridge builder, attempts
to recapture his younger, more authentic self by reviving his relationship
with a British actress, Hilda. Cather complained many years later, in her
essay "My First Novels (There Were Two)," that many liked the book because
it follows the "conventional pattern" (*On Writing* 91) and because much of
the action takes place in London, a more engaging scene than a familiar
village in America. Her second "first" novel, *O Pioneers!*, she claimed, was
written entirely for herself; it was to be a novel of the soil, in which her
impressions of prairie life, if less glamorous than those of London, were still
more authentic. She realized, as she said in the same essay, that it is useless

to follow another's manner, however interesting, if you haven't the special qualifications for it.

What she had the special qualifications for and what she discovered in her next attempt at a novel was an authentic and spontaneous talent for writing about her youth in her native Nebraska. *O Pioneers!* mapped out the direction *My Ántonia* would take a few years later, though she might lose her way once more in *The Song of the Lark*. In any event, in bringing an acquired and earned literary sophistication to bear on familiar territory she found her own way, and we might describe the results of that discovery as a sort of cosmopolitan regionalism.

Cather said in a preface to Sarah Orne Jewett's stories that the true artist "fades away into the land and people of his heart, he dies of love only to be born again" (*On Writing* 51). *My Ántonia* is surely one of Cather's happier books; perhaps she gave herself more completely to her subject than she had ever done before. In any case, by giving her narrator a successful New York law practice, an unhappy marriage, a trip to Europe (including Ántonia's native Prague), and a Harvard education, the author superbly outfitted Jim Burden with the requirements for nostalgic but learned reminiscence.

But because Cather limited herself to a story of remembrance, she likewise limited the sorts of disclosures she might make about her title character. Jim Burden's story possesses the solemnity and equipoise of memory itself, but the author's choice of point of view prohibited the sort of access James had to the thoughts and feelings of Isabel Archer. We may further distinguish Cather from James by juxtaposing passages from *Portrait of a Lady* with *My Ántonia*. When Isabel realizes that Madame Merle has "married" her, we, as readers, are allowed within the circle of her disappointment:

> She had long before this taken old Rome into her confidence, for in a world of ruins the ruin of her happiness seemed a less unnatural catastrophe. She rested her weariness upon things that had crumbled for centuries and yet still were upright; she dropped her secret sadness into the silence of lonely places, where its very modern quality detached itself and grew objective, so that as she sat in a sun-warmed angle on a winter's day, or stood in a mouldy church to which no one came, she could almost smile at it and think of its smallness.   (430)

Cather, necessarily, handles a similar sadness in Ántonia—her disappointment that she could not continue her schooling—in a very different way:

> "I ain't got time to learn. I can work like mans now. My mother can't say no more how Ambrosch do all and nobody to help him. I can work

as much as him. School is all right for little boys. I help make this land one good farm."

She clucked to her team and started for the barn. I walked beside her, feeling vexed. Was she going to grow up boastful like her mother, I wondered? Before we reached the stable, I felt something tense in her silence, and glancing up I saw that she was crying. She turned her face from me and looked off at the red streak of dying light, over the dark prairie. (123)

Cather renders the silent sadness of her character by mere suggestion, filtered through the memory of Burden, who bears within him his own disappointments in a way that affects the tonal quality of the entire novel.

Gaston Cleric introduces Jim Burden to the "world of ideas," and "when one first enters that world everything fades for a time, and all that went before is as if it had not been" (258). Yet there are "curious survivals," "figures of his old life"—among them the memory of Ántonia—that have shaped his experience. Burden eventually discovers what "a little circle man's experience is," but he would not have acquired the detachment necessary to see things anew without the larger experience of the world beyond his native soil. Having discovered the world, he may know the parish in a way that allows him to be the first to bring the muse to his country.

In a way, My Ántonia is a record of those curious survivals, memories of the legends, language, and customs of the people of Cather's native land. To the extent that these elements are preserved in her narrative, Cather is a regionalist; to the extent that she, like her narrator, escaped the "curious depression that hangs over little towns," hers is a privileged recollection of Nebraska life. My Ántonia benefits from the detached tone of patient repose that makes it a fit companion for those three books Cather thought have the possibility of long, long life—The Scarlet Letter, Adventures of Huckleberry Finn, and The Country of the Pointed Firs. "I can think of no others," she said, "that confront time and change so serenely" (On Writing 58). If students of the American novel can begin to see a network of associations between and among the novels selected for the course, they should begin to be able to make convincing generalizations about the American novel and its tradition. At all events, informed by Cather's critical statements about her own fiction and that of other American novelists, they should not have much difficulty recognizing Cather's place within the American tradition and her special contribution to it.

My Ántonia in Women's Studies: Pioneer Women and Men—The Myth and the Reality

Mary Anne Ferguson

Though the specific content of Pioneer Women and Men: The Myth and the Reality varied over the ten years that I taught it, *My Ántonia* was its central text; students read the novel early in the course and again at the end, and throughout it was our constant point of reference. Conceived as an interdisciplinary course involving literature, history, and art, the course had as its central purpose introducing students in both women's studies and American studies to the methods and limitations of the interdisciplinary approach; another purpose was to help students read on a more sophisticated level and develop writing skills appropriate to that reading level, so that the course could legitimately "count" toward the English major. In addition to *My Ántonia*, required reading usually included at least Cather's *O Pioneers!*, Charley O'Kieffe's *Western Story*, W. H. O'Gara's *In All Its Fury: A History of the Blizzard of January 12, 1888* (both memoirs written almost fifty years after the fact), and Mari Sandoz's biography of her father, *Old Jules*. All these works centered on immigrant experience in Nebraska in the 1880s, as did the slides I showed.

I first taught *My Ántonia* in the early 1970s, in the course Images of Women in Literature. The novel proved attractive to my students, but we were all puzzled by its appeal; reading as feminists, we felt it was not the earth-mother figure that attracted us, though we were all deeply moved by the image of Ántonia surrounded by her eleven children and the other fruit of her labors. We came to realize that Cather's deliberate elevation of Ántonia into a mythic hero caused our responses.

There was no time in that course for ample discussion of Cather's techniques, of the relations among myth, romanticism, and realism in the book. A planning grant from the National Endowment for the Humanities to develop Pioneer Women and Men allowed me to explore materials in history and art that I thought could furnish answers to questions about *My Ántonia*, as well as educate us all about life in Nebraska in the 1880s, about how the three disciplines represent the past, about where the "truth" might lie. From the beginning I was interested in problems of historiography; I was also wary of the reductionism inherent in attempting to compare "real life" and artistic representation.

I started the course with three short works intended to elicit discussion about distinctions among myth, romance, realism, and verisimilitude: Hawthorne's "My Kinsman, Major Molineux," Emerson's "Nature," and Cather's "A Wagner Matinée." We discussed the techniques by which Hawthorne had made Robin into a hero, as comic in his overconfidence and naïveté as was Parsifal, but serious as a personification of the young American Republic.

I introduced Richard Slotkin's definition of myth—"A myth is a narrative which concentrates in a single, dramatized experience the whole history of a people in their land" (269)—and suggested that Robin was mythical in representing the experience of the lone male in American society.

The first sentence of "Nature" ("Our age is retrospective") paved the way for Cather. "A Wagner Matinée" is a return to youth and lost dreams for an aging Nebraska pioneer woman as well as for the nephew who narrates her story. Emerson's exaltation of the beauty of nature as a teacher of ultimate truths was excellent preparation for Cather's tales of love of the land as surpassing all others. "A Wagner Matinée" served well to define verisimilitude, realism, sentimentality. Students saw easily that the male narrator's pity is sentimental; they felt that he projected his feelings that Nebraska was a cultural desert without understanding that his aunt's perception might be very different. They suggested that her tears in response to Wagner's intensity might have stemmed from a sense of passion fulfilled rather than from the suffering and loss the narrator ascribes to her; the narrator—and perhaps Cather herself—did not give enough weight to Aunt Georgianna's success as wife, mother of six, housewife, farmer. This perception was strengthened when a student played for the class and analyzed all the music Cather alludes to in the story; later, after reading *My Ántonia*, the students saw that Wagner's treatment of his heroic figures was romantic in that he exalted received myths, whereas Cather created a myth of a heroic woman who was also a realistic human being.

With these insights, I felt the students were ready to read *My Ántonia* and the other required readings and to start research into one of the categories of related works I had listed in a bibliography. Each student was to become an expert in one category for the purposes of contributing to class discussions, giving short oral reports, and writing a long paper. Always indicating parallels between their reading and our common reading, they could choose to focus on Cather's other works, her biography, or criticism of her; other fiction; other documents by immigrants; Nebraska history; theories about immigration and the westward movement; critiques of historians' views of immigration; or on art: photographs of the "sod-house frontier" as well as paintings both of women and of western landscape. Choosing a topic, writing the required précis, and composing the final paper necessitated extended conference time, but group conferences according to research category proved fruitful and timesaving. The quality of the students' work for the course continued to amaze me; some of their papers led to honors or master's papers and in one case to publication, and their sense of expertise led to lively and rich discussions.

An example of how class reading and discussion, student reports, and questions worked together occurred in our reading of Cather's *O Pioneers!*, written five years before *My Ántonia*. Students found Alexandra not only implausible but also unattractive; her asexual life made her seem more deprived than Aunt Georgiana of "A Wagner Matinée." A student review of Mildred Bennett's book on Cather's world made it clear that many of Cather's characters in *My Ántonia* were drawn from life. Slides of Bennett's illustrations and of Solomon Butcher's documentary photographs reinforced this impression. The knowledge that Ántonia was modeled on a real Annie Pavelka, who had an illegitimate child but later married happily, counteracted the credibility of the stereotype of the seduced and abandoned heroine so prevalent in American literature, as another student's report on Leslie Fiedler's work established. Cather's presentation of such a woman as heroic made her iconoclasm breathtakingly clear: students now began to see Cather's shift from the goddesslike figure of Alexandra, for whom there seems to have been no living analogue, as a deliberate move toward establishing a character who could acceptably embody the American experience of love for the land. They suggested that the omniscient voice of *O Pioneers!* distanced the reader from Alexandra as Wagner's intense music distanced his heroic figures from real historical characters, whereas Jim's perspective as a character in the story added to their sense of Ántonia as real.

Another student reported on Blanche Gelfant's "The Forgotten Reaping-Hook: Sex in *My Ántonia*," which focuses on Jim Burden's sexual confusion and fear of adult sexuality; a report on Cather biography made it clear that Jim's life experience closely parallels Cather's. These two insights led to discussion—which remained unresolved—of Cather's sexuality. They also made clear that Cather's knowledge of and close relations with immigrants far transcended those she ascribes to Jim; Jim is romantic in preferring memories to experience, but Cather is realistic in her use of Jim as narrator. We found that Cather's use of Jim was a literary strategy: a male voice is more authoritative; Jim's perspective plausibly and economically introduces the epic allusions and dimension of the book; the image of Jim as the conventional male hero (as when he kills the snake) furnishes a basis for seeing as heroic Ántonia's sturdier courage in the face of greater obstacles. Students felt they could see beyond Jim's nostalgia to the hard reality of Ántonia's life.

The interweaving of response, questions, and expert information continued as the required reading furnished additional material. *In All Its Fury*, memories written down fifty years after the fact by more than sixty survivors of the great blizzard of 1888, was particularly rich. It offered intimate details of immigrant life that often corroborated and augmented Cather's descriptions. But there were lapses in its verisimilitude: memory could not be trusted when one looked back fifty years to an incident that occured when one was very young. The "school children's blizzard" moved across Nebraska from morning recess through lunch and afternoon recess, but memories of when it occurred did not always concur with the geological charts. We learned that newspaper accounts of casualties varied from two hundred to one thousand and that a survey of school principals was suppressed for fear the truth would discourage immigration. But we found a common theme in the "eyewitness" reports and the newspaper accounts: the young women teachers were true heroes of the blizzard, often having led their students to safety at the sacrifice of a leg or even of their lives. Students felt they were watching the process of legend making, of mythopoesis, and they could apply new insights to the old questions about Alexandra and Ántonia as central characters.

A student report on Slotkin's description of how the Daniel Boone legend arose supported this insight. Sandoz's *Old Jules* furnished another view of the power of myth: Jules's vision of his ideal loner, "the man with the Winchester rifle," and his faith in the land despite years of failure kept him, unlike more than half of his fellow immigrants, from leaving Nebraska. He had heroic qualities; he was also dirty, crude, often brutal to his four wives and to his children. The question of historiography was graphically illustrated: How could the daughter he had mistreated be an objective biographer? Sandoz asserts that she relies on the mass of papers Jules himself left, but the question of her objectivity must be answered subjectively, from the tone of her writing and her selection of facts.

Discussion of these historical sources led most fruitfully into further questions of Cather's artistry in selecting, her skill in presenting a few scenes and characters vividly, the economy of her classical allusions. Against the multiple personal memories of the blizzard of 1888 and the many people involved with Old Jules, Cather's focus in *My Ántonia* on snowstorms as they affected the lives of a few people is strikingly simple. The three heavy snows of the winter of Mr. Shimerda's death are a stark background for his burial alone at a crossroads, a place Jim tells us is "the spot most dear to me"; it is no wonder that when he later makes explicit Cather's Vergilian epigraph (*Optima dies . . . prima fugit*), Jim perceives early memory as melancholy. Cather uses a snowstorm as background for what might have been only a sad memory for Ántonia: she has her illegitimate child "one day in December"; by the time Jim learns of her ordeal, it is summer. The starkness of Ántonia's life compared to Jim's memories of it establishes Cather's transcendence of her narrator's romanticism.

Student reports and my research made us appreciate the difficulty all artists had in representing American landscape. Thomas Cole, Albert Bierstadt, and Albert Pinkham Ryder struggled to show the beauty of spectacular mountains and storms; they succeeded to a degree, but any human figures they include are dwarfed. Cather's verbal images of the quiet beauty of grass and snow on the plains show the spiritual aspects of nature that Emerson emphasized and allow the human figures to assume heroic size.

Most students finished the course with a new respect for fiction as a mode of truth, but they also realized that there could be greater and lesser approximations, as with Cather's two Nebraska novels. They all learned that they could not place absolute confidence in so-called facts, that they must select and fill in the frame of reference for themselves and make informed choices. They learned that each medium had its characteristic concerns: paintings of women might well be studies of changing light rather than of women; historical works might support a subjective view of reality. We felt that the image of the lonely male as the hero of the West was the result of a male perspective that ignored the experience of women like Charley O'Kieffe's widowed mother and Ántonia. Over the years that I taught the course, new material—diaries and letters, critiques of Cather as a great woman writer, Annette Kolodny's *Lay of the Land*—refined our sense of having learned from primary materials and from sharing our knowledge. *My Ántonia* proved memorable indeed.

My Ántonia in American Studies: History, Landscape, and Memory

Barbara Bair

The narrative of Willa Cather's *My Ántonia* is permeated with a sense of passage—the movement across landscape and time, the transition from youth to age, and the juxtaposition of the present with an idealized past. As a memoir, the story is built on Jim/Cather's memory of a place and time and of a person who comes to epitomize, in a poetic sense, the force of memory translated into the history of a region. Ántonia becomes the personification of the American phenomenon of westward migration and settlement. As such, her story is transfused with heroism and with a metaphysical feeling of doubleness or transition. It is studded by visual and religious images that twin opposites in a suspended moment of time—images that mirror the narrative tracing of one form of life's being transmuted into another, just as the boy Jim becomes a man, and the rural prairie life of his (and by extension, America's) youth is exchanged for the modern adulthood of the railroad and the city. In Cather's art, history is told as allegory, as an almost mythic process of metaphorical and personal transfiguration.

My experience in teaching *My Ántonia* has been in American studies and women's studies courses. While the cultural construction of gender, women's labor, and women's roles are the focus of the discussion of *My Ántonia* in the women's studies course, the American studies course is organized around questions of the development of the American landscape and so-called American values. In this context *My Ántonia* is used with nineteenth- and early twentieth-century classics (Hawthorne, Melville, Alcott, Stowe or Twain, Faulkner, Crane, Wharton, and Lewis) to formulate definitions of the "American" character (based on race, gender, class, and ideology) and to develop ideas about regionalism and the various authors' interpretations of American history. Because *My Ántonia* falls almost at the end of the syllabus in the American studies course, we compare it with other authors' works (already read by the class) mainly in discussion sections rather than in lecture. The comparisons vary, then, according to the interests and dynamics of the different groups of students. In comparing *My Ántonia* with Hawthorne's *The Scarlet Letter*, for example, I may ask the class for a comparison of Ántonia's place in the Black Hawk community and on the prairie with Hester Prynne's status in the woods and the Puritan town. This discussion raises the issues of the changing value sets placed on the classic wilderness-civilization dichotomy through time and asks the class to explore definitions of individualism and collectivism, freedom and social control, as manifested in the two literary-historical situations. With Melville, Stowe, Twain, and Faulkner, the questions turn to the issue of race. With these authors, the class is asked to reread closely Cather's passage featuring Blind d'Arnault. The discussion then begins with the issue of authorial perspective, with an ultimate goal of working toward a dual question: (a) How closely do Cather's and Jim's narrative identities coincide? and (b) If Jim's prejudices are Cather's, can the depiction of Blind d'Arnault be fairly described as racist? The class recalls that in Melville's *Benito Cereno*, the reader is given not Melville's but Amasa Delano's—the American's—view of Babo and the other slaves present on the European slaver. That view in turn is loaded by patronizing prejudgments not only about blacks but about European Catholics. In Twain's *Huckleberry Finn*, much of what we know of Jim is presented through the special eyes—and changing consciousness—of young Huck. Indeed, *My Ántonia*, *Huck Finn*, and Faulkner's "The Bear" have in common a youthful male protagonist and the theme of initiation into a landscape and into a value system that landscape is made to reveal or represent. In Faulkner's story, Sam Fathers, who is of mixed Afro-American and Native American heritage, personifies for young Ike McCaslin the ancient values of the wilderness, also embodied in the bear. Tom, a Christ figure in *Uncle Tom's Cabin*, is presented by Stowe as a personification of an entirely different set of values (e.g., piety, forbearance), shared not only by some of her oppressed blacks (men and women) but by many of her white women.

After the class retraces these varied images of blacks, they debate what Cather is doing with her blind piano player. Most decide that Cather's technique of characterization falls somewhere between Faulkner's (Blind d'Arnault as a personification for Jim of values and attributes—sensuality, instinctual genius, expressiveness, barbarism, or primitivism—that represent an alternative world to the repressed thin-chestedness of Black Hawk, which he is in the process of repudiating) and Stowe's (where the attributes assigned to black characters, however metaphorical, often carry negative connotations of racial stereotyping). I also refer to *Sapphira and the Slave Girl* to provide a different example of Cather's characterization of black people.

The comparison of Cather and Stowe makes for a smooth transition from race to gender as a primary subject, and additional discussion time is given to a comparison of Alcott's and Wharton's work with *My Ántonia*, specifically to the question of women's culture (the relation of Jim and the Harlings, and Jim and the immigrant girls, versus Laurie and the Marches in *Little Women*) and women's roles (the options open to women in *Summer* or *The House of Mirth*, versus in *My Ántonia*, as well as the differences that class and the absence or presence of a network of women make in creating these options). The depiction of urban immigrant tenement life in Stephen Crane's "Maggie: A Girl of the Streets" is usually worked in later during discussion of the Shimerdas as a rural immigrant family, and Sinclair Lewis's *Babbitt* (with its modernizing midwestern city and its images of the bourgeois lifestyle and a boosteristic commercial value set) is also used after the initial comparisons discussion takes place, in a lecture and discussion on Cather's theory of history. Bringing in Crane and Lewis helps tie together the themes of settlement, westward migration, and modernization dealt with from the beginning of the course. The remainder of this essay addresses Cather's thematic approaches to the latter elements—her vision of history and her depiction of the West, and the related subthemes of passage, memory, and the symbolic landscape.

The cyclical structure of the narrative of *My Ántonia* (Jim's arrival in the West, his departure and return, and the corresponding pattern of closeness, separation or repudiation, and reconciliation in his perceptions of Ántonia) mirrors the many specific forms of passage Cather depicts in the novel, and translates her theory of history into art. The theme of movement, one of the versions of passage presented in the novel, is impressed on the reader early on. It appears in Cather's introductory image of the train speeding through the western landscape with her fictional self and alter ego–narrator aboard and in the actual beginning of "Jim's" story, where we find the simultaneous migration of the young Virginian (personally enacting the westward movement of native-born Americans from the East Coast) and the Shimerda family (similarly serving as representatives of transatlantic immigration and homesteading). The landscape that is the background for this allegorical journey by rail is to the prepubescent Jim a kind of tabula rasa —"There was nothing but land: not a country at all, but the material out of which countries are made" (7). For the recently orphaned boy, the whole experience of coming West is also otherworldly. He has "the feeling that the world was left behind, that we had got over the edge of it, and were outside man's jurisdiction" (7). This feeling of alienation and newness is tempered by his introduction to the social milieu of the prairie and the security of the pastoral landscape of his grandmother's garden and kitchen. There, disorientation momentarily halts, as does the passage of time. Jim lies on his back beneath the sun and feels "entirely happy. Perhaps we feel like that when we die and become a part of something entire, whether it is sun and air, or goodness and knowledge. At any rate, that is happiness; to be dissolved into something complete and great" (18).

A similar juxtaposition of loss and a redefined sense of place are found in the story of Mr. Shimerda, who brings Old World values with him into a new land. The Shimerdas' marriage in Cather's novel may make readers recall that of Per Hansa and Beret in another midwestern masterpiece, O. E. Rölvaag's *Giants in the Earth*. Beret, like Jim, experiences the openness and loneliness of the prairie; like Mr. Shimerda, she longs for the collectivity and traditions of her native village, and experiences a melancholy in America. She projects a religious interpretation on her western experience, associating the straying from rootedness in a former culture and a former landscape with a straying from God—a loss of both heaven and home. Mr. Shimerda's feelings of isolation and degradation are worsened by his memories of Europe, by his longing for his friends and their shared knowledge of "music, and the woods, and about God, and when they were young" (236). The American ethos of individualism and materialism so readily grasped by his wife is of no comfort to his aesthetic nature. Cather and Rölvaag use similar devices to resolve their immigrant characters' unhappiness: resolution and peace are found through Christian imagery of birth, death, and rebirth—another form of cyclic passage in Cather's novel.

In *Giants in the Earth* Per Hansa and Beret's child Peder Victorious is born on Christmas day. His birth ushers in the second part of the novel, which ends in the surrogate sacrifice of Per Hansa in the snow. In *My Ántonia*, Mr. Shimerda is associated with Christmas—he worships at the Burdens' beautifully decorated tree the winter of his death. The extreme alienation of his suicide (taking place, ironically, in a stable) and the harsh judgment inherent in the manner of his burial are offset by young Jim's conviction of his soul's release, and the peace he feels as he senses the older man's spirit passing through the Burden kitchen on its return home to Bohemia. It is Jim who lends Mr. Shimerda's death a spirit of redemption and solace, as if the death of the body has also meant an end to the displacement so upsetting to the immigrant's psyche.

The cyclic pattern of religious imagery continues when Cather has Mr. Shimerda's first grandchild born at Christmas time. The baby's father's absence from the novel enhances the sense of parthenogenesis or virgin birth, making Ántonia a madonnalike figure despite the social stigma attached to the illegitimacy of her maternity. Jim's secondhand knowledge of this period of Ántonia's life (through the Widow Steavens's memory and retelling of the events) is paired with his visit with her in the fields, and her confession that her recollections of her father make him "more real" (320) to her than are most living people. This feeling of the sustaining of the past in the present is accompanied by a magical natural phenomenon. The sun lay "like a great golden globe in the low west" (321), hanging momentarily on the horizon, while "the moon rose in the east. . . . [T]he two luminaries confronted each other across the level land, resting on opposite edges of the world" (322). This powerful planetary twinning of day and night, birth and death, brings Jim back to a psychic state similar to that he felt in his grandmother's garden as a child: "I wished I could be a little boy again," he tells us, "and that my way could end there" (322).

The feeling of return and redemption that Jim feels after Mr. Shimerda's death and again years later in the field with Ántonia is also the dominant emotion evoked in the last section of the novel, when he returns to the scenes of his childhood after an absence of twenty years. The open prairie of his youth had long given way to wheatfields and cornfields "and the whole face of the country was changing. . . . [A]ll the human effort that had gone into it was coming back in long, sweeping lines of fertility" (306). The fruitfulness of the landscape is personified in the now middle-aged Ántonia, who like the earth itself is "a rich mine of life" (353). She is to Jim an earth mother, or Demeter, a goddess of fertility and harvest. The imageries of Christian and pagan myth come together in Jim's description of the sod fruit cave, whence Ántonia's many children come tumbling forth from darkness into light—a scene emblematic of a womblike mass birth, a release from the underworld, and a rising from the dead. This image of rebirth recurs in Ántonia's favorite son Leo, born on Easter. The sequence completes the cycle of religious symbolism—begun with Mr. Shimerda's icy and lonesome death—at the exultant point of resurrection, and it lends the adult Jim a positive sense of reconciliation and closure similar to that which he wished for Mr. Shimerda as a boy. This cyclic passage is underscored for us when Jim relates that he "had the sense of coming home to myself, and having found out what a little circle man's experience is" (371–72).

While Jim, in returning to the scenes of his boyhood, discovers the permanence of the past as retained in memory, his idealization of that past also contains elements of tragedy and romantic antimodernism. His glorification of the land and the associations of his youth carries with it connotations of diminishment and historical eclipse. The theme of passage in Cather's work, then, is manifested not only in the rituals of the life cycle—initiations to adulthood, to sexuality, and to the processes of production, birth, and death—in religious and mythical metaphors of cycles of death and resurrection and images of the revolution of the planets, or in literal movement and migration, but also in a sense of the development and passing away of an entire historical era.

The symbolic equivalent of the narrative realizations Jim comes to in the "Cuzak's Boys" section is Cather's image of the plow magnified against the setting sun, presented earlier in the novel. Jim and the immigrant girls witness the plow

> . . . within the circle of the disk; the handles, the tongue, the share —black against the molten red. There it was heroic in size, a picture writing on the sun. . . . Even while we whispered about it, our vision disappeared; the ball dropped and dropped until the red tip went beneath the earth . . . [and the plow sank] back into its own littleness somewhere on the prairie. (245)

Rich in overtones of sexuality and fertility, this brief transfiguration of the pastoral image, writ large and glorious against the sun, remains only in memory. Memory becomes its own reality—indeed, Jim tells us that "some memories are realities, and are better than anything that can ever happen to one again" (328).

The sense of diminishment and passage Jim feels in visiting Nebraska relates not only to the disconnectedness and sterility of his adult life in comparison to Ántonia's productive fruition but to the contrast created earlier in the novel between his boyhood on the prairie (the end of the pioneering period of the West) and his adolescence in Black Hawk (a microcosmic indication of the Babbitry of development to come). Like most images in *My Ántonia*, the social milieu of Black Hawk is described using metaphors of the landscape—specifically, the use of animal imagery that equates the social divisions of the prairie town with that of the inhabitants of the prairie-dog town Ántonia and Jim liked to visit as children. The social matrix of the prairie-dog town is composed of the dogs, the earth owls—who, in a land of few trees, share subterranean burrows with the rodents—and the rattle-snakes, who prey on the others, who "were quite defenseless against them; [they] took possession of their comfortable houses and ate the eggs and puppies." Jim and Ántonia feel "sorry for the owls" when they observe the prairie-dog town, but they also feel that "winged things who would live like that must be rather degraded creatures" (30).

The first direct analogy Cather draws from this exploitative animal relation is that of the Shimerdas living like badgers in their sod dugout, cheated by that "snake" of a fellow countryman, Krajiek, their landlord, who preys on them financially and at one point moves into their earthen home (32). A similar version of class control occurs in the prairie town, where tripartite divisions exist between the town's capitalists, the petty bourgeoisie, and the immigrant women who work as domestic servants. In Black Hawk, Wick Cutter, the rapacious moneylender with his reptilian bald head and rough skin, is presented as a snake of the community, making his living off the vulnerability of others. Like the warm-blooded and sociable dogs and the winged but tragically earthbound owls, the immigrant women appear as "almost a race apart" (198) from the native-born women whose homes they share. Ántonia, Lena, and the others display "a positive carriage and freedom of movement" (198) as a result of their "out-of-door work" (198) that contrasts with the "round-shouldered and hollow-chested" (199) Black Hawk girls, who are as confined in their physiques as in their homes, where they live "like the mice in their own kitchens . . . furtive and repressed" (219). Fittingly, the local masonic club is named the "Owls" (220).

The petty self-limitation and prejudices Jim finds in his movement into Black Hawk life combines with his passage away from the strength and heroism he finds exemplified in the immigrant women of his youth. Those pioneers become increasingly emblematic for him of a previous, superior era of history. Cather's art idealizes the moment of transition or passage—

the magnified sun before it descends into night, the boy before he becomes a man, an epoch of western history before it is transmuted into the parochialism of Black Hawk or the entrepreneurial modernism of the railroad and the distant city. Jim finds sustenance not in modern progress but in the personified, transfigured past—in Ántonia with her peasant qualities, and in the prairie she has come to represent. Just as Ántonia is lent a kind of apotheosis in Jim's eyes, so the prairie landscape she is associated with is, at sunset

> . . . like the bush that burned with fire and was not consumed. That hour always had the exultation of victory, of triumphant ending, like a hero's death—heroes who died young and gloriously. It was a sudden transfiguration, a lifting-up of day.   (40)

This complex theme—an individual life as symbol of a historical period or cultural milieu, personal death as a signal of an end of an era, and the preservation of an emblematic life through translation into art or memory— recurs in much of Cather's fiction. In *My Ántonia* the West—Cather's *patria*—is transfigured into allegory, into myth, and Cather's epigraph becomes a terse judgment of American history, a short treatise of antimodernism: *Optima dies . . . prima fugit* ("the best days are the first to flee").

My Ántonia in the Freshman Writing Class

Jennifer Bradley

In both subject and style, *My Ántonia* serves the objectives of freshman composition. Though provincial in setting, it ranges widely through topics from folklore, theater and music history, geography, education, women's studies, American history, political science. Though few of today's college freshmen know either the *Georgics* or the difference between badgers and gophers, like Jim and Ántonia, they all know how it feels to live in a new environment. And even if they are not foreign or immigrant, like the Shimerdas, they want to learn its language. While Cather's prose does not model the structure of biology lab reports and anthropology observations, its clean yet evocative style inspires students to write with simple elegance and to develop assertions rigorously.

For the teacher, *My Ántonia* inspires a course that is practically effective and intellectually exciting. Hence I aim not to present a model syllabus but to discuss curricular principles and representative assignments and, by implication, to encourage teachers to develop materials and procedures of their own.

Despite the advice of many currently marketed freshman readers and rhetorics, my composition syllabus stresses neither inventing topics nor writing about personal experience. Of course the assignment bulletin almost always provides choice among comparable tasks, and from time to time students may help to design a writing project. But most topics for exposition are assigned; until well along in their majors, undergraduates rarely propose their own topics for writing. And in few disciplines is the personal essay's autobiographical testimony considered evidence. Making analytical connections does not of course preclude informal response; "freewriting" about personal impressions encourages fluency and provides an opportunity to articulate inchoate intuitions (Elbow). But writing from text demands that these hunches be developed with data and for readers who want critical analysis, not impressionistic musings. When students speculate informally on the implications of the title of Cather's novel, for example, on the function of the quotations from Vergil, or on the introduction's service to the novel as a whole, this meditation becomes a usable resource for formal analysis of the novel.

Instead of topic selection and autobiographical reminiscence, the study and writing skills that college requires and rewards are what inform the freshman composition course. Readings resemble the challenging texts students encounter at college. Writing exercises develop a wide repertoire of expository skills that students can rely on, so that in future they will know which ones work best for particular critical tasks. Learning styles differ, however, and no single linear gradation of tasks or modes best suits all students' growth. Rather, the design is spiral and "recursive" (Kiniry and

Strenski). Few students master a technique or mode after a single unit of study, so the syllabus introduces increasingly complex skills yet provides generous opportunity to fine-tune each of those skills and to combine them. Resulting assignments replicate what obtains in students' other college courses.

Along with usable notes, apt paraphrase, accurate definitions, and the ability to classify data and provide examples, summary is presented as a serviceable academic skill. It aids close reading and prewriting, and during revising, it helps student writers test intentions against the draft itself. It is also the basis for entire essays; I believe that many university writing assignments, which at first seem more complicated, are in fact elaborate summaries of lectures, books, and other course materials. When My Ántonia is the focusing artifact for the freshman composition course, students begin by creating simple plot synopses or by summarizing accessible passages from related scholarly articles; as the course continues, summaries become more challenging and incorporated into longer assignments. Tracing the fortunes of one or a few characters (Lena and Tiny, for example) builds a focused summary, and students complete it more fruitfully if they have already learned to organize simpler summaries. As summary writing becomes more difficult, students must make decisions about selection and arrangement for readers with various interests and needs.

Most college writing requires the student not only to understand a primary text but to connect it with others. Professors from many disciplines assign comparative papers; even more prominent in undergraduate classes is analysis. Students of the social sciences, for example, might well face the task of applying some theoretical definition to an assigned collection of data. As with summary, such an analysis is easier for them—and they learn more from doing it—if they know the moves. An easily manageable assignment sequence works this way: Students paraphrase Margaret Mead's definition of "anxiety" from a 1956 New York Times Magazine article; because this definition is not explicit, they must work carefully to tease out Mead's point. They then summarize two sections of My Ántonia, one about farming and one about the town. The next step is to analyze each of the two passages in light of Mead's definition; a cooperatively composed analysis allows students to teach one another before they tackle the second on their own. They then draft and finally revise for an academic audience a comparative essay about anxiety in both settings.

A more challenging assignment sequence of graduated activities employs medical anthropologist Pamela J. Brink's four-stage model of culture shock. Because her collection of readings, Transcultural Nursing, is edited for professionals working with patients, students writing about My Ántonia must ignore her application to the health-care setting and inventory only the basic model: (1) honeymoon—delight in new surroundings; (2) alienation—

depression and anxiety because of strange surroundings; (3) *acceptance*—adjustment to values, customs, and pace of current surroundings; and (4) *reacculturation*—acceptance so total that returning to the indigenous culture would cause another culture shock. Simple comparative exercises ensure that students control the sometimes subtle distinctions between successive stages of shock. To prepare for analysis, they write short in-class treatments of their own experiences of the stages of shock; this work is especially liberating for foreign and immigrant students. To focus on the novel, students work in groups to propose characters to whom the model might apply. Some choose characters they find interesting and wrestle with the constraints of the analytical framework; Mr. Shimerda becomes a convenient choice, for though he advises and promotes acceptance (bk. 1, chs. 3, 10), he doesn't himself achieve it. Other students begin with the model. A project about Ántonia forces choice because of the sheer weight of information about her; Otto, Jim, Cleric, and the other Shimerdas challenge because analyzing them also requires precision about Brink's categories. Finally, after much productively "messy" brainstorming, the class is ready for a formal academic treatment of the novel, an anthropological analysis.

Other series of assignments work toward the same goal: familiarity with reliable writing processes and with disciplines other than literature. Students who analyze their experience according to Nietzsche's definitions of Apollonianism and Dionysianism from *The Birth of Tragedy* can use the autobiographical exercise to model an academic treatment of the institutions and individuals Cather describes. Students eagerly create a Jungian analysis of female archetypes in the novel. Passages from "Psychological Aspects of the Mother Archetype" (especially paragraphs 148–186) serve as the analytical framework; the description of Mrs. Wick Cutter provides a short in-class pump primer. Treating male characters is a more difficult task, so for Jung I substitute my own list culled from Frye's *Anatomy of Criticism*. I've developed other clusters of assignments using *My Ántonia* in conjunction with pieces by Marx, Maslow, and Frederick Jackson Turner. At this point, students need to think critically about their own educational process, and, in the context of Jim's, selections about education from Mill, Cardinal Newman, and Montaigne work especially well.

So that students feel some degree of success in their work, texts must be chosen with care; students' academic interests and new feelings of independence govern these choices. If the class is to analyze the power of place in *My Ántonia*, budding cultural geographers may analyze winter on the farm using selections about plains weather and climate, or they may refer to Robert Redfield's basic definitions in *The Little Community* (chs. 1–3) to describe the farmers and Black Hawk. Prospective English majors, however, may prefer to examine Jim's study room in Lincoln (bk. 3, ch. 2) as a "border country" of romance or to gauge the novel's fairy-tale structural motifs by applying Vladimir Propp's thirty-one sequential narrative functions (selections from *Morphology of the Folktale*, chs. 2–3).

Because students are all this time analyzing and developing their writing styles, a rhetorical approach often colors the discussion of academic writing. Students imitate short passages from *My Ántonia* (e.g., the boy Jim's first view of Nebraska or the tableau of young Cuzaks gathered around their mother), using for content their personal histories or another writer's ideas. These exercises become a usable resource for a multiple-draft essay. During the prewriting stage of composing, the constraints of another's style allow students to discover ideas they might not have discovered on their own; as they revise, they polish their prose actively in ways that simple discussion of style might not have encouraged. Style study is particularly crucial at this point in students' lives, for they are being socialized to the university, learning what counts as evidence and what decorum is expected on papers and in class. As Richard A. Lanham says, young people speak "with literal accuracy" of going to college to "find" themselves (115). Despite Jim's self-effacing assertions about the way he composes, he plays out a similar quest as he uses writing—even his final revision—to discover "my Ántonia."[1]

NOTE

[1]For support and suggestions as I prepared this article, I am grateful to UCLA Writing Programs Directors Mike Rose and Lynn Batten, Freshman Preparatory Program Coordinator Malcolm Kiniry, Carol L. Edwards, Jeanne Gunner, and Shari Zimmerman.

Teaching *My Ántonia* to Adults: An Interdisciplinary Approach in a Community College

Constance Mierendorf

I teach *My Ántonia* in a ten-week course called Introduction to the American Novel for the College for Working Adults (CWA), an interdisciplinary, Associate of Arts degree program at Minneapolis Community College. In addition to the novel course, the theme-based curriculum, entitled "The American Experience," includes Freshman Composition and Art America, an introductory art-history survey. Students attend classes on weekends and evenings and watch a weekly telecourse in conjunction with Art America. The goals of the CWA humanities curriculum are to build on students' life experiences, to teach them critical thinking skills, and to link the three courses in "The American Experience" to maximize students' learning time and potential. *My Ántonia* works as the core of an "American Experience" unit where students learn how to apply Cather's artistic theory to their own writing and discover how visual art and literature complement each other. I will begin with some observations about the unique characteristics of adult learners and why *My Ántonia* appeals to them and then focus on how I integrate *My Ántonia* with other works in the novel course, the composition course, and Art America to meet the objectives of the CWA program.

Benefiting from their multiple roles as students, workers, and parents, adult learners bring a wealth of experience to the classroom. I use an integrated approach to critical thinking in the College for Working Adults that draws on both the personal and the academic knowledge of students (Chaffee). Being able to apply their practical experience to their studies strengthens adult learners' confidence and encourages active learning. Thus the College for Working Adults provides a forum for personal growth as well as a path to an Associate of Arts degree. Adults find the themes and characters in *My Ántonia* particularly accessible on a personal level.

The values Ántonia embodies and Jim embraces have special appeal for mature students. Most are returning to college after having been out of school for a number of years, and they see themselves as pioneers of sorts. Committed to academic success, they identify with and admire Ántonia's determination. Like Jim Burden they have reached the age where they are able to reflect on the patterns of their lives; adult learners comprehend and relate to the reminiscence on a level of maturity that Cather herself had achieved when she wrote *My Ántonia*.

Among the themes in *My Ántonia* adults grasp most readily is the preeminence of family, heritage, and community. Unlike younger, traditional students, adults in the CWA program tend to form support groups within the classroom and transform the class itself into a community of sorts. Discussions of how society functions in the novel and what value Cather placed on community and family successfully tap students' interests.

Cather's style and her turn to the past also captivate CWA students. They comment that her clarity and her nostalgic descriptions of nature and life on the prairie are renewing. While CWA students juggle full-time careers, family life, and their studies, they find reading about Ántonia's world to be a retreat. They become caught up in Jim's memories and, on a psychological level, identify Black Hawk and the farms on the divide as their own home. Adult learners understand the reality of the past that Cather creates in a way that younger students do not, primarily because adults have a keener sense of their own history. In fact, CWA students cite their ability to relate to Jim's look backward as key to their rating *My Ántonia* their favorite work in the novel course.

I teach *My Ántonia* using an inductive, thematic approach. The novel appears midway in the quarter, preceded by *The Scarlet Letter* and *The Adventures of Huckleberry Finn* and followed by *The Great Gatsby*. One challenge of any introductory literature course is to present widely disparate works and still retain some unity in the course. Since CWA students are enrolled in three classes in "The American Experience" and possess a limited knowledge of literature, unity becomes even more crucial. I meet this challenge by asking students to apply a set of discovery questions to each of the novels they read: How does each novel treat American individualism? What attitude does the work present toward tradition and the past? What tensions or conflicts arise in the story?

Students build on their knowledge of *The Scarlet Letter* and *Huckleberry Finn* when they consider the moral conflicts in *My Ántonia*, the contrasts between life in Black Hawk and life on the divide, and Cather's romanticism. Jim's personal conflict also emerges as a point for discussion: he desires to return to the past and recognizes, as the story unfolds, that this is impossible, that *optima dies . . . prima fugit.*

Following *My Ántonia* with *The Great Gatsby*, students readily compare Jim's knowledge that he cannot recapture the past with Jay Gatsby's insistence that he can. The treatments of Ántonia and Daisy as embodiments of the past also lead to fruitful comparisons. Each of the discovery questions results in provocative analysis of the novels and encourages students, giving them confidence in their critical reading abilities. Reading *My Ántonia* in this historical sequence helps establish Cather's place in the evolution of American fiction.

At the beginning of each novel session, I reinforce the integrative critical thinking method and assure class discussion by asking students to write for five minutes on a modified discovery question that includes application of students' life experiences and knowledge of their previous readings to *My Ántonia* (Coles).

In coordinating the novel and composition courses, I translate Cather's literary theory and examples from *My Ántonia* into usable strategies and models for student writing. Like the progression in the literature course, the sequence of assignments in Freshman Composition builds on students' successes. CWA students begin by writing a short narration followed by a descriptive essay. The next assignment, the personal reminiscence, combines the two. *My Ántonia* serves as a model for this assignment, and application of Cather's writing theory contributes to student mastery of the writing process.

Cather's imagistic technique suggests a helpful prewriting activity for the reminiscence as well as an approach to reading *My Ántonia*. I begin the reminiscence component with Jim Burden's recollection of Ántonia as he lay awake in the hay cave on the Cuzak farm (352–53). I ask students to recall images from their pasts that remain strong in their memories, thus generating topic ideas for their writing.

One example I use from *My Ántonia*, in addition to being an excellent reminiscence, also allays students' fears about how dramatic their writing need be. Their reservations that they have nothing worth writing about are answered in Jim's memory of his grandmother's garden (16–18). In this rich passage, Jim admits "nothing happened," yet the garden scene invites readers into Jim's world, introduces them to his grandmother, and reveals Jim's insights into the peace he had made with the new land.

Another brief example from the book includes a myth that pervaded Jim's childhood memory of his first autumn in Nebraska (28–29). The passage establishes the sunflower as the central image, describes the openness of the land, and then goes on to tell Fuchs's story about how the Mormons scattered sunflower seeds across the prairies as they traveled west. The paragraph ends with Jim's association of sunflower-bordered roads with freedom; the sunflowers had become a personal symbol that stuck in his mind through adulthood.

Jim's recollection of Grandmother Burden's garden and the prairie sunflowers takes students beyond image and description to interpretation. Like the novel as a whole, these examples conclude with observations about life. The personal reminiscence as a writing exercise meets the criteria of the integrative approach as well as James Britton's strategies for expressive writing. Students progress from describing a scene, person, or event to understanding and explaining its significance to their lives.

My Ántonia's lucid style also serves as a model for student writing. Adults respond positively to Cather's language, noting that she writes for contemporary audiences. The technique of simplifying during revision and the importance of tone, voice, and audience can be addressed in the composition class as students read *My Ántonia* for the novel course. To illustrate editing for strength and clarity, I show the series of sketches for *The Sower* by Millet that Cather discusses in "On the Art of Fiction." The final picture visualizes what Cather meant when she wrote, "art, it seems to me, should simplify. That, indeed, is very nearly the whole of the higher artistic process; finding what conventions of form and what detail one can do without and yet preserve the spirit of the whole . . ." (*On Writing* 102).

The myth that "good" writing is complicated and that "good" writers always use polysyllabic words is exploded when the class analyzes Cather's style. Students conclude that effective prose is vivid, and, like Jim's recollections of Ántonia, it leaves a strong impression on the reader. Indeed, readers come away from *My Ántonia* with images like the black plow silhouetted against the sky and the eruption of the Cuzak children from the fruit cave etched in their memories. Using *My Ántonia* as a model for a writing assignment not only provides students with methods for sound communication but also brings them to an appreciation of Cather's art on a technical level.

Cather acknowledged her indebtedness to visual art in *My Ántonia* and in her planning of *The Professor's House* and *Death Comes for the Archbishop*; she also often borrowed critical terms from painting to discuss writing. The images in *My Ántonia* lend themselves to comparisions with art and interdisciplinary study. Additionally, visual examples help students whose learning styles are nonverbal and bring all students to a holistic understanding of "The American Experience" (Arnheim; Edwards).

The Art America component of the curriculum progresses historically through the quarter in concert with the American novel course. Students consider the same questions about values and tradition in Art America that they explored in Introduction to the American Novel, and they apply standards of style and structure that they had become familiar with in Freshman Composition to the paintings in the art course. Students soon discover that many themes and techniques in American visual art parallel those in American fiction.

In many ways, the nineteenth-century genre artists William Sidney Mount and George Caleb Bingham share Cather's vision of rural America. Their works extol the charms of everyday life in America, depicting scenes one might encounter in a Cather novel. Like Jim Burden and his tale of the Nebraska past, the genre artists painted affectionate images of country life.

To help students understand how form affects subject matter and how Cather's modernist style offers an original treatment of the past, I contrast the genre artists' versions of the country and its people with those of the twentieth-century regionalists Thomas Hart Benton and Grant Wood. (Wood is the artist whom Ferris Greenslet, Cather's editor at Houghton Mifflin, proposed to illustrate a deluxe edition of *My Ántonia*.) The careful attention to detail in a work like Mount's *Bargaining for a Horse* (1835), for example, contrasts sharply with the simplified, almost geometric rendition of *Dinner for Threshers* (1934) by Grant Wood. Bingham's *Boatmen on the Missouri* (1846) presents similar subject matter to Benton's *The Young Fisherman, White River* (1940–60), but the highly stylized Benton painting creates a different mood and illustrates the importance of form and technique in the presentation of a subject. By studying these visual examples, students gain insight into the significance of Cather's style in relation to her subjects.

Through its varying perspectives, this interdisciplinary approach to *My Ántonia* enhances students' appreciation of the novel. Exploring *My Ántonia* from a variety of disciplines, placing it in the tradition of the American novel, using it as a rhetorical model, and discovering its pictorial analogues bring students into full view of Cather's artistry. This pedagogical method approaches Willa Cather's vision of the interrelations among the arts.

Teaching *My Ántonia* as a Plains Novel

Robert Thacker

As a person, Willa Cather was affected by the plains landscape; she knew it intimately and never escaped its imaginative pull. Recalling her introduction to the plains as a child, newly arrived from Virginia, she speaks of its effect on her imagination as "a kind of erasure of personality"—she saw herself as one "thrown out into a country as bare as a piece of sheet iron" (*Kingdom* 448). She also admonished a friend for not understanding the imaginative effects of western space, protesting "You have not seen those miles of fields. There is no place to hide in Nebraska" (Sergeant 49). At the beginning of *My Ántonia*, of course, Cather dramatizes her experience as Jim Burden's retrospective memory of arriving in Nebraska; however Jim adjusts to the plains after his first night there, his memory of his initial feelings of erasure never leaves him as he writes his reminiscence. As the novel concludes, he takes us back along the same road he and Ántonia traveled their first Nebraska night, recalling once more his feeling of being "overcome by that obliterating strangeness" the plains landscape offers (8, 371). Thus to Jim, the pioneer plains he and Ántonia share lies at the core of their relation, their "freemasonry" (i).

I teach the novel as being both about the plains landscape and derived from it; in addition, since it dramatizes pioneering, *My Ántonia* offers a story particularly important in the American westering experience. Because I teach in an eastern university, I usually have to provide my students with background materials on the Great Plains. This need lends itself to my approach, however, since I see *My Ántonia* in direct relation to the literature of westward expansion; as such, I offer my students a variety of background materials—slides, maps, and readings—sufficient for the course's focus.

In the plains-literature course, which treats Canadian as well as American works, I begin by having the students read first-person accounts excerpted from the writings of plains explorers and travelers (ca. 1540s through late 1870s). At this point, I ask the students to notice the type, extent, and degree of personal reactions to the "new land" of the plains. Then we examine two books, Wallace Stegner's *Wolf Willow* and N. Scott Momaday's *The Way to Rainy Mountain*, that offer considered descriptive, historical, and personal evocations of the plains as a writer's landscape. We then go back to beginnings, taking up two key nineteenth-century texts, Cooper's *The Prairie* and Parkman's *The Oregon Trail*. I encourage a wide-ranging discussion on these works, for we use them to understand the lure of the West in nineteenth-century America, the myth of the garden versus the great American desert, the image of the Indian, and other relevant topics. To demonstrate the appeal of the West during the nineteenth century, I bring up its effect on the writers of the American Renaissance, most particularly Melville, whose *Moby-*

116

Dick bears extended evidence of his interest in the West generally and his reading of *The Oregon Trail* in particular. Both Cooper and Parkman reveal, too, that the effects of the plains—as a new, unfamiliar region—were felt most acutely by individuals, who found themselves uncertain, forced to adapt to a drier climate and to a landscape that offered none of the usual characteristics of landscape: no trees or elevations, only a dreary flatness.

From Cooper and Parkman we turn to the fiction proper, considering Rölvaag's *Giants in the Earth* and Frederick Philip Grove's *Fruits of the Earth* (a Canadian counterpart to Rölvaag's novel) before taking up *My Ántonia*. I teach these novels before Cather's because each contains detailed expository description of plains pioneering amid plots that emphasize the individual pioneer's heroic confrontation with the land, quite like Cooper's depiction of Bumppo. After *My Ántonia*, which comes next, we consider plains fiction dealing with the postpioneering era, discussing such works as Sinclair Ross's *As for Me and My House*, Wright Morris's *Ceremony in Lone Tree*, N. Scott Momaday's *House Made of Dawn*, W. O. Mitchell's *Who Has Seen the Wind*, and Robert Kroetsch's *The Studhorse Man*. Throughout the course, the major theme that emerges is imaginative adaptation to the land, its transformation from unknown land to—in Morris's phrase—the home place.

My Ántonia plays a crucial role in defining this theme in fiction. I try to differentiate between Rölvaag's and Grove's novels and *My Ántonia*, because Cather offers a far more complex vision of plains experience. While they see the plains as land to be conquered, Cather presents it as a fundamental, even symbiotic, part of her protagonists' very beings, their "freemasonry." Thus we begin by discussing the various ways Cather's treatment of plains pioneering differs from Rölvaag's and Grove's; because of the subjective value Jim assigns to the landscape as it relates to his memories of Ántonia, this topic inevitably leads us into the novel's introduction, where we try to isolate the role played by the plains in "setting up" the narrative that follows. We note the initial image of the hot plain that Cather's unnamed narrator and Burden see from the train window, and follow it ultimately to Ántonia, who symbolizes for them "the country, the conditions, the whole adventure of our childhood" (ii). These three elements, we decide, encompass the whole of Jim's narrative and—I usually add—all relate to the landscape, since the plains country at the time of pioneering makes possible Jim and Ántonia's adventures and so their "freemasonry." This discussion, which usually broadens to include most of book 1, also allows me to ask questions about the narrative's point of view and so to point up how Cather dramatically situates the reader in the strange plains landscape, which, as Jim's memories explain, always piques the imagination and, at the same time, both frightens and delights. Throughout the novel, we discover after we see how frequently

Jim alludes to the landscape and his first night in Nebraska, the new land is a perpetual presence that never escapes our view for long, just as he keeps it always in mind himself.

Thus by concentrating on the introduction and book 1 we discover the plains landscape as an organic presence that informs the characters' relations and, as is evident in Jim's sense of "erasure," serves as a basis for Cather's imagery. At the same time, we explore Cather's structure, noting the images she offers, whether symbolic tableaux—like the plow against the sky in "The Hired Girls" or inset stories such as those of Pavel and Peter or the Cutters. Late in the novel, Jim makes a comment that defines this technique: "Ántonia had always been one to leave images in the mind that did not fade—that grew stronger with time," and continues to see in them "immemorial human attitudes which we recognize by instinct as universal and true" (353). Through this series of carefully selected and precisely drawn images, the novel gains an imaginative power that seems to exceed the narrative itself (Miller, "American Dream"; Peterman).

After exploring the relations between Jim and Ántonia in the first two sections of book 1, we turn to a scene that seems to me to encapsulate the essence of Cather's response to and use of the salient features of the plains in *My Ántonia*. In book 4, Burden visits Ántonia after the birth of her daughter, but before she marries Anton Cuzak, and walks with her across the plains (321–22). Examining this scene, we decide that this passage makes the plains' organic relation to Cather's tale precise and vivid; it symbolically defines the relations between Burden and Ántonia by embodying the novel's essential romantic conceit, their shared experience and attraction. As Jim sees Ántonia in his story, she is "his" Ántonia, a symbolic being illuminated by his reminiscences; each is a luminary, the polar opposite of the other, turning a bright being toward the other "across the level land." The land, we discover, is the third element in Cather's symbolic configuration and is as necessary as the other two, for the characters are conjoined through their shared plains pioneering experience and their sympathy with Nebraska.

Referring back to Castañeda and the other first-person commentators we examined, we see that Cather's use of plains images is both consistent with and rooted in the tradition of imaginative response to the plains; her images give to the narrative its affecting quality—for they are, indeed, images in our minds "that [do] not fade"—a point we discuss repeatedly as we look at a succession of key images. Returning to Jim's introduction to Nebraska, we follow his reactions and thoughts through the first two chapters of book 1, which culminate in his pumpkin-patch transcendence in his grandmother's garden. Jim's growing delight over the landscape allows us to question Cather's technique in her introduction of the plains and to define her expository purpose—since through Jim's experience she is both explaining the plains and dramatizing the way it makes a person feel, the way it made Cather feel, initially and throughout her life.

We increasingly see that Cather achieves such effects through her creation of Jim as first-person narrator and putative author; he and Ántonia arrive in Nebraska on the same night, and the land informs their relation from first to last. As had Rölvaag and Grove, in *O Pioneers!* she had dramatized through imagery and diction the relations among land, sky, and human structures, but in *My Ántonia*, the students decide, the same impression is given immediacy by way of first-person narration. Here the emphasis is on the felt quality of landscape, seen in late summer or early autumn and made articulate by Jim Burden's filtering sensibility. They discover that, by locating us in the landscape along with Jim, Cather forces us first to reckon with his sense of erasure, of the sense of strangeness the landscape engenders, and then, like him, to adapt to it.   *Arizona*

These points made, we then look at the way Cather's plains images are orchestrated, noting particularly Jim and Ántonia's meeting on the wild plains during a beautiful autumn day with Mr. Shimerda in book 1. I notice how this scene begins where Jim's pumpkin-patch experience leaves off— with nature as beneficent—Jim speaking of the day glowingly, as "that magnificence!" (40), but we note that it ends with a looming awareness of transience—of the coming of winter and, through Shimerda's melancholy (symbolized by Jim and Ántonia's flitting shadows), his impending suicide. Cather uses this doubleness, of romantic delight and melancholy, to underscore her characters' relations and emphasize the fragility of being—and she defines the correspondence through plains images. In so doing, she seizes on those elements that affected European commentators like Castañeda, whose imaginative reactions fluctuated between delight and terror, depending on an observer's purpose, vantage point, and the season. Cather carefully uses the landscape's features to define her characters' relations, depict action, and move her narrative. Another scene we use in the same way is at the end of book 1, when Jim and Ántonia watch a thunderstorm on the distant plains—it too encapsulates both poles of reaction wrought by the landscape.

But the scene that we realize most vividly defines the role played by the plains in *My Ántonia* occurs when, picnicking with the hired girls out on the plains just before he leaves for college, Jim recounts the apocryphal story, which he believes, that Coronado's expedition traveled as far north as the Republican River in present-day Nebraska. To prepare my students for our discussion of Cather's scene, I ask them to look again at Cooper's introduction of Natty Bumppo in *The Prairie* (9–17) and to recall, as well, a parallel passage from Grove's *In Search of Myself* (259) we had discussed when we studied his *Fruits of the Earth*; in it, the author describes a newly arrived immigrant he saw plowing a round against the setting sun on the very day he arrived in Manitoba—this image gave Grove the idea for his novel. (A third analogy, though not as explicitly thematic as the others, is a passage from *The Way to Rainy Mountain* in which a cricket is seen across the plains against a full moon.) Returning to Cather and reminding the students of their readings from Castañeda, we see Jim alluding to Coronado's failure and comparing his sufferings to Mr. Shimerda's; he describes the plains at its most glowing and beautiful:

> Presently we saw a curious thing: There were no clouds, the sun was going down in a limpid, gold-washed sky. Just as the lower edge of the red disk rested on the high fields against the horizon, a great black figure suddenly appeared on the face of the sun. . . . There it was, heroic in size, a picture writing on the sun. (245).

Examining this scene, we note how Cather orchestrates it toward this plains-induced spectacle: the refrainlike repetition of golden and glowing landscape description; the discussion of Coronado and the country's romantic past that sets the atmosphere; Coronado's strivings and tragedy as parallel to Mr. Shimerda's; finally, the whole is encompassed in as fine a use of the plains mirage as Cooper's introduction of Natty Bumppo in *The Prairie*. We decide, as well, that Cather's use closely parallels Cooper's, for the symbolic plow, rendered "heroic in size" by the landscape, encapsulates Jim's vision of the pioneer spirit; although the heroic figure soon fades, the vision it evokes— embodied in an image made luminous by the landscape—lingers.

When thus placed in the context of the literature of the plains, stretching back to the person Cather invokes, *My Ántonia* offers a completely felt and sympathetic rendering of Jim's personal plains—one that points up the land's beauty while dramatizing its effect on the imagination. So the students see that Cather was the first to apply romantic strategies to the plains landscape, at the moment of its transformation, and that doing so dramatically involves the reader with Jim's feelings. Cather's techniques, which adjust the traditions of literature to the landscape's characteristics, are rooted in and amplify the basic elements of plains landscape description. Her view of the land, which commingles a romantic fancifulness (Burden's golden sentiments, seen from the vantage point of his empty present) with its more threatening aspects (Mr. Shimerda's suicide), recognizes both poles in the history of response to the landscape and presents them powerfully personalized, as elements of Jim's character.

I ask my students to refer to *My Ántonia* for a final description of this process. We turn to the opening of book 3 and read that, away at the University of Nebraska, Jim recognizes his connection to "the places and

people of my own infinitesimal past. They stood out strengthened and simplified now, like the image of the plough against the sun" (262). Just after,
looking out his window on the edge of Lincoln one March evening, Jim
notices that over "the prairie, where the sun had gone down, the sky was
turquoise blue," and he turns to his Latin text, Vergil, two lines of whose
Georgics Cather quotes; the first offers an apt description of Jim's romantic
point of view, "the best days are the first to flee," and the second describes
her position in plains writing as the author of both *O Pioneers!* and *My
Ántonia*: "for I shall be the first, if I live, to bring the Muse into my country"
(264). After we discuss Jim's description of his romantic point of view here,
I ask my students to consider whether other plains novels have used similar
methods, what passages from other books we've read describe moments in
which the ordinary becomes momentarily heroic. We begin by talking about
Cooper's and Grove's symbolic use of the setting sun as parallel to Cather's,
but then I ask the students to look briefly at Rölvaag's and Grove's depiction
of their heroes' relation to the land. They find a real difference and usually
decide that in each case the author was offering us a protagonist of heroic
stature, fitted especially for confrontation of the plains. In contrast, when I
continue and ask them to consider their readings of Stegner and Momaday,
the students respond by seeing their works as much closer to what Cather
offers in *My Ántonia*—they too reveal an authorial attachment to the plains
as a closely held, personal landscape.

This is, we discover finally, just what Cather accomplishes in *My Ántonia*:
she offers us the plains as a luminous landscape—one aglow with human
understanding and awe, with romance, and one captured in the novel, and
in Burden's mind—through images dependent on "the level land" that "do
not fade." The Nebraska plains is Jim and Ántonia's land—just as it was
Cather's—in an essential, vital way. We find in *My Ántonia* a succession of
images drawn from the land itself as Cather experienced them, objectified
them through her detached perspective in time and place. By following
these landscape-based images, we see in *My Ántonia* the whole of the plains
literary tradition in microcosm; just as Willa Cather's subject was plains
pioneering, so too was she the plains' foremost literary pioneer.

Teaching *My Ántonia* to
Non–English Majors from Spanish-Speaking Homes

James L. Evans

In 1967, I accepted a position at Pan American University at Edinburg in the semitropical Lower Rio Grande Valley of southeastern Texas. About three-fourths of the inhabitants of this four-county area were of Mexican ancestry, and most of them either had immigrated to the United States after the Mexican Revolution (1910–20) or were descendants of those who had.

The fall 1967 enrollment was 3,821, and more than eighty percent commuted daily from their Spanish-speaking homes. Enrollment continued to increase, and it is now about 8,500. Although the social and economic level of Mexican Americans has improved greatly since 1967, the area is still bilingual and bicultural and most students are from Spanish-speaking homes.

Each semester I ordinarily teach a class of English 2303—Readings in American Literature, a course designed for nonmajors; consistently, more than ninety percent of my students are Mexican Americans. Among the 80 who completed the course with me in 1985–86, 72 were Mexican American, 6 foreign (including 4 Oriental), 1 Anglo-American, and 1 American black. In my class of 41 during the fall semester of 1986, 39 were Mexican American.

I have used *My Ántonia* in this course for about ten years. The sentence structure and diction of *My Ántonia* are appropriate for young adults who are intelligent but communicate mostly in Spanish, and the lives of immigrants on the Divide have many parallels to the lives of Mexican Americans here. Also, I know the Red Cloud area well. Numerous times during summer vacations I have walked the streets of Red Cloud, visited the Willa Cather Pioneer Memorial and the Cather childhood home, driven around Catherton, stopped in the town of Bladen, and loitered on the Divide.

I spend nearly four seventy-five-minute periods on *My Ántonia*. In the introductory material presented before students begin reading the book, I use a map showing Webster County and pass around photographs, including one showing Highway 281 in downtown Red Cloud. Since the same 281 runs through Edinburg less than a mile from campus and is the only major highway north from this county, students feel drawn to the locale of *My Ántonia* before they begin the book. I mention that when Cather and her characters arrived in Nebraska in the 1880s, it was primitive land, just as our region was then, but whereas ours was endless brush and chaparral, Webster county was nothing but land, "not a country at all, but the material out of which countries are made" (7).

We spend two meetings discussing the content of the book. During these days I make the story realistic by circulating such items as Mildred Bennett's *The Red Cloud Chief*, Cooper-Skjelver's *Webster County* with bookmarks in selected places, pictures of a dugout and a sodhouse, and magazines with illustrated articles (e.g., Howarth).

In class I treat the book as an account of persons (both real and fictitious ones) who lived in Nebraska in the early days and as a story to be enjoyed. I point out that much of the novel is based on actual persons, places, and situations Cather knew when growing up in Webster County. Since the character of Ántonia is based on the life of Anna Sadilek Pavelka, who came from Bohemia to Catherland in 1880 and spent her remaining seventy-five years there, I always tell about her and her family, using information I have learned from conversations in Webster County. These personal facts make the story genuine as well as realistic to students. I emphasize that the book includes much biographical material (especially about Cather in the role of Jim and Anna in the role of Ántonia) and that perhaps it seems so realistic because Cather was picturing actual persons and events. But I also stress that the book is fiction; thus, Cather was free to alter facts, as she did when combining two Sadilek sons in the character of Ambrosch. I always include a few anecdotes that students will remember, such as Mr. Pavelka saying, "I am the husband of My Ántonia."

Since not all Mexican immigrants find instant prosperity or happiness in the United States, students know the reality of the problems faced by immigrants in *My Ántonia*. Every month literally thousands of Mexicans illegally attempt to enter this *county*. Every PAU sophomore knows that some of them drown in the Rio Grande, some are caught and deported on arrival, and some who do succeed in entering the country not only have economic problems as great as the Shimerdas did their first winter but also live in constant fear of arrest by immigration authorities. Dire poverty is also faced by many who enter legally. Thus, the role of Ántonia's father suggests the stark tales students have heard from their ancestors and stark incidents they still observe about the problems of finance, language, and adjustment in a foreign land.

Minute details in *My Ántonia* are significant to my students. For example, Ántonia's difficulty in asking Jim the word for *blue* is typical of language problems; the dried mushrooms show the great value of little things from the homeland; and the use of Bohemian words (*mamenka* and *tatinek* for mother and father) have emotional appeal for readers who often use two languages in one sentence.

Nevertheless, the economic and social progress of Cather's immigrants surely offers encouragement to students here. The American farmers on the Divide never let their daughters become hired girls and Mrs. Burden feels disgraced that Jim attended dances with the hired girls; by the end of the story, however, descendants of the early immigrants are often prosperous farmers. Nearly all first-generation Mexican Americans in this area were victims of poverty and prejudice, but usually by the next generation, often by drudgery in the fields, they had a better life. Though a few PAU students do live in abject poverty today, every profession in the area now includes persons whose Mexican ancestors (like the hired girls in Black Hawk) knew very little English and subsisted on the bare necessities.

The role of Ántonia Shimerda Cuzak (or Anna Sadilek Pavelka) is the greatest value of the book to my students. With the factual information I give about Anna and her children, students are able to know Ántonia long after Jim's visit in "Cuzak's Boys." They imagine Ántonia not only as a mother but later as a widow who lives on the Divide and then in the small town of Bladen till 1955. Especially after I show the picture of the stately Anna on her eighty-fifth birthday (Day) and tell about the prizes she won shortly before then at the county fair on her handwork and baking, they can visualize her and regard her as a person they love and admire in her old age. She becomes "our Ántonia." Until the present generation, Mexican American women (like Ántonia and Anna) often had a dozen or more children and outlived their husbands by thirty years. Obviously Ántonia (Anna) causes students to think of those women who labored throughout their lives and whose descendants now prosper in the same country those women immigrated to years before.

On the last day we go over two letters and look at slides. In the Willa Cather Pioneer Memorial I once copied the 26 December 1933 letter of Anna Pavelka to Carrie Miner Sherwood (the Frances Harling of the novel). In this newsy letter in poor English, Anna thanks Carrie for delivering the coffee Willa had ordered for her, gives an update on her children, and vividly pictures the hardships of farm life in a drought year of the depression. The letter enables the students to see her life as a widow with married children, to feel her family love, and to recall accounts of hardships they have heard from their own elderly relatives. Then we read the letter Anna wrote to an Omaha schoolgirl in February 1955. This letter in Anna's handwriting gives autobiographical material Cather used in the novel. The contents restate material I have already given, but the actual handwriting and the actual words of the real Ántonia give further realism to the book and to the character of Ántonia. The ungrammatical English not only makes the character of Ántonia more genuine but also reminds students of letters from persons whose native language is Spanish. Students might be amused to read that most persons on the ship the Sadileks took to America were "pollish" and the family "boght 10060 acker farm," but their laughter is not ridicule; it is the devoted feeling they have when reading the words of a loving grandmother who scarcely knows English.

I then show about forty slides. I begin with the Divide; then I show pictures of Red Cloud, including ones of the early streetcar, the streetcar in Streetcar Days parade of 1982, the Miner store of the 1890s, the street sign for 281, the two Cather homes, and the Willa Cather Pioneer Memorial, where Silas Garber once had a bank. (The last enables me to digress slightly and to suggest *A Lost Lady* as further reading.) I return to the Divide and show pictures of the George Cather house, the modern fields, and the Pavelka farm on which Anna lived for years. I also show one of downtown Wilber (the Czech capital of Nebraska where Ántonia's husband attends the fair in "Cuzak's Boys"). That the signs in Wilber are in Bohemian is quite important; every community near PAU has stores with signs in Spanish, and students realize that Cuzak's trip would logically be to a Bohemian community just as their trips are usually to San Antonio, Mexico, or some other place where their native language is used. I always encourage questions at any time, and the answers often lead to digressions. The first time I showed slides of the Pavelka barn (where Jim and the Cuzak boys slept) and the backyard with the cellar, students asked: "What does a cellar look like inside?" I then realized that I had never seen a cellar in south Texas. To students at PAU, my offhand description of the inside of a cellar is more useful than an exposition on the Vergil quotation on the title page of *My Ántonia*.

At the next meeting I make a few concluding comments and mention that surely Ántonia was happier than Jim Burden. I add that Cather has no descendants but Anna Pavelka has numerous ones, mostly in southern Nebraska. This concluding statement reminds students that prosperous Anglo settlers here have often left few descendants but the poverty-level Mexican ones have left many. It also reechoes the parallels that I have mentioned and the many that need no mention between the lives of characters in *My Ántonia* and the real persons of the Rio Grande Valley.

For Mexican Americans attending an open-admissions university in this bilingual and bicultural area, *My Ántonia* is an ideal book to use.

TEACHING SPECIFIC ASPECTS

Art and Apparent Artlessness: Self-Reflexivity in *My Ántonia*

Blanche H. Gelfant

Whatever the context for teaching Willa Cather, whether a general course on modern American fiction or a specialized one on women writers, I have approached her work through two phrases from *A Lost Lady*. Invariably I find they lead me where I hope to go, though I have sometimes gone in different and even opposite directions. I quote them here to introduce a relatively oblique approach to *My Ántonia* that may complement the various approaches this volume shows are necessary and illuminating. The phrases to which I refer are Niel Herbert's succinct but ambitious definitions: they describe the books he is reading as "an almost inexhaustible resource" and the charm of Marion Forrester—her "tantalizing" and elusive "something"—as "seemingly so artless, [but] really the most finished artifice" (80, 100). Though art and apparent artlessness pertain to a woman and inexhaustibility to books, both phrases act self-reflexively within the novel, calling attention to literary values it idealizes and would possess and distinguishing them from the moral values of fidelity, chastity, and honor it thematizes. To note Cather's self-reflexivity means seeing her as a sophisticatedly modern writer, and a highly conscious as well as controlling one. Clearly she is aware of her guiding aesthetic principles, and in making these explicit through the novel's self-reflexive comments, usually attributed to a character, she seeks to control the way the reader thinks about her art. Niel Herbert's apparently unmotivated digression on reading—as he describes what he reads, how and why, and the radical effect of literature on his life—would be intrusive if it were not instructive, his way of telling us and our students to read *A Lost Lady* as he reads the *Heroides*—"over and over." Through rereading we should discover as he did the inexhaustibility of great writing and the art that underlies the illusion of its artlessness, an illusion of naturalness and ease, of charming, unstudied simplicity, that Cather cultivates as fastidiously as Marion Forrester and expects to have appreciated.

An awareness of Cather's self-reflexivity can indeed foster appreciation as students see the text itself (not only the teacher) urging them to understand its art as well as its themes. I am assuming, of course, that students will discuss Cather's themes extensively and from a variety of approaches—through consideration of genre, gender, historical, literary, and mythic backgrounds, to name a few. I am suggesting that they also consider how the themes become persuasive because of literary qualities within Cather's novels that the novels define and attribute to themselves as works of art—qualities that may have a particularly poignant appeal to undergraduates. For in a world that seems as ungraspably complex as ours, they may be drawn to the simplicity and accessibility of Cather's fiction, to its apparent artlessness; at a time when this world's natural resources are being exhausted, they may respond to an inexhaustible resource that human hands, a recurrent Cather image, have created rather than despoiled. Moreover, as Cather's texts give their assurances that rereading will leave them not depleted, as undergraduates often fear, but immensely enriched, they discourage mere browsing and invite study, serious and actively attentive reading. In effect, students would learn from Cather's close readers, college-going characters with whom they can identify, like Niel in *A Lost Lady*, Vickie Templeton in "Old Mrs. Harris," and Jim Burden in *My Ántonia*. By serendipity, such characters become our teaching assistants, a pedagogical role I believe Cather herself assigns as she turns her students into exemplary readers.

In *My Ántonia*, Jim Burden is both a student and reader and a writer, the fictional author of memoirs whose form he defines as formlessness, the first of many self-reflexive comments that in their totality constitute nothing less than a poetics of fiction. What I would wish students of *My Ántonia* to see is the presence of a poetics inscribed in the text, of intercalated theoretical propositions that define a general view of narrative and govern the particular aesthetic design of Cather's novel. Students easily overlook this design not only because Jim obscures its presence by calling his memoirs formless but also because his claim seems correct, appropriate to a personal account of the past so casual in structure and conversational in style, so seemingly free and easy, as *My Ántonia*. Unlike, say, William Faulkner's

"The Bear," which students perceive as having been made—as a *work* of art with a dense linguistic surface and strained narrative technique that demand critical analysis—*My Ántonia* seems simply to have happened, as Jim claims, and to ask only that it be enjoyed. Like many of my colleagues, I have heard undergraduates complain that their enjoyment of a book is "ruined" when they are forced "to take it apart." I have wondered how to refute this complaint without seeming to deny a student's felt experience, and I have turned with relief to the text for an oblique but effective rebuttal. For its self-reflexive remarks both support and constitute acts of critical analysis, while its poetics dispels many naive notions students have about fiction, the process of reading, and the function of criticism.

One naive view subverted by *My Ántonia* is that every story has a "true" meaning that can be handed over intact from one reader to another, from teacher to student. Indeed, many students would attend a class on *My Ántonia* in order to hear a teacher tell them what it means. Then they will know, once and for all. Instead, a study of *My Ántonia*'s self-reflexivity shows that meaning is often implicated in the reader's desire and seldom validated by reference to an external "truth." Students see this point for themselves when they look at the many examples of indeterminacy in the novel and try to determine meaning. How are they to tell what the story of Jim's encounter with the rattlesnake really means? Does it mean, as Ántonia says, that Jim had crossed the threshold to manhood, or does it mean, as Jim believes, that he had engaged in a "mock-adventure" with a lazy old snake that left his courage unproved? What is the "truth" about the sunflower-bordered roads that Jim follows through the prairie (29) or about the "great circle where the Indians used to ride" that he discerns still "faintly marked in the grass" (62)? The text gives different versions and shows Jim choosing the romantically heightened one. Thus he prefers to believe that the flowers formed "roads to freedom," though he knows that "botanists do not confirm" Otto Fuchs's story about the fleeing Mormons sowing a sunflower trail for their followers. He is "sure" that Indians made the grass circle when they galloped around in its ring torturing prisoners, though he knows his grandfather thought the Indians "merely ran races or trained horses there." The Mormons and the Indians belong to America's historical past, and yet neither Jim nor the reader can learn the "truth" about them: history seems to have produced not verifiable facts but only a legacy of stories, variant versions of what happened. One chooses to believe a particular version for one's own reason. This modernist view of history as a product of subjective choice rather than objective necessity may not surprise politically minded students, but it may surprise readers of *My Ántonia* lulled by Jim's pleasant but authoritative memoir into security about the American past. For while they are being told what happened, they are also being told, quietly and parenthetically but insistently, that the meaning of what happened, the "truth," is unascertainable.

What are the implications of these instances of indeterminacy that Cather slips into her text? What literary purposes might they serve? Each instant is inconsequential for Jim and Ántonia, a trivial notation that could be expunged—except that it helps support a view of fiction, and arguably of history and of "truth," that makes Jim's memoirs more problematic, more complex and provocative to read, than they first seemed. For if stories of the past lack clear and unequivocal referents for their facts so that variant versions compete, then Jim must be choosing his preferred version of Ántonia from others equally as possible and cogent. Cather's introduction obviously wants the reader to see Jim's personal bias, insisting on it by reiteration of the personal pronoun *I*: "I remember . . . I amuse . . . I finished . . . I didn't . . . I simply . . . I suppose. . . ." The *I* leads to the significantly possessive *my* that Jim places before Ántonia, a word that "seemed to satisfy him." If satisfaction is the writer's reward, according to the text, it follows on an act of appropriation involved in writing that the reader reproduces in the process of reading. For just as Jim appropriates Ántonia for his story, we as readers appropriate him, taking over his memories and making them so integrally part of our consciousness that we can legitimately call his Ántonia our own.

What is at stake for the student in these acts of appropriation that *My Ántonia* reveals as central to writing and reading? Once Jim Burden becomes *My Jim*, each student might ask, does his romanticism become mine, his choices and evasions mine, his oversights, his sexual and racial prejudices, even his ways of reading? Perceptive students will see that the text itself raises these questions as it distances first the introduction's narrator and then Frances Harling from Jim as a person of "romantic disposition." The narrator's ambiguous statement that Jim's youthful romanticism has remained untouched by time can be interpreted as a compliment or criticism, a sign of stability or of stasis and eventual regression. Thus the novel quickly poses its hermeneutic question: How can we interpret? How do we determine what something means? Ántonia is important to Jim only because he has imbued her with romantic meaning. She is not close to him in reality, though he says he would have liked to have her "for a sweetheart, or a wife, or my mother or my sister—anything that a woman can be to a man" (321). She is a symbol, a girl who "seemed to mean to us the country, the conditions, the whole adventure of our childhood." Clearly, she does not embody this meaning for Frances Harling, who has told Jim that he "put a kind of glamour" over the hired girls: "The trouble with you, Jim," she said, "is that you're romantic" (229). If Frances is warning Jim, she may also be alerting the reader that his way of seeing is slanted and requires scrutiny, the test of a reality which, paradoxically, the novel itself has made elusive and perhaps even unnecessary. For in its famous statement declaring some memories better than realities, it places illusion at the core of Jim's story and the novel (328). In the elided twenty years, when Jim remained apart from Ántonia, he clung to his illusions about her, dreading the possibility of their loss if he saw her again. He had learned how powerful and pleasurable illusion could be when as a student he had attended the theater in Lincoln and believed in the "dazzling loveliness" of Camille, brought to the stage by an "infirm old actress" with a "ravaged face" and "curiously hard and stiff body" (274). She "wrung" his heart and "twisted" his nerves more than any real woman could do, more than the really dazzling Lena Lingard.

By such problematic episodes the text questions the mysterious relationship between activities of the mind—remembering, imagining, believing, dreaming—and those of the person in "real" life. Since reading engrosses the mind, placing illusion above reality at least for a time, it raises an issue important to itself and to its reader: What role should literature properly play in life? Jim responds to this question by describing (and prescribing) his reactions to the stories he hears and reads. For example, the horrific story that Pavel tells Mr. Shimerda, and Ántonia tells him, and he in turn tells the reader, produces "a painful and peculiar pleasure" as its emotional aftermath. Stories please and pain Jim in a "peculiar" way because they enter his consciousness and become inseparable from his own memories. Pavel's story becomes Jim's nighttime dream, intimately, personally, and inextricably part of his consciousness as *he* rides the bride's sledge, not through snowy Russian fields but "through a country that looked something like Nebraska and something like Virginia" (61). Stories have made Pavel's past experiences autonomous—free to move into anyone's imagination and mingle with his or her memories. Stories also release Mr. Shimerda's past from his person, making it appropriable by Jim. Thus "Mr. Shimerda's memories, not yet faded from the air" (102), turn into "pictures" in Jim's mind. These memories had become animated, free and footloose, when Jim recalled the stories he had heard about Mr. Shimerda, "all that Ántonia had ever told me about his life before he came to this country" (102). Just as death releases Mr. Shimerda's "spirit" to wander and return home to Bohemia, stories release his memories to seek and find a sympathetic imagination.

My Ántonia thus blurs the boundary between self and others as its stories objectify and transmit what is in human consciousness, turning personal memories into verbal objects, works of literary art to be given away and received, written and read—and it tells its readers it is doing so, asking them, in effect, to consider the nature of art. Moreover, it self-consciously blurs the boundary between history as the collective memory of the past and literature as the cultural artifact left behind by history. Implicitly it raises questions about its own genre: is it a historical novel, a personal memoir, a romance? Why is it self-declaredly formless, when the essence of art, we are commonly told, is form? It is life that may be formless. Is the novel then declaring itself true to life or realistic even though it has described itself as the artifact produced by a romanticizing mind? Indeed, Jim seems to make discriminations between life and romance murky, not only as an adult more impassioned by a woman on the theater's stage than one in his life, but also as a child when he saw literature reified into life. The "real" Otto Fuchs had seemed to him to have stepped out of the pages of *The Life of Jesse James*, "one of the most satisfactory books," he says, "I have ever read" (4). In the first pages of *My Ántonia*, Jim is already concerned with fiction, and he will continue to be so, sometimes finding its pleasures greater, other times less, than those of his immediate experiences. Robinson Crusoe's "life on the island seemed dull compared" to his (100) and that of the Swiss family Robinson no more "adventurous" (66). The popular children's books he reads as a boy imbue his life with excitement as they show him what adventure is and that he is experiencing it—a winter like that of the Swiss Robinson family, isolation like Crusoe's. More subtly, they show the reader that Jim's story has the heightened emotional qualities of perennially thrilling stories. Literature thus prepares Jim for life, and the reader of *My Ántonia* for "adventure" in the mundane setting of Nebraska. Paradoxically, it precedes and takes precedence over "real" experiences, and it enhances them: they become pleasurable because they resemble fiction. Otto Fuchs, with his desperado air, his vicious scar that gave his mouth a "sinister curl," and his "ferocious" look, might have frightened a sleepy displaced boy, but he pleased Jim because he resembled a storybook Jesse James. Illness and the isolation of dark wintry days and nights might have discomposed Jim if their hardships had not seemed as "adventurous" as those in *The Swiss Family Robinson*.

The novel's most enigmatic and involuted representation of how literature and life interact, its most heightened self-reflexive moment, occurs when Jim is studying Vergil's *Georgics* and seductive Lena Lingard appears, showing up first in person and then as a "picture" on a page of poetry in Jim's dream. Lena's visit calls forth memories of the hired girls Jim had known, not Ántonia but the sexually charged Bohemian Marys and the Danish laundry girls. "It came over me, as it had never done before, the relation between girls like those and the poetry of Virgil" (270), Jim thinks, making laundresses and housemaids the muses of poetry. This "revelation" is "precious" to him but must be puzzling to us; it is also pedagogically invaluable as it leads us to ponder what poetry means in the novel, how it relates to everyday life and, specifically, working women, and how context provides clues to interpretation. One contextual element is the classroom in which Gaston Cleric had explicated a line of the *Georgics*: "Cleric had explained to us that 'patria' here meant, not a nation, . . . but the little rural neighborhood . . . where the poet was born" (264). At this point, the novel's self-reflexivity is obvious and self-serving, since it evokes a great literary tradition to support its own material, rural Nebraska, as a significant literary setting. Though Jim romanticizes everyday life in Nebraska and imbues ordinary people like Ántonia with historic importance, he endorses literary realism (if that involves writing about ordinary everyday life), indicates its relevance to *My Ántonia* as a rural novel, and indirectly praises Cather for her pioneering efforts as a midwestern artist. For she could say of herself what she has Jim imagine Vergil saying: "I was the first to bring the Muse into my country" (264). *My Ántonia* thus becomes a pioneer novel in a double sense: in its portrayal of pioneer life and in its self-conscious decision to be the first to create art out of material that American writers had conspicuously overlooked.

Perhaps I have said enough about how approaching *My Ántonia* through its self-reflexive remarks reveals the conscious artfulness of this seemingly artless text and how it reveals Cather's underlying poetics, which is more comprehensive and ranging than space has permitted me to show. If I could say more here, I would go on to examine the role that voice plays in the novel and its poetics, citing how Grandfather Burden's voice was "so sympathetic," its intonations so awesome, that it made words Jim did not understand sound "oracular" and "sacred," and the biblical past seem "like something that had happened lately" (13, 84); or how the "fervour" of Cleric's voice communicated the passion of poetry (265); or how the lament in the Widow Steavens's voice evoked compassion for the fallen and disgraced Ántonia; or how Ántonia's husky, breathy voice made everything "she said seem to come right out of her heart" and everyone enjoy her stories (176). This project would initiate an attempt to define Jim's voice and, more elusive, Cather's, and to relate both to music and sound, so essential to Cather's lyrical language. I would examine also Cather's criterion for creating and recognizing a "perfect utterance"; that is what Jim calls the *Georgics*, a work in which "the pen was fitted to matter as the plough is to the furrow" (264). Jim's own brief utterance establishes "perfection" as a literary ideal; appropriateness of style to material, or form, as the means to this ideal; and the modulation of many narrative voices as essential to the form of a novel that has defined itself as formless. The modulations in voice are paralleled by variations in literary mode as *My Ántonia* mingles romanticism with melodrama and its violence, love story and its stock characters, history and its uncertainties, popular fiction and its adventures, and parody. Where, how, and why Cather introduces these variations, incidentally slipping into her putatively celebratory story instances of violence, seduction and abandonment, attempted rape, murder, and suicide, we can encourage students to discover for themselves by a study of the novel's self-reflexivity.

Any approach to the novel, including one through its self-reflexivity, leads to critical possibilities that begin to seem inexhaustible. As students realize this, they can appreciate the unfathomable depths that lie beneath the surface of the artful artlessness in *My Ántonia*. Seeking it, they come upon the inexhaustible pleasures and uncertainties of reading. They may have moments when they feel about their Ántonia as Jim Burden felt about Lena Lingard's "mellow, easy laugh," that was "either very artless or very comprehending, one never quite knew which" (266).

My Ántonia as Double Bildungsroman

Charlotte Goodman

Like most women of my social class and generation, I got married soon after I graduated from college, and, giving birth to three children, I, like Ántonia, became "a rich mine of life" (229). Twenty years elapsed before I had completed my doctorate and had begun to teach English at Skidmore College. In 1975, as I selected the texts for an introductory fiction course, I made sure to include a number of works by women, among them *My Ántonia* and George Eliot's *Mill on the Floss*.

The juxtaposition of these two bildungsromans proved to be serendipitous, for in the process of teaching them I discovered that both Eliot and Cather had substantially revised the conventions of the male bildungsroman. Unlike, let us say, *Great Expectations*, *Portrait of the Artist as a Young Man*, or *Sons and Lovers*, both *The Mill on the Floss* and *My Ántonia* trace the growth and development not of one character but of a pair of characters, one a male and the other a female. The structure of these two bildungsromans also differs from that of the traditional bildungsroman: Whereas the structure of the traditional bildungsroman is linear, beginning in childhood and progressing toward the moment when the mature male protagonist, casting off the restraints of earlier life, contemplates the future, the structure of *The Mill on the Floss* and *My Ántonia* is circular. Eliot and Cather both begin their novels with a description of the shared childhood experience of a male and a female protagonist who inhabit a prelapsarian edenic world in which these children are companions; then they dramatize the separation of the male and the female character in adolescence and young adulthood, when the male, as does the hero of the typical male bildungsroman, journeys forth to seek his fortune, while the female is left behind; and finally, these novels conclude when the male protagonist is reunited with his female counterpart.

A similar pattern is also found in Emily Brontë's *Wuthering Heights*, Jean Stafford's *The Mountain Lion*, and Joyce Carol Oates's *Them* (Goodman). While one can hardly make the claim that these five double bildungsromans constitute a major literary tradition for women writers, the similarities among these novels are significant nevertheless: The double form of the bildungsroman, with its focus on both a male and a female protagonist, appears to be a particularly congenial form for the woman novelist who wishes to emphasize the ways in which a society that rigidly differentiates between male and female gender roles limits the full development of men and women alike. Unusually close, the paired male and female protagonist in each of these novels function, I believe, as psychological "doubles," for each character is intensely involved in the psychic life of his or her counterpart. Each character may also embody a separate aspect of the female author's own psychic life, the female character representing the author's identification with those women who have conformed to traditional female gender roles, the male character, the author's quest, like that of many males, for learning, power, mobility, autonomy. Together the male and the female character suggest the possibility of androgynous wholeness, that is to say, the combination in a single individual of traits that usually have been considered male and traits that usually have been considered female. For Cather and other women writers as well, androgynous wholeness is imaginable only in a mythic prelapsarian world of nature before a patriarchal culture gained ascendancy. Offering a critique of a patriarchal society in which gender roles ordinarily are rigidly defined, the male-female double bildungsroman, then, traces the way in which a harmonious and balanced androgynous self, one that combines both "male" and "female" traits, is fractured by a culture that traditionally assigns radically different roles to men and women. Only in the final scene of each novel is the fragmentation of the self momentarily healed as the male and the female protagonist are reunited.

After I have described the characteristics of the male-female double bildungsroman, I consider the double structure of *My Ántonia* in particular, emphasizing Cather's choice of a male narrator to tell a woman's story and establishing parallels between *My Ántonia* and other novels of this type. I then discuss Willa Cather's life in order to suggest why she might have found the double structure of the male-female bildungsroman to be useful when she wished to dramatize some of the central conflicts of her life. Focusing on her most important conflict, which might best be described as a gender conflict, I point out that in her youth Cather chose to call herself William, to cut her hair short like a man's, and to wear masculine attire (see O'Brien, " 'Thing Not Named' " 580–81). Subsequently, Cather was reluctant to ridicule domestic women, especially working-class women like Ántonia; nevertheless, she recognized that artistic women like herself or her protagonist Thea Kronborg, an opera singer in *Song of the Lark*, had to eschew the domestic if they wished to pursue an artistic career.

Another issue I mention in connection with Cather's gender conflicts is her putative lesbianism. I describe her close friendships with Louise Pound, Isabelle McClung, and Edith Lewis, and I point out that *My Ántonia* was written soon after Isabelle McClung, perhaps the most important woman in Cather's life, married. According to James Woodress, Cather experienced a "profound emotional crisis" when Isabelle McClung announced that she was planning to get married, bringing to an end an intimate relationship between Cather and herself that had begun in 1899 (Woodress, *Life and Art* 172–73). The marriage of her friend probably forced Cather, who was then forty-three years old, to reconsider the advantages and disadvantages of the way of life she herself had chosen.

Cather's ambivalence about Nebraska, where she lived in her youth after her family moved there from Virginia, is also worthwhile to discuss. Although she had many pleasant, even transcendent memories of Nebraska and was fond of a number of people she had known there, including Annie Pavelka, the Bohemian girl on whom Ántonia is based, Cather herself chose to leave Nebraska and ultimately to make her home in the East, as her character Jim Burden does. When discussing Cather's ambivalent feelings about Nebraska, I have my students read her moving short story "A Wagner Matinée," which describes the way a cultured woman, like Cather herself, reacts to life on the prairies. Jim Burden's retrospective account in *My Ántonia* of life in Nebraska when he was a child is in part a celebration of its pastoral pleasures: the fecund earth, the warm yellow pumpkins, the sun and air. In contrast, "A Wagner Matinée" emphasizes the enormous sense of deprivation that an educated woman, formerly a music teacher at the Boston Conservatory, experiences after she marries a farmer and is exiled to his bleak farm in Nebraska. Based on one of Cather's aunts, the story's protagonist is an analogous figure to Ántonia's fiddle-playing papa, who is driven to commit suicide by the harsh life on the prairies.

Conflicts about gender identity and gender roles, ambivalence about whether the western world of nature or the eastern world of culture is preferable— these are the tensions Willa Cather dramatized again and again in her fiction. To emphasize her divided allegiances, I have found it useful to quote two passages, one from *My Ántonia* and one from her essay on Katherine Mansfield. In the former, Jim Burden meets Ántonia's husband Cuzak during a visit to Nebraska. Jim says that Cuzak, "a city man," now lives on a farm "in one of the loneliest countries in the world" (366), and imagining that Cuzak spends his evenings "listening to the silence," Jim Burden observes: "This was a fine life, certainly, but it wasn't the kind of life he had wanted to live. I wondered whether the life that was right for one was ever right for two!" (367). The second passage appears in Cather's essay on Katherine Mansfield:

> One realizes that even in harmonious families there is this double life, which is the one we can observe in our neighbour's household, and, underneath, another—secret and passionate and intense—which is the real life that stamps the faces and gives character to the voices of our friends. Always in his mind each member of these social units is escaping, running away, trying to break the net which circumstances and his own affections have woven about him. One realises that human relationships are the tragic necessity of human life; that they can never be wholly satisfactory, that every ego is half the time greedily seeking them, and half the time pulling away from them. (*On Writing* 108)

Differing human needs, the impulse to cleave to other human beings and the contrary impulse to "break the net which circumstances and . . . affections have woven"—it is these "tragic" and irresolvable conflicts that Cather dramatizes in *My Ántonia*. The male-female double bildungsroman, tracing a "double life," was an ideal vehicle for inscribing such conflicts.

To emphasize the double focus of *My Ántonia*, I begin my discussion of the novel itself by asking who its protagonist is, Ántonia or Jim Burden? Once we have established that both characters play an equally important role in the narrative, we then look carefully at the introduction, comparing the introduction in the 1918 edition to the more abbreviated one appearing in subsequent editions. I suggest that the introduction is important because it supplies some important clues about Jim Burden's character and life that help the reader assess his reliability as a narrator. Among the questions we consider are the following: Is the "I" who narrates the frame story male or female? What is this narrator's opinion of life on the Nebraska prairies? How does the fact that the narrator mentions Jim Burden's "romantic disposition" affect the reader's response to Jim Burden's account of Ántonia's life? What significance is there in the narrator's remark that Jim Burden changed the title of his manuscript from "Ántonia" to "My Ántonia"? What is the difference between the kind of document that is normally carried in a legal portfolio and the manuscript that Jim Burden's portfolio contains? Why does Cather have Jim Burden rather than Ántonia tell Ántonia's story? How might Ántonia's account of her life have differed from Jim Burden's? At this juncture I mention how unusual it is in fiction for a male narrator to describe the life of a woman, a narrative device Cather employs not only in *My Ántonia* but in *A Lost Lady* and "A Wagner Matinée." What Jim's narrative makes evident is that the circumstances of Ántonia's life have not equipped her to recount her own experience in the elegant English prose that Jim himself writes, for even though Ántonia tells many stories to her children in Bohemian during her later years, she admits sadly to Jim that she has all but forgotten the English she learned in her youth (335). Once they have considered the implications of Cather's introduction, however, my students are aware that Jim Burden's account of Ántonia's life may not be as objective as the legal briefs he ordinarily writes. Cather's introduction causes the reader to deconstruct Jim's romantic view of Ántonia and to see Ántonia somewhat differently than Jim Burden does.

During our discussion of the novel, I also emphasize the underlying pattern of union, separation, and return that characterizes this male-female double bildungsroman. When Jim and Ántonia are children and live in a rural environment, they function as equals: "We drifted along lazily, very happy, through the magical light of the late afternoon," Jim says, recalling a day when he and Ántonia had explored the Nebraska countryside together (40). Jim teaches her to speak English, and she, in turn, amuses him with tales of the Old World. All too soon, however, this edenic period comes to a close. Black frost appears, and hundreds of miles of yellow sunflowers are "transformed into brown, rattling burry stalks" (43). To signify the end of childhood innocence, Cather introduces a loathsome phallic snake that threatens Ántonia and Jim. By killing the snake, Jim is initiated into adulthood, and this ritual act also allows him to gain ascendancy over the older Ántonia. Whereas he had formerly been annoyed by Ántonia's superior tone, now he observes, "She liked me better from that time on, and she never took a supercilious air with me again. I had killed a big snake—I was now a big fellow" (50). This episode with a snake that lay "in long loose waves, like a letter 'W' " (45) prefigures the later episode in which the villainous Wick Cutter, who planned to assault Ántonia sexually, encounters Jim Burden instead. Jim Burden is so revolted by this incident that he hates not only Wick Cutter but also Cutter's intended victim, Ántonia. "She had let me in for all this disgustingness," Jim Burden says (250).

The gulf between Jim and Ántonia widens when they move to the town of Black Hawk, leaving the pastoral world behind them. Here the differences between them in class and gender become more pronounced: Jim goes to school, while Ántonia becomes a "hired girl." In book 3 the separation between Jim and Ántonia is complete. As other heroes of the male bildungsroman do, he goes off to further his education and embark on a career; she remains in the provincial town of Black Hawk until she runs away with a railway conductor, a person who perhaps represents mobility to her, and when she is abandoned by him, she returns to the country to bear a child alone out of wedlock.

The pattern of the male-female double bildungsroman is not completed until the male and female protagonist are reunited. In *My Ántonia* this reunion occurs when Jim returns to Nebraska twenty years later. During an earlier visit, he had wished that he "could be a little boy again" and that his way "could end there" (322); now, visiting the flourishing farm of Ántonia and her husband Cuzak, he asks if he can "sleep in the haymow with the Cuzak boys" (344). Returning to the scenes of his childhood, when he and Ántonia were undivided, Jim completes his journey. "I had the sense of coming home to myself . . . ," he observes (371).

The question I pose as we conclude our discussion of the novel is who had a better and more satisfying life, Jim or Ántonia? Does *My Ántonia* really celebrate the "heart" over the "head," as John H. Randall III maintains that it does (*Landscape* 106–08)? To those that insist on romanticizing Ántonia's life, I point out instances in the novel where Cather suggests that Ántonia's life has not, perhaps, been as idyllic as Jim makes it out to be.

For example, during Jim's earlier trip to Nebraska when he visits Ántonia and her illegitimate daughter, Ántonia tells him, "I'm going to see that my little girl has a better chance than I ever had" (320–21), and at the end of the novel Ántonia remarks that the children of Mary Svoboda, the finest butter maker in the area, "will have a grand chance" (226). These passages imply that Ántonia herself does not necessarily advocate her or Mary's way of life for the next generation. Toothless, gray-haired, and flat-chested, Ántonia confirms Tiny Soderball's observation to Jim that his old friend has had a "hard life" (327). Moreover, while Jim honorifically describes Ántonia's large family as "a rich mine of life," Ántonia's friend Lena Lingard expresses a different point of view about large families. Coming from a large family herself, Lena vows never to marry, for she bitterly remembers home as "a place where there were always too many children, a cross man and work piling up around a sick woman" (291).

I believe that instead of celebrating the "heart" over the "head" in *My Ántonia*, Cather is lamenting that a single individual cannot experience the female maternal fulfillment of an Ántonia and the male intellectual satisfactions of a Jim Burden. It is true that Jim, childless and married to a woman who is irritated by his quiet tastes, is incomplete, but Ántonia's life in rural Nebraska would hardly have satisfied him either. The double structure of *My Ántonia* allows Cather to travel two roads, that of the male intellectual who lives in the urban East and that of the earth mother who lives in the West. The tensions in the novel remain unresolved, however, until Jim, through his narrative, repossesses "the precious, the incommunicable past" when he and Ántonia were undivided (372).

Gender, Sexuality, and Point of View:
Teaching *My Ántonia* from a Feminist Perspective

Sharon O'Brien

Like most of us, I vary the interpretive and pedagogical strategies with which I approach texts depending on the academic context—the focus of the course, the surrounding texts, the level and background of the students. So there is no stable text of *My Ántonia* that I unvaryingly present to my classes. If I am teaching the novel in a lower-level survey course in American literature, for example, I usually approach it as a story about the American writer's attempt to find the materials for art in the texture of American life and juxtapose Cather's intermingling of memory, desire, and storytelling with Hawthorne's similar interweaving of these creative powers in *The Scarlet Letter*. When I teach the novel in my upper-level course on women writers or my senior seminar on Cather—courses in which I employ a more sophisticated intermingling of feminist and psychoanalytic theory as well as biographical and literary analysis—I focus in a more concentrated way on issues of gender and sexuality. The approach I am about to describe would be one I would take in either of these two courses.

Students in both courses approach *My Ántonia* having read and discussed feminist theory. I generally introduce them to the importance of considering gender in assessing women's fiction by assigning sections from part 1 of *The Madwoman in the Attic* (Gilbert and Gubar's attention-getting opening sentence—"Is a pen a metaphorical penis?"—tends to give them the motivation to keep reading) and often supplement this material with essays by other feminist critics, many from Elaine Showalter's useful anthology *The New Feminist Criticism*. Because I want to help students make careful links between writer and text (instead of engaging in unfounded biographical speculation) I also have them read some recent psychoanalytic accounts of female development and identity by Nancy Chodorow and Jane Flax; I also find useful Carol Gilligan's analysis of female moral development in *In a Different Voice*, since Gilligan draws on Chodorow's model but writes in a style that students find more accessible.

This reading gives my students a set of questions rather than answers, theoretical issues that can help them assess Cather's purposes and accomplishments in *My Ántonia*. They will be prepared to view Cather not as a genderless, disembodied being but as a woman writer who had to struggle to integrate those seemingly contradictory identities. They will be ready to debate what I consider the important, and perhaps finally unresolvable, questions about the novel: does Cather fully free herself from patriarchal definitions of gender and narrative in *My Ántonia*? Or does she unwittingly reinforce them? Or—and this is my own view—does she create a novel filled with contradictions and ambiguities, at times speaking in a woman's voice, at other times employing a male perspective?

Having read Gilbert and Gubar's analysis of "palimpsests," those subversive, angry subtexts in nineteenth-century women's fiction in which female rebellion is both disclosed and concealed, the students are also ready to tackle a currently controversial question: Is there a lesbian subtext in *My Ántonia*? I would like to give students the necessary historical and biographical contexts for approaching this question by having them read Carroll Smith-Rosenberg's classic article "The Female World of Love and Ritual," a short story or two by Sarah Orne Jewett, the exchange of letters between Jewett and Cather, and a theoretical article on defining lesbianism, but so far I have decided, because this reading is so time-consuming, to cover these issues in lecture. I discuss with them the interpretive issues involved in defining a writer as lesbian and present the case for viewing Cather as a lesbian writer (which I develop at length in my essay " 'The Thing Not Named': Willa Cather as a Lesbian Writer" as well as in my biography of Cather). Then we have both the biographical and the historical grounding for asking whether Jim Burden is a "mask" for a lesbian perspective.

So I spend a good part of each course preparing the theoretical groundwork, raising issues that can be asked of *My Ántonia* as well as of other novels in the course. I tend not to assign students specific essays on Cather, because I generally find that they are so impressed by the critic's seemingly invulnerable argument that they then cannot think for themselves. So I prefer to have them read feminist theory that they then can test out against a specific text; that way I both encourage originality in their papers and allow for debate and controversy in class, particularly important when dealing with a novel that has prompted as many varying readings as has *My Ántonia*.

After discussing these theoretical questions and before moving to an analysis of the novel, I present what seem to me to be the key interpretive problems in approaching *My Ántonia*—problems that I think are central to a feminist reading—and in doing so I draw on the work of critics like Blanche Gelfant, Susan Rosowski, Jean Schwind, and Judith Fetterley. The first interpretive crux is whether we are to consider Jim Burden a reliable narrator: Is Cather identified with his romantic (and male) viewpoint, particularly at the end of the novel, where he celebrates the earth mother Ántonia as a "rich mine of life"? Or does she consistently and subtly undercut his perspective? Cather's readers differ on these questions. I believe her point of view is unstable: at times she is ironically distant, at other times identified with his construction of "my" Ántonia—and her wavering is connected with her alternate acceptance and criticism of male views of women in her portrayal of Jim's point of view.

I should confess that my perspective is quite a difficult one to convey to my students, who have a good deal of trouble even in questioning a narrator's authority. And to suggest that at times even the author may be ambivalent and conflicted—this idea can be very disturbing and raises some resistance. And yet I think that students in upper-level classes need to confront such difficult questions of authorial intention—considering even the impossibility of our retrieving a determinate, unconflicted authorial intention. And I think that when we are looking at women writers or lesbian writers who cannot always speak openly and directly, such interpretive problems need to be raised.

The second interpretive difficulty has to do with Jim Burden's sexual identity—and thus with Willa Cather's. Is he a "mask" or "cover" for a lesbian writer who cannot write directly, in such an autobiographical narrative, of desire for her "lost ladies"? Or is he a male character created by a lesbian writer who wants to explore male desire? Or is he a male character created by a woman writer whom we assume to be heterosexual—or whose sexual identity we assume to be irrelevant to the text? Not surprisingly, critics of *My Ántonia* have embraced all these views, and the differences of opinion can generally be traced to whether Cather is viewed as a lesbian writer or not.

Once again, I find myself faced with a difficult interpretive and pedagogical issue in teaching *My Ántonia*. My view, which I develop at some length in my biography, is that although we do not know whether Cather had sexual relationships with women since most of the vital correspondence has been destroyed, she nonetheless—given the correspondence we do have—possessed a lesbian identity. And thus, unlike Sarah Orne Jewett, she could not write unself-consciously about love between women, even though such love was the emotional center of her life. So as readers of Cather's novels —*My Ántonia* in particular—we have to consider Cather's possible use of camouflage, encoding, and metaphor to express what we might call "the thing not named," choosing a male alter ego in *My Ántonia* simply because she could not follow Sarah Orne Jewett's nineteenth-century advice and cast a narrator who loves another woman as female.

Hence in teaching the novel I raise with my students the question of the lesbian subtext, and once again I find myself asking them to consider indeterminate meaning as a reasonable interpretive resolution. I find myself unable to view Jim Burden as either an unproblematic male character—the view of those who do not consider Cather a lesbian writer—or a simple mask for a lesbian consciousness, a character who is not "really" male at all. My unwillingness to view Jim simply as an unconvincing mask is connected with my belief that the "lesbian subtext" is an extremely complex matter in Cather's fiction.

I think that the word *subtext* may be an unfortunate one in that it posits a hierarchical distribution of texts—an acceptable surface text superimposed over a hidden, subversive text, a kind of literary-archaeological layering in which the submerged text is assumed to be the "real" story the author would have written had she been able. There are two problems, I think, with this view: we cannot assume that Cather was not invested, imaginatively and emotionally, in the "surface" text; and to argue that her sensitive or sexually maladjusted male characters are "really" female and that her heterosexual plots are merely covers for homosexual desire is to simplify both Cather's texts and her literary imagination. So when I teach *My Ántonia* I present a view that my students find even more problematic than the notion of a subtext that is the "real" story: I suggest that authorial intention (and thus literary meaning) may oscillate back and forth between overt and covert, surface and hidden, heterosexual and homosexual plots, and that the best metaphor for thinking about meaning in *My Ántonia* is the continual interplay between figure and ground.

I find this a difficult viewpoint to suggest to students, most of whom want to know the "real meaning" of the text, in part because our pedagogy often encourages the idea that we can recover, with assurance, authorial intention and literary meaning ("What Cather is *really* saying here is . . ."). And I admit that I do not introduce this subversive notion in my entry-level course, largely because freshmen and sophomores—if introduced to the notion of textual indeterminacy without enough preparation—will eagerly embrace a kind of anti-intellectual relativism, assuming that whatever they then say about a text is acceptable. And of course my upper-level students can also embrace this temptation.

So I proceed carefully in presenting this view of *My Ántonia*, and in fact I don't introduce the notion of the "oscillation" I see in intention and meaning until we have looked at the text carefully, although I have prepared my students to think about ambiguity and contradiction. So after this somewhat sophisticated introduction to the novel, we do some old-fashioned close reading.

I first focus on the question of gender, centering on the problematics of point of view: Do Cather and Jim share the same social and narrative assumptions? We then analyze a number of passages in which Cather seems to be ironically undercutting Jim's point of view, thus calling into question his unexamined myths about women (and masculinity): the original and the 1926 introduction, the battle with the snake, the romantic interlude with Lena, his return to Ántonia, and "Cuzak's Boys." Although I haven't taught the novel since Jean Schwind's interesting article appeared, in the future I'll also draw on her juxtaposition of the visual and the verbal texts.

We then turn to passages in which Cather seems allied with Jim's romanticism: early sections in which he responds both to Ántonia and to the beauty of the Nebraska landscape, and the last (and to me the most problematic passage) in which he celebrates Ántonia as the "rich mine of life" and archetypal mother (of sons, not daughters). Here he is taking on the privilege of the male subject and speaker to define (and thus confine) an individual woman by transforming her into a symbol, and yet at this point Cather does not seem to undermine his perspective.

And finally, to add one more layer of ambiguity to Cather's point of view, we consider ways in which Ántonia nevertheless escapes the inherited narrative and social assumptions with which Jim (and, at times, Cather) would confine her. We talk about Ántonia's revision of the "fallen woman" plot and, most prominently, about her role as storyteller throughout the novel, discussing the fact that Jim is also a character in *her* story, as we discover in "Cuzak's Boys." By this point we generally have the basis for some lively debates: some students will be arguing for Cather's consistent ironic detachment from Jim, others for her identification with him, others for her ambivalence. Although the latter view is mine, I do not present it to my students as the only "correct" one, although I do insist that if they want to argue either for Cather's ironic detachment from Jim's point of view or for her identification with it, they need to take account of those passages that seem to suggest an alternate reading.

I conclude by turning to the second key issue, that of sexuality, explaining that although questions of gender and sexuality are intertwined in this novel, as they are in life, for purposes of analysis we will examine them sequentially. In considering the presence (or absence) of sexuality in *My Ántonia* at times I have assigned two short stories in which I think Cather is using an unconvincing male mask when she is exploring desire for an unattainable woman: "The Burglar's Christmas" and "On the Gulls' Road." Using these stories for contrast and comparison allows us to ask whether Jim may function simultaneously as a mask and as a fully realized male character.

We then look closely at scenes in which Cather's attitudes toward sexuality, and Jim's sexual identity, are most evident: once again, the snake-killing scene; Wick Cutter's attempted rape of Ántonia/Jim; Jim's dream of Lena; the picnic scene, where Jim flees from Lena. We debate whether Cather is portraying male fear of female sexuality, or conveying her own ambivalence, or encoding lesbian desire. My own view, as I have suggested, is that she is doing all these things, but once again the complexity and ambiguity in the novel allows for good class discussion.

As must be clear, in looking at Cather's representation of gender and sexuality in *My Ántonia* I am not guiding my students to a settled definition of unified, coherent, stable textual meaning. Rather I try to open their minds to a text that I see as shifting and indeterminate, encouraging them to think in terms of "both/and" rather than "either/or." I want them to question the binary oppositions that are our cultural heritage—male-female, heterosexual-homosexual, subject-object—since I think that Cather herself questioned these oppositions in her life and in her art.

In many courses students find it very hard to address such epistemological uncertainties; they want the professor to tell them the truth, not to convey a way of thinking critically. But I find that in my courses on women writers students are more receptive to this approach to *My Ántonia* than are students who read the novel in more conventional and "canonical" courses, possibly because courses on women writers themselves call into question the categories of meaning and value we generally use to evaluate literary texts.

NOTE

There are many definitions of *lesbian*, ranging from an insistence on sexual activity to a more broadly conceived focus on "woman-identified" experience. It is important to point out to students that one's definition naturally shapes the conclusions one comes to. In my view, a historically grounded definition that stresses identity rather than behavior is essential, since what we want to capture is the writer's self-definition. For a discussion of these issues, see my article " 'The Thing Not Named.' "

Jim Burden: A Rare Modern

Glen A. Love

In teaching *My Ántonia*, I like to emphasize that Jim Burden is one of Cather's consequential moderns. He is a westerner, of course, as are all of Cather's main contemporary figures, and he shares the westerner's sense of possession of a primal creative energy, emanating from the land itself. But Jim has also left the West, like Cather's other new Americans, and has gone east. To go east, both for Cather herself as a young writer and for her striving fictional figures, is to take up one's part in the larger modern world, to find a meaningful role in society, to attempt to reach one's fullest human potentiality. This new role characteristically must allow individuals to combine their obligation to society with the obligation to the unmodified and essential western core of selfhood. It is an uneasy union for the Cather hero and heroine. Nevertheless, they are carried forward into the great world to face its threatening challenges.

The character of Jim Burden, then, I suggest to my students, is what helps to make *My Ántonia* a more significant book than *O Pioneers!* Without Jim, Ántonia's story would be simply another tribute to the immigrant pioneer on the mid-American frontier. With Jim's presence in the novel, we have a more deeply textured work, a rendering of not only the old pioneering, but the new.

Cather's introduction marks out immediately and unmistakably the essential elements of Jim's life and career: He is a westerner, like Ántonia, whose love of his home country is deep and strong, but he has left the West and followed a modern career in New York as legal counsel for a western railroad. Despite an unhappy marriage, he has achieved success in his work, which brings him back west, allowing him to revivify his contemporary "eastern" self at the wellsprings of his youth. Finally, and most important, we know that Jim has also become an artist, a writer. He has, from the powerful memories and feelings associated with Ántonia and his youth, shaped a work that may break through the closed circle of "freemasonry" (1) that has not only identified but also isolated this unstoried western country and its representative figures, like Ántonia, from the wider world.

When one considers all that Jim Burden does and represents, he becomes a central and protean fictional figure for Cather. The destructive or limiting forces of contemporary life, the conflicting demands of society and self, reach a productive tension in Jim, to form a more complex personality than has emerged in Cather's novels up to this time. The book, then, might be seen also as Jim Burden's story, as his insistence on the word *My* in his manuscript title indicates. Ántonia Shimerda, for all her vitality, must be seen, too, for what she does to and for Jim Burden, who, out of the undeniable potency of her influence on him, still essentially creates her for himself and for the reader. Students may wonder—in this regard—why so many incidents and sections in the book seem unrelated or only remotely related to Ántonia (the Wick Cutter episode, Blind d'Arnault, the Lena Lingard segment, etc.). But if Jim Burden is seen as the artist who composes his story as something other than a purely objective portrait of Ántonia, then these events, as John J. Murphy points out (*Teacher's Guide*, n. pag.), take on importance in revealing the shaping of Jim's personality.

Jim is a boy of ten at the opening of the novel when he journeys to Nebraska from Virginia—as had Cather herself as a child—and first meets the Shimerdas, who are also newcomers to this huge and unfamiliar land. Jim comes to find Ántonia interesting because, like himself, she had "been early awakened and made observant by coming at a tender age from an old country to a new" (131). With her European heritage and her fresh awareness of life, she expands Jim's education beyond that provided by the narrow and spiritless town of Black Hawk. Ántonia and her artistic and sensitive father help to arouse in Jim's mind the desire for wider understanding that is part of his growing wish to shape the wild, chaotic, and unstoried Nebraska landscape, "not a country at all, but the material out of which countries are made" (8), into meaningful form. We see an intimation of Jim's later desire, like Vergil in the *Georgics*, to "be the first, if I live, to bring the Muse into my country" (171), in the opening pages of the book, when Jim, the writer-to-be, confesses that he felt "erased, blotted out" (9) as he arrived in Nebraska. Ántonia helps Jim to sense the heroic potential of the life around him, to turn the blots and erasures into meaningful symbols, to emulate the "picture writing on the sun" (159) that pioneer farm life suggests.

Perhaps Ántonia's greatest contribution to Jim as the potential writer is that she arouses in him the powerful and deeply felt impressions and pictures of his own youth. Ántonia "leave[s] images in the mind that did not fade—that grew stronger with time," as she also touches elements of the most memorable human importance. ("She lent herself to immemorial human attitudes which we recognize by instinct as universal and true" [228].) Thus Ántonia calls up in Jim the most powerful reverberations of private and common experience, which he must possess and unite if he is to become a true artist. (Other complementary relationships in the novel are pointed out by Stouck, "Marriage.")

But Ántonia is more than a rich source of human images and expressions for Jim. She also encourages him directly in his early efforts at communication, as if she realizes that he possesses an ability that she cannot command but that she instinctively recognizes as precious and worth nurturing. When Jim gives the high school commencement speech, Ántonia is deeply stirred. At this point, and once more when Ántonia implores Jim to tell the girls the story of the early Spanish explorers (" 'I've tried to tell them,' " says

Ántonia, " 'but I leave out so much' " [158]), we sense that Ántonia's encouragement of Jim helps to initiate his desire to write and to shape his growing conception of the responsibilities of the writer. Like George Willard of Sherwood Anderson's *Winesburg, Ohio,* with which students may be familiar, Jim takes up the "burden" of the artist: to communicate the truths of the inarticulate to the great world. In doing so, the artist reveals the heretofore unrealized significance of the voiceless ones to a wider audience, which is itself graced by this sympathetic enlargement of its understanding.

Another figure joins Ántonia in furthering Jim's education. Attending the new state university at Lincoln, Jim meets a brilliant young scholar, Gaston Cleric, who introduces him to the Greek and Roman classics. Reading Vergil, Jim discovers that his feeling for his native country is part of a timeless and universal search for one's place in the world. Cleric nourishes Jim's intellectual growth as Ántonia had his emotional nature.

Both Ántonia and Cleric warn Jim against diversions from the high road of idealism. Both caution him against the soft and beautiful Lena Lingard. Yet both Cleric and Ántonia become victims of the self-destructive personal relationships against which they warn Jim. Cleric never becomes the great poet he might have been because he spills out his power in brilliant conversation, talking his gifts away (169). Ántonia is left pregnant and abandoned by her lover.

Ántonia recovers herself after the birth of her baby through her marriage to a young Bohemian, Cuzak, and then raises a large family. But the lesson of her experience has not been lost on Jim, who follows the familiar Catherian path of avoiding the potentially destructive passionate sexual relationship. (See Gelfant on this issue.) Jim eventually marries, but the relationship becomes a loveless one, and there are no children. Still he is free to pursue his own interests. Jim professes his admiration for the exuberant and warmhearted farm girls like Ántonia and Lena, but in retrospect it appears that he fears sex. It is the nonthreatening asexual union with Ántonia that meets the requirements of the Catherian hero. Thus, Jim follows the pattern of a number of Cather's main characters in finding that their marriage means much less to them than their career.

Jim expresses precisely Ántonia's proper role in his life when he tells her, "I'd have liked to have you for a sweetheart, or a wife, or my mother or my sister—anything that a woman can be to a man" (208). Here it is clear that Ántonia as Jim's lover would have been less than satisfactory. She must be his muse instead. Had they married (as some students will wish), the results might have been disastrous. One can imagine the relationship repeating the mismatch of Ántonia's parents: the earthy mother, grasping for a better life for her children, and the introspective, artistic father, driven to despair by the collapse of his dreams. No, Ántonia's most crucial relationship to Jim is that she "lent herself" to his artistic requirements. At the end of the novel, when Jim meets Ántonia after a number of years, she is a "battered" woman, a mother of many, a "rich mine of life" (228–29), selflessly serving her husband and her many children, her farm, its animals, its encircling orchard, the activities of planting, cultivating, and harvesting, just as she has served Jim's artistic hunger for representative human attitudes.

Jim has distanced himself from the batterings of close human relationships. That is both the price and reward of his artistic creation. His failures on Ántonia's familial and personal level free him from the self-effacement that results from submersion into the human swarm. Ántonia achieves immortality because she nurtures life, and Jim because he creates a work of art. She has her children and he his book. To judge Jim as a failure because he is landless, childless, and unhappily married is to ignore Cather's compelling loyalties to the achievements of art. (Students may feel that this view undervalues Ántonia's achievements. The teacher may expect very lively discussions on this crucial matter. Susan J. Rosowski, in "Willa Cather's Women" [263–68], best makes the case for Ántonia's defying and triumphing over Jim's myths of male transcendence to become her own person.)

Jim has had a true marriage in his life: the chaste and vicarious one that has finally linked him to his idealized Ántonia, to his treasured past, and thus to his own deepest sense of himself. The novel closes with a graceful interweaving of these connections, as Jim remembers his first night in Nebraska as a boy (240). Ironically, the "incommunicable" past has, in the power of Jim's narrative, been communicated. And in this communication, Jim has fashioned a response to the "obliterating" cancellation of personality that had overcome him as a young boy crossing the prairies for the first time.

Although Jim looks back to the past in the book's final passage, we remember that he also has a present and a future. On the personal level, he has his newfound relationship with the Cuzaks to look forward to. He anticipates hunting trips with the boys. He wants to know Cuzak better. His mind is filled with "pleasant things" (239) as the novel closes. The completion of his manuscript marks his birth as an artist. His work with his railroad is important and satisfying, helping to nurture the growth of his home country. It enables him to carry on the positive values of pioneering that he has recorded in the life of Ántonia.

Thus Jim is an active, functioning new American, a figure that we may overlook in Cather if we consider her vision to be only retrospective. As one who finds a point of balance between the conflicting pulls of West and East, past and present, individualism and social obligation, Jim Burden is one of Cather's most significant moderns.

The Doctrine of the Open Road in *My Ántonia*

Paul Comeau

One challenge for me in teaching *My Ántonia* is to define for the students the greatness of this apparently simple regional novel. My response is to meet the challenge head on, as it were, to teach the book in terms of the intrinsic qualities that make it what James E. Miller, Jr., has called an enduring commentary "on the American experience, the American dream, and the American reality" ("American Dream" 112); in short, the qualities that make it an American classic. I take as my starting point D. H. Lawrence's study of the early classics of American literature, in which he analyzes works by Hawthorne, Melville, and Whitman, among others, to discern the soul or essence of America. Whitman, he concludes, best exemplifies the "American heroic message" in his doctrine of the open road, the road of destiny down which every soul must travel alone, "accomplishing nothing save the journey, and the works incident to the journey . . . the soul in her subtle sympathies accomplishing herself by the way" (173). In addition, Lawrence identifies three principal thematic and stylistic features as fundamentally American: the escapist impulse, the questing hero, and the symbolistic style of writing. These elements provide the students with a helpful focus for their reading.

I begin teaching *My Ántonia* with a detailed reading of the introduction, which profiles Jim Burden's character in relation to the woman of the book's title. He is a man of "romantic disposition," and Ántonia has come to symbolize to him "the country, the conditions, the whole adventure of . . . childhood." Jim is further depicted as a perpetual traveler, endlessly crisscrossing the country by train in his capacity as legal counsel for a great railway. The journey motif informs the narrative throughout, enhancing the sense that Jim's life is a pilgrimage in which Ántonia is the central force. Here, then, is the first indication that Whitman's doctrine of the open road applies to Cather's novel, with additional evidence immediately forthcoming as book 1, "The Shimerdas," opens in the midst of Jim's "interminable journey" west.

The primacy of the journey is underscored by the imagery describing it, which is less that of dislocation than of symbolic birth into "a new world" (3) following a nine-year gestation period. In his metaphoric infancy, Jim does not recall his "arrival" but first awakens to the ministrations of a mother figure who promptly bathes and feeds him. All notion of the past recedes into the background, like some embryonic dream: "We did not talk about the farm in Virginia, which had been [grandmother's] home for so many years" (11). Indeed, Jim's identity is so undeveloped that when confronted with the vast sky and prairie he feels "erased, blotted out" (8), and readily succumbs to the somewhat prenatal urge "to be dissolved into something complete and great" (18). The effect of his nascent personality is a muted perception of destiny, an inability to distinguish the open road: "If there was a road, I could not make it out in the faint starlight" (7). The inescapable sway of destiny, however, is prefigured in grandfather's sympathetic reading of the Psalms: "He shall choose our inheritance for us, the excellency of Jacob whom He loved" (13).

Initially, Jim identifies closely with the people around him, particularly with Ántonia and her family. His impressionable imagination translates their adversity into a romantic adventure, as David Stouck suggests (*Willa Cather's* 49–50), and as his relationship with Ántonia grows, he develops a child's imitative empathy for her plight, even to the point of calling Virginia his "old country" (81). Yet his sympathy remains emotionally and intellectually naive, because he cannot comprehend the misery of dislocation and deprivation underlying the Bohemians' bitterness. It is in the unromantic context of human suffering, however, that the reader understands Pavel's torment and Mr. Shimerda's suicide, and in this context that we apprehend the truth of Ántonia's closing words to Jim in book 1: "If I live here, like you, that is different. Things will be easy for you. But they will be hard for us" (140).

The reality Ántonia alludes to is the immigrant experience, the twofold struggle of human beings against a new land and against one another. Both concepts are central to the American consciousness in Lawrence's estimation, since immigration is as much escapist as it is reformative: "That's why most people have come to America, and still do come. To get away from everything they are and have been" (3). Mr. Shimerda and his Russian friends illustrate Lawrence's thesis. Pavel and Peter flee from their home in the Ukraine to elude their reputation as murderers, and Mr. Shimerda forsakes good wages and dear friends in Bohemia to placate his nagging wife. In their haste and ignorance, they unwittingly enslave themselves to creditors and to the land itself. They see their dreams of freedom and prosperity die with the first snow but lack the fortitude to persevere, because they have left their hearts and their identities behind. They are nameless exiles in a land which is "not a country at all, but the material out of which countries are made" (7). That this same experience produces the classic American hero is betokened in Mr. Shimerda's Christmas blessing, which in Dorothy McFarland's words marks Jim "in some way as a spiritual heir" (43): "I felt as if he were looking far ahead into the future for me, down the road I would have to travel" (87). The introduction suggests that his journey has led Jim to a more profound understanding of the immigrant experience and, by extension, of the American psyche. As Miller correctly observes, in re-creating "the story of his and, in part, the country's past, he envisions it through the disillusion of his—and, in part, his country's—unhappy present" ("American Dream" 116).

For the present, though, Jim's road ends at the town of Black Hawk, where his grandparents move at the beginning of book 2. The move signals his transition from childhood to adolescence, and indeed he first sees the town as a "new world" fraught with opportunities to develop his latent social skills. At school he learns to play children's games, while at the Harlings' he experiences the joys of family life with children his own age. His devotion to the Harlings is temporarily secured when Ántonia arrives as their hired girl, but her influence soon redirects his attention to the primacy of the immigrant legacy, causing him to question his new-fledged allegiances.

The hired girls' various positions in town—Ántonia keeps house for the Harlings, Lena Lingard sews for Mrs. Thomas the dressmaker, and Tiny Soderball waits on tables for Mrs. Gardener at the Boys' Home Hotel— imply an extension of the bondage that impelled Mr. Shimerda to suicide. Their triumph is that they transcend servitude in their zest for life, but the price of their exuberance is the town's hatred and, in Ántonia's case, Mrs. Harling's indignation. The decline of Ántonia's fortunes centers around the Vannis's dance tent, which touches a primitive chord and precipitates in her a nightly flurry of feverish dancing and impetuous behavior. Though similarly caught up in the festive climate the tent promotes, Jim responds more moderately, relying on it primarily to relieve the tedium and general tyranny of small town morality. Consequently, he is only mildly rebuked for his recklessness, while Ántonia is dismissed for hers.

Jim's immediate reaction is "to get away as soon as possible" (227), whereupon he resolves to escape to the university in the fall. He interrupts his preparatory studying just once during the summer to go on a picnic with the hired girls. Meditatively silent throughout much of the afternoon, he listens to them reminisce about the hardships of moving to a new country. The somber tone of these recollections notwithstanding, the prevailing mood of the picnic is not melancholy, for the sense of exile and alienation is mitigated by the effects of heredity and regeneration invested in the girls themselves. They believe, for example, that Selma Kronn became a teacher because "she was born smart" and that Lena is wild because her grandfather "married a Lapp" (242).

The resulting tension between the despair of alienation and the hope of renewal is the creative tension at the heart of the American spirit, as Jim intuits when he compares the vibrant hired girls with their anemic Black Hawk counterparts. On a developmental level, this tension informs Jim's personality by virtue of his close identification with the immigrant experience. On a broader symbolic level, it defines the paradox of human achievement, which is further exemplified in the heroic image of the plow magnified in the setting sun. Projected against the fiery backdrop, the plow evinces the promise of regeneration, but as the light diminishes the picture fades, leaving merely a haunting awareness of insignificance and mutability (245).

Another kind of tension comes to the fore in the next two books, which seemingly depict opposite sides of the inner conflict facing Jim as he continues his journey into the competitive adult world. Book 3, "Lena Lingard," ostensibly highlights his romantic attraction to Lena and the world of art, whereas book 4, "The Pioneer Woman's Story," assesses his abiding loyalty to Ántonia in relation to his quest for social and economic success. The disparity inheres in the girls' characters and emerges in their respective dance styles. Lena's romantic, languid approach contrasts with Ántonia's lively, inventive one; and although Lena's poverty-stricken childhood leads her to reject for herself a future of marriage, children, and farming, a parallel history prompts Ántonia to seek fulfillment in the very things Lena renounces. Nevertheless, Jim's apparent dilemma is resolved in the context of the novel as a whole, wherein books 3 and 4 signify progressive stages in his psychological and emotional development that better equip him for his fated odyssey. He must first come under Lena's influence before he can fully comprehend what Ántonia means to him as a person and as an idea.

At the university Jim encounters a "world of ideas" (259) in which life is perceived abstractly through art. In Vergil's *Aeneid* and *Georgics* he discovers antique worlds where heroic virtues thrive. When Lena arrives unexpectedly to visit him, the chivalric principles of amour propre and noblesse oblige come alive in the present, inspired by her engaging personality. He concludes that Mr. Ordinsky's exaggerated courtly behavior toward her is comparable to Ole Benson's clumsy devotion, which in turn supports his hypothesis that poetry could not exist without girls like Lena. It is in the light of poetic inspiration, then, that Lena's influence on Jim must finally be understood, as Paul Olson argues ("Epic" 281). She recalls to him the people and places of his "own infinitesimal past" (262), making him aware that, like those of the authors he admires, his life can be expressed only in terms of "his own naked land and the figures scattered upon it" (262). America is his land, and Ántonia the central figure in his past with whom he must ultimately be reconciled.

The possibility of reconciliation seems remote at the outset of book 4, with Jim condemning Ántonia for being compromised by Larry Donovan and becoming an object of pity. Conversely, he is impressed by the success of Lena Lingard, who has become a reputable seamstress, and by the prosperity of Tiny Soderball, who was deeded a mine claim in the Klondike, invested her money wisely, and returned a wealthy woman to San Francisco, where she has convinced Lena to open a dressmaking shop. Yet even Jim can see that the relation between Tiny and Lena—"Tiny audits Lena's accounts occasionally . . . and Lena, apparently, takes care that Tiny doesn't grow too miserly" (328)—though functional, is not enlivening. They more or less limp through life together, devoid of the inner spark that once inspired him to poetry. His reunion with Ántonia is pure poetry by comparison.

The Widow Steavens's sensitive account of Ántonia's betrayal touches Jim's heart and encourages him to visit her again. Their meeting is one of those quiet moments in Cather's writing that testify to her ability to create lasting images in the mind: "We met like people in the old song, in silence, if not in tears. Her warm hand clasped mine" (319). The warmth of her touch dissolves any thoughts in his mind of Lena or Tiny. In Ántonia, as in the vast prairie on which they stand, the changes wrought by time seem "beautiful and harmonious . . . like watching the growth of a great man or of a great idea" (306). Jim is in fact witnessing both simultaneously, since his renewed perception of his old friend fuses the idea of the woman with that of the land she represents, a land cultivated and enriched by the heroic pioneers who sought it out, claimed it, loved it. Moreover, his wish to be a boy again and to have his road end here on the plains with Ántonia is a spontaneous tribute to both, but one he quickly acknowledges to be unrealistic and vain. He therefore continues his journey alone, promising to come back when time permits.

When after twenty years Jim does return, he finds Ántonia to have aged physically, but thus divested of youthful beauty she is more immanently Ántonia, "a rich mine of life, like the founders of early races" (353). Her recent history substantially parallels that of the immigrant founders of America (342). Jim notices at once, however, that she has not lost the fire of life, so that the "idea" of Ántonia he has carried with him over the years is vindicated in the present. He sees, too, that her husband Cuzak has been "the instrument of Ántonia's special mission" (367) in an immediate and practical way that Jim could never be, despite his earlier wish to have her for "a sweetheart, or a wife, or my mother or sister—anything that a woman can be to a man" (321).

The doctrine of the open road, in its purest form, precludes such exclusive personal attachments in favor of a more catholic approach to human relations based on spiritual empathy. Lawrence describes as "true democracy" this condition of "sympathy" to which the pilgrim soul naturally aspires (177). In the spirit of true democracy and in fulfillment of his destiny, Jim must leave Ántonia's farm to proceed with his travels, but he remains faithful to his ideal, to Ántonia, in his empathy with Cuzak and the boys. He is also fortified in his pilgrimage by a clearer perception of the circularity of human experience, which for all time has linked him spiritually with Ántonia, as with the country she embodies. The narrative itself is a celebration of this special union, a glad recognition of a greater soul and a communion of worship. Thus the essence that Lawrence detected in the early classics is writ large in *My Ántonia*, according to the criteria he outlined.

Teaching the novel from this perspective is rewarding for students, because it reminds them to look for substance behind critical labels like "American classic." More particularly, it enriches their understanding of the text on several levels. First, it highlights Jim Burden's archetypal quest for value, establishing him as a representative American literary hero. Second, it illuminates Willa Cather's symbolistic style of writing and her unique interpretation of the immigrant legacy, both of which place the novel in the forefront of American literary tradition, following not only in the legacy of Whitman but also in that of Sarah Orne Jewett and other women writers. And third, it reveals the book's heroic message by identifying the true democratic principle underlying American idealism—the glad recognition of great and greater souls in the open road. Indeed, this message pervades much of Cather's subsequent work, receiving its most direct expression in "Old Mrs. Harris," in the quotation Mrs. Rosen ascribes to Michelet: "Le but n'est rien; le chemin, c'est tout" (158). The primacy of this message is what ultimately qualifies *My Ántonia* as an American classic, transcending the compass of a personal or even a regional study to personify the consciousness of a nation.

Kindling the Imagination:
The Inset Stories of *My Ántonia*

Michael Peterman

As a teacher of literature working mostly with undergraduates I am regularly reminded of the emotional power—what I have elsewhere called the "charm"—of Willa Cather's *My Ántonia*. It matters little whether the course concerns American writing, western fiction, or the novel as genre. It matters little whether the students are freshmen or seniors. Most students are drawn to the novel. They are, however, often frustrated in their attempts to articulate the nature of its power.

In suggesting that my students read Cather's essay "The Novel Démeublé" along with *My Ántonia*, I provide a kind of aesthetic agenda for what is at first a free-ranging discussion. I begin simply by asking students to share their responses to the novel ("What kind of book is this?" "If it 'works,' how does it work?"), thereby testing my own ability to remain silent while the group establishes its particular mood. Only as opportunity allows do I begin to direct attention to Cather's idea of "the emotional penumbra," the importance of what "is felt upon the page without being specifically named there," of what is "created" (*On Writing* 40–41). Where better to turn for specific application than those adventures or "vignettes" or "inset stories" that figure largely in the novel's first two sections? Usually some students have already remarked on these vignettes, a clear sign that these episodes have something to do with the bond Cather establishes with her readers. In particular, the story of Peter and Pavel galvanizes student attention. "What does it mean?" they ask. "Why is it there?" "How does it relate to the novel as a whole?" So haunting and powerful is the wolf story that, as Susan Rosowski has recently observed, "it is often the single episode people remember years after first reading *My Ántonia*" (*Voyage Perilous* 80).

I find it useful at this point to introduce into the discussion David Daiches's view that the "structural pattern" of the novel is flawed. Convinced that *My Ántonia*'s central theme is "the development and self-discovery of the heroine," Daiches argues that, while episodes early in the narrative are "full of life," they bear "little if any relation to the story of Ántonia's development." The "remarkable little inset story" of the Russians, he notes, has a "somewhat uncertain [relation]" to the novel as a whole (37–47).

How "random" are these vignettes? (Gelfant 99). One should, of course, acknowledge Cather's own wryly self-conscious remark, "If you gave me a thousand dollars for every structural flaw in *My Ántonia* you'd make me very rich" (Bennett, *World* 212). At the same time one can direct students to the careful and challenging interpretations of recent critics like David Stouck and Blanche Gelfant, both of whom see imaginative patterns at work in the vignettes.[1] Focusing particularly on Cather's use of certain of these episodes or inset stories in the novel's first two sections, this essay sees such experiences as implicit steps, or building blocks, in the shaping not only of the individual imaginations of Jim and Ántonia but also of the special relationship between them on which later, often disturbing events crucially depend.

In directing specific attention to these inset stories, I begin by calling attention to the description of the cedar tree that Jake brings home for Jim's first Nebraska Christmas. Decorated in the unexpected splendors from Otto's cowboy trunk, "Our tree," as Jim recalls, "became the talking tree of the fairy tale; legends and stories nestled like birds in its branches" (83). The image is, I suggest, a clue to what Cather aims to make of the early stages of her narrative—the book is to be the talking tree of the shared immigrant experience of Ántonia and Jim. It is explicitly a story about the "freemasonry" of youth, designed to encompass vividly and suggestively "the country, the conditions, the whole *adventure* of *our* childhood" (emphases added). "Freemasonry," the crucial word in the introduction, establishes the emphasis on instinctive sympathies and fellowship, on those shared adventures, be they experiences undergone or stories heard, that draw Ántonia and Jim ever closer together emotionally and imaginatively.

For both Jim and Ántonia, Nebraska offers so violent a change from past experience that, though they are ten and fourteen respectively when they arrive, their adventures come to them freshly, with the force of first things. Nebraska is their Robinson Crusoe's island, their Swiss family Robinson's jungle. While Ántonia's disjunction is cultural and linguistic, Jim's is severe enough that, faced by a landscape very different from Virginia, he feels that "I had left even [the] spirits [of my dead parents] behind me" (8). As new friends in "a new world," they share experiences and adventures with an openness, freshness, and passion that is at once believable and deeply affecting. By age as well as by the Old World distinction represented by her father, Ántonia has an advantage that sufficiently distances her from Jim in sexual matters, rendering her more like an older, watchful, and sensitive sister. Moreover, she is his entrée into the realities of immigrant experience. By circumstance, Jim is initially her teacher of English and her guide to the confusing labyrinth of American ways. Each has much to offer the other. As their lives unfold and develop, this continues to be true. The beauty the novel celebrates is the relationship they create and, against the march of time, sustain.

From the cedar tree, I find it useful to move to Bruno Bettelheim. In *The Uses of Enchantment*, Bettelheim argues that the sustaining sense of "meaning in our lives," what constitutes "a secure understanding of what the meaning of one's life may or ought to be," is the product of a long development: psychological maturity, like wisdom, "is built up, small step by small step, from most irrational beginnings" (3). Though in *My Ántonia*

Cather is not precisely concerned with either children or fairy tales—the absence of the healthful experience of unsugared fairy tales in the experience of most modern children is Bettelheim's major concern—she brings to her presentation of Jim and Ántonia's Nebraska experience a sensitivity to the process of psychological development that Bettelheim is helpful in explicating. Fairy tales and mythical stories have throughout human history constituted much of a child's intellectual life. Avoiding overt didacticism, such stories "relate to all aspects of the child's personality," presenting human problems in so simplified and typical a manner that they give full credence to the seriousness of children's predicaments and allow them the opportunity to begin to understand themselves, to create a sense of order sufficient to sustain them in life. The implicit message of fairy tales is one that the child discovers independently:

> that a struggle against severe difficulties in life is unavoidable, is an intrinsic part of human existence—but that if one does not shy away, but steadfastly meets unexpected and often unjust hardships, one masters all obstacles and at the end emerges victorious.   (8)

In her depiction of the episodes that define the relationship between Ántonia and Jim, Cather anticipates Bettelheim while avoiding his solemnity. She recognizes that certain stories or experiences can facilitate the growth of personal identity, especially if they are assimilated as experience. As Bettelheim notes,

> Explaining to a child why a fairy tale is so captivating to him destroys . . . the story's enchantment, which depends to a considerable degree on the child's not quite knowing why he is delighted by it. And with the forfeiture of this power to enchant goes also a loss of the story's potential for helping the child struggle on his own, and master all by himself the problem which has made the story meaningful to him in the first place.   (18)

The Peter-Pavel episode provides a striking case in point. Cather implicitly establishes its importance by giving it early prominence in the narrative. Also implicitly, she suggests that such a story, while not formally a fairy tale, has a tremendous emotional and imaginative power for both Jim and Ántonia.[2] The immediacy of suffering and death and the horrific details deeply fascinate them. Later in the novel Cather is careful to remind us of this capacity in young people to entertain the gruesome when Ántonia's children greet a retelling of the Cutter murder-suicide with cheers of "Hurrah! The murder!" (361). More significant still, the Peter-Pavel story has a special place in the "freemasonry" of Ántonia and Jim's relationship. As Jim recounts, "we talked of nothing else for days afterward" except "our Pavel and Peter" (56). Later he adds,

> For Ántonia and me, the story of the wedding party was never at an end. We did not tell Pavel's secret to anyone, but guarded it jealously—as if the wolves of the Ukraine had gathered that night long ago, and the wedding party been sacrificed, to give us a painful and peculiar pleasure. (61).

It is a measure of Cather's fine judgment, her artistic tact, that she nowhere tries to interpret what, if anything, Pavel's story might mean. We know that Pavel is delirious when he tells it to Mr. Shimerda. Realistically, we might well question the story's assertions in that it would be a rare pack of wolves that would run down seven sledges one by one. But as preposterous as the events appear to be, the story is the more powerful—and must have seemed so to Cather—because of its "awful" elements and because of the conditions in which it is heard. The death-bed raging and confession, the despair of dying so far from home, the sense of innocence betrayed, the ferocious urge · to survive, the awe of entering into dark and forbidden secrets all contribute to the effect on the young people.

Because critics generally rise to the challenge of explanation, they have found it difficult to accept Cather's tact and restraint at face value. Blanche Gelfant, for instance, gives this episode special prominence in her interpretation, arguing that Pavel's action in throwing the bride to the wolves constitutes a "grisly acting out of male aversion" (108; see also Kroetsch, "Fear"). But how supportable is such a reading? While Pavel intended to throw out the bride, he did not hesitate to push both bride and groom off the sledge when the latter naturally resisted. If anything, the story seems to allegorize Pavel's profound sense of exile and alienation, dying so far from the homeland and church in which and against which he defined his personal existence. By earlier noting his "wild-looking" appearance, "rebellious manner," and reputation as "an anarchist" (33–34), Cather seems to suggest a personal history of uneasy radical behavior that haunts Pavel in the empty and foreign spaces of Nebraska. Certainly, the sparse imagery of bride and groom (Church and Christ) and of distant monastery bells is more suggestive of a religious and ascetic than of a sexual emphasis.[3]

At the same time, to the impressionable Jim, Peter and Pavel seem to be dogged by a relentless destiny. "Misfortune," he notes, "seemed to settle like an evil bird on the roof of the log house, and to flap its wings there, warning human beings away" (51). Theirs is above all a story of immigrant defeat. It is especially telling on Ántonia's father, whose misfortune it is to bear the full weight of middle-aged exile and whose gruesome suicide is anticipated by the Russians' conspicuous failure.

For Ántonia and Jim, by contrast, the story becomes something quite different. It is a part of their mutual treasure hoard. Without this shared and haunting episode we would have far less sense of why Jim feels so strong a kinship with Ántonia. Few of their experiences would seem to have united them more. And, if we accept Bettelheim's notion that young people learn in their own ways through undidactic tales, we might well argue that the lesson implicit in the tale is to avoid jettisoning the bride and groom, to avoid, in short, betrayal of one's closest friends. Jim's concluding remarks about the vignette subtly suggest the way in which the story has taken a special hold on his particular landscape: "At night, before I went to sleep, I often found myself in a sledge drawn by three horses, dashing through a country that looked something like Nebraska and something like Virginia" (61).

Another vignette of similar gruesomeness is Ántonia's account of the tramp's suicide in the threshing machine. It belongs in the narrative to Ántonia's days in Black Hawk with the Harlings and gives a special warm flavor to Cather's presentation of life in that home. Through its telling Ántonia emerges still more clearly in her role as powerful storyteller, as agent of the oral tradition Cather carefully integrates into the freemasonry of an early Nebraska upbringing. We remember that it was Ántonia who translated and told Pavel's story to Jim, who recounts Jim's killing of the rattlesnake (another episode worth attention) "with a great deal of colour" (49), and who, through her "stories and entertainment" (351), later inspires a similar kind of excitement in her children. She tells her stories engagingly and innocently, as if somehow, however great their intrinsic fascination, they cannot be explained. (The same qualities are apparent in Rudolph's telling of the Cutter murder [361–63].) For Jim, "Everything she said seemed to come right out of her heart" (176).

In looking closely at the details of the tramp story, one is again struck by Cather's care in her placement of the episode as well as by the restraint of her presentation. Pavel's story is told in late autumn with winter approaching, anticipatory of Mr. Shimerda's suicide. Though its event occurs in the heat of harvest, the tramp story is a winter's tale that anticipates the different kind of madness to be found in Wick Cutter.

The tramp comes upon the threshing at Ole Iverson's. Seeing him first, Ántonia senses from his eyes, which were "awful red and wild, like he had some sickness," and his sardonic remarks, that he is "crazy." Ignoring her warnings, Ole allows the tramp up on the thresher, whereupon, after cutting a few bands, "he waved his hand to me and jumped head-first right into the threshing machine after the wheat" (178). What fascinates about the story is at once its power to shock, its economic use of detail, and its innocent mode of telling. Ántonia recounts her adventure directly to Mrs. Harling, effectively dramatizing the "basic harmony" between hired girl and mistress, and the special place Ántonia has won in her home. The few details—the tramp's expression of disgust with immigrants in "Americy," his wave, the fact that the machine never worked right thereafter, and the contents of his pockets—provide apparent clues to his action but allow for no coherent explanation. Why, we wonder, did his possessions include only an old pen-knife, a wishbone, and a worn copy of "The Old Oaken Bucket"? Gelfant adapts this story to her argument by stating that in the tramp's pockets, "the threshers find only 'an old penknife' and the 'wish-bone of a chicken' " (110). What happens, we wonder, to the poem that is, in the story's aftermath, the one detail that transfixes the listeners?

The power of the tramp story lies as much in its gruesomeness, which causes Nina Harling to cry, as in its mysteriousness. Innocently Ántonia herself voices the question, "Now, wasn't that strange . . . ? What would anybody want to kill themselves in summer for? In threshing time, too! It's nice everywhere then" (179). There is no available answer. Alcoholism, failure, despair, and alienation suggest themselves, but only partially. Ántonia's response, which implies Jim's as well, is a healthy one. The experience, transmuted into a story, has, if anything, deepened her commitment to life. Much as Bettelheim suggests in *The Uses of Enchantment*, disquieting realities serve to develop or reinforce positive, healthful ideas and beliefs.

The episodes that play a prominent part in the early sections of *My Ántonia* are not mere inset stories or fascinating digressions. They are delicately placed steps or building blocks that image and characterize the rich and enduring relationship between Ántonia and Jim. They provide a sense of that special cohesiveness, so much so that these memories live as freshly for Jim in the present as they originally did. In such episodes, so often related to story telling, Cather captures not only the felt appeal of adventures shared but the instinctive sympathy between Jim and Ántonia that is near the novel's center. And while such episodes give amplitude to the pastoral paradox that David Stouck develops in detail, Cather's control is such, I would argue, that she does not "romanticiz[e] disturbing and unpleasant memories" (*Willa Cather's* 46). Rather, she allows the reader to infer from their presentation the healthful ways in which Ántonia and Jim imaginatively transmute such experiences. The novel offers stages in growth, not instances of evasion.

"Art is a concrete and personal and childish thing after all," Cather wrote in her unfinished essay "Light on Adobe Walls" (*On Writing* 125). Those properties are evident in the narrative steps by which she unobtrusively and evocatively takes us into the feel of events and stories—things done and things heard—that together engender the extraordinary sense of friendship and kinship at the heart of *My Ántonia.*

NOTES

¹ Stouck has convincingly argued that, "with its rural setting and its journey through memory," *My Ántonia* conforms to the pastoral mode. At its heart the novel confirms "the paradox that what is being celebrated can never be experienced again, that its reality is only a memory." To this end Cather strives to create "a sense of timelessness and spacelessness" in the novel's early sections. The result for Stouck, a "romanticizing of time and space," is "part of an imaginative process at work throughout the novel which either eliminates unpleasant memories or converts them into romantic vignettes" (*Willa Cather's* 46, 47, 49). Blanche Gelfant, by contrast, challenges the twin assertions that the novel is unsatisfactorily structured and that it is America's "chief affirmative novel." Putting the emphasis on Cather's "strange involuted" avoidance of sex, she argues that *My Ántonia* is a "brilliantly tortuous" work, its episodes "falling together to form a pattern of sexual aversion into which each detail fits." The novel is for her characterized by a "Romantic mystique of childhood [that] illuminates the fear of sex in Cather's world" (95, 99–100, 113–14).

² Stouck notes that in the early stages of the novel, events with the flavor of the old country "are charged with romantic suggestion of times and places full of wonder to a child, like the magic of fairy tales" (*Willa Cather's* 49). According to Paul Schach, the story is (Cather's) version of a folktale prominent among Great Plains settlers who came from Russia or Germany.

³ I am indebted to Peter Sullivan of the University of Indiana in Pennsylvania for suggestions concerning the Russian church and peasantry.

Teaching the Illustrations to *My Ántonia*

Jean Schwind

At the end of *My Ántonia*, we learn that the "central figure" of Jim Burden's story has been diligently recording her own history for over twenty years. Ántonia has preserved the "characters of [her] girlhood" in a collection of pictures that constitutes a vital "family legend," and when Jim visits the Cuzak farm Ántonia entertains him with her "big boxful of photographs" (349–50). That these tintypes and photographs fill Jim's mind as he falls asleep after viewing them testifies to their imaginative power; however, the simile Jim uses to describe the pictures—they are like the "old woodcuts" of school primers—has an opposite effect. By identifying picture stories with children's stories, Jim trivializes the authority of Ántonia's pictorial memoir in a way that anticipates the critical response to *My Ántonia*. Like the books of his childhood, Jim's text is illustrated. Jim Burden's narrative has been accompanied by a series of eight pen-and-ink drawings by W. T. Benda since the first edition of *My Ántonia* appeared in 1918, and until recently the illustrations have encouraged the naive misreadings of critics who have praised the novel for its childlike simplicity (Gelfant 94–95).

This persistent misconception of *My Ántonia* as a "simple" novel undoubtedly has many roots. The superficial simplicity of Cather's clear prose style and the status of *My Ántonia* as a "woman's novel" have both invited simple readings of the novel, and the Benda illustrations have largely worked to confirm this critical misperception. The illustrations have encouraged the equation—picture books are children's books—implicit in Jim's memory of the woodcuts in his school primers. To consider the illustrations as a critical part of Cather's text that complicates, contradicts, and generally illuminates Jim Burden's narrative—as I do, and as I try to get my students to do when studying the novel in class—is thus difficult because such a consideration not only seems to violate the artistic simplicity of the illustrations themselves (which do indeed have the minimal form of "old woodcuts"; unlike the highly detailed and allusive drawings of more famous illustrators like John Tenniel, Benda's spare sketches neither demand nor seem able to support close critical scrutiny) but also challenges the persistent assumption that *My Ántonia* is "easy reading."

I admit, then, that I have usually found it difficult to provoke students to think about the Benda illustrations as an essential part of *My Ántonia*. I have also found, however, that time spent in studying the illustrations is justified by a substantial payoff: studying the novel's pictures brings into sharp focus the questions about narrative point of view, formal structure, and figurative language that are essential to understanding the novel as a whole. As I have argued at length in an earlier essay, Benda's illustrations provide an important subtext in pictures which subverts the words of Jim's text (Schwind).

In the central narrative fiction presented in the introduction to the novel, an "old friend" of Jim's speaks as the editor of *My Ántonia* and explains how his manuscript came into her possession. By claiming editorial authority over *My Ántonia*, the speaker of the introduction simultaneously suggests that Jim's narrative is inadequate (specifically, she implies that Jim's "romantic" vision of the past is extremely partial and in need of correction) and assumes responsibility for emending Jim's faulty account. This central fiction of *My Ántonia* as a critically edited or supplemented text emphasizes the importance of the novel's pictures. Of the textual supplements that can be attributed to Jim's editor (the short introduction, the single footnote about the pronunciation of "Ántonia," and the pictures added to illustrate Jim's story), the Benda illustrations stand out as the most extensive editorial addition to Jim's manuscript. The illustrations are implicitly presented as the editor's most significant attempt to compensate for the narrative deficiencies hinted at in the introduction to *My Ántonia*. The Benda illustrations are critically important because they function as a visual textual supplement that Jim's editor includes in the published version of Jim's memoir to correct the "romantic" bias of his account.

To understand this pictorial correction it is first necessary to understand the faulty narrative vision the illustrations are designed to emend. Logically, then, discussing the illustrations should be saved for final class sessions on the novel, when students are well acquainted with Jim Burden and have some sense of the strengths and limitations of his story about Ántonia. Getting students to read Jim's text critically enough to see the romantic misperceptions that Benda's more realistic illustrations are intended to offset is hard work, because Jim's narrative skill blinds readers to the serious flaws in his portrait of Ántonia and "all that her name recalls." In particular, the lyrical beauty of Jim's depictions of the western landscape—his description of the "great black figure" of the plow against a golden sunset, for example, or his equally rhapsodic account of a "beautiful electric storm" (245, 139)—is so impressive that it disarms us critically, making us uninclined to weigh Jim's eloquent words. Admiring the poetry of these passages, even the most wary critics (much less susceptible undergraduates) have either ignored or pardoned the descriptive clichés and outmoded conventions that pervade Jim's "picture writing" (245). To stay with the same examples, Jim's description of the "heroic" plow and the lightning storm are both rooted in Old World traditions of classical landscape painting that seriously misrepresent the New World Jim strives to represent. Just as Mediterranean cityscapes incongruously shape Jim's vision of a storm in landlocked rural Nebraska ("the mottled part of the sky was like marble pavement, like the quay of some splendid seacoast city doomed to destruction" [139]), the famous golden glow of Claudian pastorals explains why Jim's "heroic" plow scene and other literary landscapes are illuminated by gentle "horizontal rays" rather than the blazing, high-noon sun characteristic of the western plains (letter to Bishop).

While Jim's narrative is undeniably eloquent, it is often an uninspired, unoriginal, and archaic eloquence that fails to reflect a strange new world that demands new forms of language ("Down to the kitchen" instead of "Out to the kitchen" [9]) and new ways of life (the treeless plains produce a new "degraded" breed of owls that nest underground; the hard life on family farms creates a new breed of women like Ántonia who take pride in working like men). The fundamental problem involved in launching a discussion of the novel's illustrations—how to make students suspicious of Jim's artistry even when he's at his most lyrical and using the richly metaphoric and allusive language that they have learned to regard as the marks of great literature—is a version of the more general pedagogical problem that Robert Scholes describes in *Textual Power*. Distinguishing between reading, interpretation, and criticism as the three related skills of literary study, Scholes notes that teaching students to make the critical "shift from reading to interpretation" is a matter of teaching them to beware of "hitches" that disrupt reading. According to Scholes, acts of interpretation depend on "failures of reading" (e.g., an unfamiliar word, ambiguity of meaning) that cause a "feeling of incompleteness on the reader's part" (22).

A good example from *My Ántonia* of the "hitch" Scholes describes—a snag in the smooth flow of reading that raises important interpretive questions—occurs at the end of Jim's first extended description of the Nebraska landscape. This passage is worth considering in class because its simple, one-word hitch is emblematic of the inadequacies of Jim's narrative and so provides an excellent point of departure for discussing the illustrations as a supplement that corrects Jim's text.

The passage begins as Jim recalls his first journey to Nebraska and the shock of encountering a landscape incommensurable with that of his childhood. Devoid of the familiar landmarks of his Virginia homeland (there are "no fences, no creeks or trees, no hills or fields"; Jim describes the prairie in emphatically negative terms, noting all that it lacks [7]), Nebraska seems like "nothing" to Jim, as "[t]he wagon jolted on, carrying me I knew not whither" (8). " 'Whither'? What's with this 'whither'?" The question posed by one of my students isolates the signal hitch in this key passage where Jim introduces us to his new world. Jim's quaint poetic diction (the archaic "whither" and the inversion "knew not") belies his claim that he has left his old world in "spirit" as well as in fact. In telling contrast to Ántonia, who eagerly learns the new language demanded by her adopted country, Jim clings to old ways of speaking and seeing.

That Jim concludes *My Ántonia* with precisely the same stilted and discordantly old-fashioned words that he begins it (in his final paragraph Jim again recalls the night he and Ántonia first entered Black Hawk as "wondering children, being taken we knew not whither" [371]) emphasizes their importance as a narrative hitch. Implicit in Jim's "knew not whither" are the many outmoded conventions that constrain his life in Black Hawk and his re-creation of that life in *My Ántonia*. The social conventions that govern Jim's relationship with Ántonia (the southern-belle standards of ladylike delicacy that prompt him to object to her fieldwork, for example, and the class distinctions that forbid serious romance between a "young man of position" like Jim and the town's "hired girls") are matched by the artistic conventions that rule his narrative.

"Knew not whither" effectively opens the question of Jim's success in describing a new woman in a new world because the phrase sounds antique even to students unfamiliar with the specific classical conventions that shape Jim's story: Homeric epithets (the "wine-coloured" sea of grass [15]); epic similes (prairie winds recede like "defeated armies, retreating"; a sunset has the "exultation of victory, of triumphant ending, like a hero's death—heroes who died young and gloriously" [53, 40]); and stock pastoral laments for a past golden age ("Whatever we had missed, we possessed together the precious, the incommunicable past" [372]). More accessible to students than the stylistic devices that Jim derives from classical poetry are the conventions he borrows from a contemporary, American, and popular literary genre— the dime-novel western. As Jim travels westward to live with his grandparents, he is absorbed by a *Life of Jesse James*, which he recalls as the "most satisfying book" he's ever read. The stereotyped characters of *My Ántonia* (Otto Fuchs is a cowboy straight "out of the pages of 'Jesse James' "; Jim's sinister villain, wicked Wick Cutter, bears an "evil name throughout the county" [6; 50]) and Jim's romantic, "Badlands" vision of the West as an arena of male freedom are as clearly indebted to "Jesse James" as his language is influenced by Vergil.

Emblematic of the traditional literary forms that rule Jim's writing, "knew not whither" signals Jim's primary failure as a storyteller. Jim never manages to "get a picture" of Ántonia because his narrative art depends on irrelevant conventions. The footloose lone rangers and "wild West" of Jesse James are as psychologically and sociologically remote from Ántonia's settled world as Vergil's Arcadia and Homer's wine-red seas are historically and culturally remote.

As it must now be evident by the length of my "preliminary" comments, most of the work in teaching the illustrations to *My Ántonia* is textual rather than pictorial: considering the illustrations as an important supplement to Jim's story presupposes a basic understanding of why Jim's text is inadequate and in need of supplement. Jim's failure to respond creatively to his new world in either his art or in his life provides an essential framework for studying the novel's illustrations because the artistic innovation that distinguishes Benda's drawings dramatically counterpoints the conventionality of Jim's narrative.

Of the eight illustrations in Benda's series, only one—the woman gathering mushrooms "in some deep Bohemian forest" (illus. 3)—is set in Ántonia's European homeland. The mushroom gatherer serves as a good starting point in discussing the illustrations because it highlights the way Benda's art—unlike Jim's literary art in *My Ántonia*—revises Old World traditions in response to the New World of the American West. Benda's "Mushroom Gatherer" depicts the Bohemian world that Mrs. Shimerda describes when she gives a bag of dried mushrooms to Jim's grandmother: the mushrooms are from a land where good "things for eat" can be collected like manna (78). The bowed branches of the tree in Benda's picture follow the same curve as the stooped form of the woman beneath them, a harmony of line that suggests the essential harmony between human life and nature in the mushroom gatherer's world. In Benda's Bohemian landscape, nature is maternally providential, supplying both food (the mushrooms) and shelter (the protective shade of the tree) gratis.

Since the remaining seven pictures of Benda's series are all New World scenes that variously revise and repudiate the conventions of his single European landscape, asking students to compare "The Mushroom Gatherer" to his Nebraska scenes invites them to make connections between the illustrations and to "read" them as a series of related pictures that tell a dramatic story. Among the iconographic details that relate Benda's mushroom gatherer to his prairie pictures, two are particularly notable: the radical difference between Benda's Bohemian peasant woman and the dominant female figures of his American scenes (Mrs. Shimerda in the group portrait of the Shimerda family [illus. 1]; Ántonia plowing [illus. 5] and driving cattle [illus. 8]; Lena knitting while watching her father's herd [illus. 7]) and the corresponding difference in the landscapes surrounding these central female figures.

In pointed contrast to the humble stoop of the peasant woman, Benda's immigrant farm women are powerfully upright and commanding in posture. Hugging a tin box against her breast "as if it were a baby," Mrs. Shimerda is appropriately the central figure in the group portrait of the Shimerdas because she is the family's moving force. As an emblem of Mrs. Shimerda's fiercely ambitious maternal love (she hopes for "much money [and] much land" for her sons and "much husband" for her daughters [90]), the tin-box "baby" underscores the difference between worldly Mamenka Shimerda and the heavenly mother of traditional madonna-and-child paintings. The strong resemblance between Ántonia and her mother in the group portrait (the only figures presented full-face rather than in profile, Ántonia and her mother wear identical scarves and are identically posed with their left arms across their chests) anticipates Benda's final portrait of Ántonia. Growing up her mother's daughter, Ántonia completes Mrs. Shimerda's revision of the Old World madonna. If Mrs. Shimerda's material ambitions distinguish her from both the otherworldly madonnas of conventional holy-family portraits and the submissively bowed mushroom gatherer, Ántonia's final portrait constitutes an even more radical departure from these traditional female types. Dressed in "a man's long overcoat and boots and a man's felt hat with a wide brim," her steps heavy with the weight of her advanced and illegitimate pregnancy, Ántonia has an integrity that transcends the conventions of family portraiture. Uniting father, mother, and child in a single commanding figure, Benda's final portrait of Ántonia proudly challenges the inherited rules of order and decorum that tyrannize Jim Burden.

The difference between Benda's final portrait of Ántonia driving cattle homeward in a December blizzard and his Bohemian woman is informed by the different landscapes these women inhabit. While the sheltering tree in the foreground of "The Mushroom Gatherer" evokes a protective and naturally hospitable landscape, the stark background of Ántonia's portrait emphasizes natural opposition to human life. In contrast to the harmoniously bowed forms of the woman and the branch above her, human and natural forms are sharply discordant in Ántonia's portrait. Ántonia's figure is clearly opposed to the prairie landscape both in color (the heavy blackness of her hat, coat, and boots sets her apart from the surrounding whiteness of the snow) and in linear orientation (her strong vertical stance opposes the flat horizontal expanse of the prairie). The utter featurelessness of the landscape in this final illustration, where the snowstorm obliterates even the bare distinction between earth and sky that defines the landscape in Benda's prairie portrait of Lena (illus. 7), not only contrasts with the strongly featured figure of Ántonia, but finally explains her strength. This land filled with "nothing"—a land where all "things for eat" must be wrested from the soil by brute force (illus. 6: two immense horses strain to pull Ántonia's plow through tough prairie sod) and where arboreal shelters are the products of human art rather than natural munificence (illus. 5: the young pine Jake carries home for a Christmas tree is the first fruit of the Burdens' efforts to "civilize" treeless Nebraska)—shapes Ántonia into the antithesis of the humble mushroom gatherer. Our final image of Ántonia is the image of a woman of unbowed strength, authority, and power.

While numerous other aspects of Benda's illustrations are worth examining (I would hope, for instance, that students would comment on the sexiness of the full-length portrait of Lena Lingard; realistic where Jim Burden is most romantic—in his vision of women—Benda shows Lena fairly bursting from her scanty dress; a carefully delineated nipple pressing against her bodice is the portrait's most salient detail), my comments here are intended to be suggestive rather than exhaustive. How students read Benda's illustrations is finally less important than making sure they don't overlook them, and perhaps there's no better evidence that we need to read Benda's pictures as carefully as we read Cather's words than the unillustrated edition of *My Ántonia*. An inexpensive edition of the novel published in 1930 without the Benda illustrations infuriated Cather, and in an angry letter to her editor at Houghton Mifflin she repudiated the 1930 text as an incomplete and unauthorized version of *My Ántonia* (letter to Greenslet). Cather's comments on the unillustrated *Ántonia* are definitively instructive: she clearly regarded the illustrations as an indispensable part of her novel, and we should do likewise.

The Functional Beauty of Style in *My Ántonia*

Stephen Tatum

Jim Burden has the duty in book 1 of teaching Ántonia to speak and read English. Although Jim regards Ántonia as a "good" student—curious, energetic, uncomplaining, motivated—his narrative is virtually silent about their lessons together, preferring instead to dwell on the incidents and the stories that interrupt or occur after the lessons are over. As a result, while Jim's task in teaching a person named Ántonia stands as a figure for our burden in teaching a novel entitled *My Ántonia*, we understand instead that it is Ántonia who teaches Jim through her presence and storytelling abilities, who comes closest to realizing what the novel sets forth as the ideal of teaching, namely, as Jim says later of his classics teacher's talent, to "quicken consciousness" by "bring[ing] the drama of antique life before one out of the shadows" (261–62).

How does one best quicken students' consciousnesses or bring the drama of pioneer life before them out of the shadows, particularly, as is often the case, if students lack Ántonia's necessity to learn or Jim's special feeling for the prairie landscape? While the essays in this volume obviously are collected to address this question, my approach tends to turn Jim's ideal back upon the students. That is, I ask students if there is anything about *My Ántonia* that quickens their consciousnesses in the way Jim is affected by his classics teacher. In this regard students—like seasoned Cather readers—typically remark that the novel contains several moments during which Cather's prose unleashes a lyrical power, one that sustains its impact long past the duration of their reading experience. Here students often refer for an example of this heightened intensity to the scene near the end of book 2 when Jim and "the hired girls" see the black plow imaged darkly against the setting sun.

When students note such significant junctures in the narrative they are getting onto Cather's heightened interest in presenting the language out of which novels are made, an interest paralleled by Jim's attraction to the Nebraska landscape "out of which countries are made" (7). During such exemplary moments Cather's verbal artistry charges words with resonant significance, infuses sentence sequences with larger meanings, and transforms mere seeing—to use one of the novel's major images—into visionary insight. As a result, when teaching *My Ántonia* I find it absolutely essential to discuss just how this happens and how deceptively simple and yet how beautifully functional this style is at such moments. Thus we settle to discuss a scene or passage and our burden becomes figuring out how it works and how it connects with the larger elements of the novel.

To accomplish this goal, I focus close readings on several features characteristic of what we can call Cather's "rhetoric of transformation": the accent on counterpointing image patterns, the management of rhythm and verb forms, the repetitions of sounds and sentence patterns, and the strategic use of ellipsis (the paring away of adjectives, adverbs, and conjunctions). While these features can be seen at work in several different passages, I most often proceed by discussing their interaction in a single pivotal passage. In any event, prior to our classroom discussion we select a passage for analysis, one that has remained vividly present after the reading experience is over. The class is then divided into smaller groups assigned to cover a particular stylistic feature and to speculate (a) on the relation between style and the passage's content and (b) on its role in illuminating the novel's larger issues, in particular its thematic concern with temporality and its characterization of Jim Burden's romanticism. Finally, I also ask the students to note as they read how a passage progresses in time and space and to look especially at those moments in the passage when an established pattern changes or something unexpected arises.

To be sure, this approach introduces some initial difficulties for students unable to recognize and name a passage's grammatical, syntactical, and rhetorical features—and in fact a review of or a handout on these features is often necessary. Nevertheless, I have found this approach has several pedagogical advantages—not the least of which is that it provides a convenient focus for a single classroom period. While close textual reading can improve the student's ability to recognize and name a passage's stylistic components, I want to stress that this procedure's major contribution emerges not only as students learn to appreciate Cather's narrative poetics but also as they learn a process, a series of questions, to draw out the significance of the details noticed for comment. In effect, this emphasis means that I usually engage the issue of Cather's verbal style after the novel has been read entirely and discussed at least preliminarily, for then the connections we make between the passage and the rest of the novel will seem not mystical but rather the result of careful reading and thorough preparation.

In order to illustrate this procedure of reading for the novel's style and the potential rewards it offers, we can examine the often-noticed two-paragraph description of the moment when the black plow appears magically against the setting sun near the end of book 2. On a Sunday morning in the July prior to his departure for Lincoln, Jim dresses and leaves home early in order to take a swim in the river before meeting the hired girls for an afternoon picnic. Near the end of the day, Jim tells the girls the story of Coronado and his search for the Seven Golden Cities, of the Spaniard's dying in the wilderness of a broken heart. This theme concerning the disparity between dreams and reality is connected by Ántonia to others, like her father, who also died in this fashion. At this point our discussion pauses to emphasize three things: how this episode foregrounds the inherent human tendency to think mythically and to be involved with story telling; how the cloistered imagery surrounding Jim's swimming hole and the metal imagery suggested by the fragments of Spanish spurs found on the prairie should be held in mind; how the episode under discussion occurs after Jim's high school graduation and just prior to his pummeling by Wick Cutter and his leaving for college studies in Lincoln.

As the group murmurs assent to Ántonia's remark, Jim's prose then shifts to describe the group view as they sit (244). We ask "what" questions: What is being said here? What feeling does the paragraph create? While the former question causes no problems, the latter question can of course be as problematic as describing the taste of a fine wine. To build a vocabulary to describe the effect of words, I often ask students to think of alternative ways of stating an idea or to draw comparisons to other authors they have read. In the end some wonder whether the clipped quality of the prose or the uninspired use of fire imagery here means Cather is a less accomplished writer than, say, a Faulkner. Before resting with this response, however, we consider whether there is anything about Jim's description of this common event that disrupts our expectations, varies the pattern established, or at least seems puzzling. Is there any reason for Jim's prose to avoid lengthy, flowing Faulknerian sentences? At this point attention is called to the slight rhythmic shift signaled by the sixth sentence ("The breeze sank to stillness."), to the unhurried progression of sentences, and to the paragraph's sparing use of adjectives and adverbs. This route challenges us to make a more precise articulation of the passage's texture and feel, and we end up realizing that a stately, decorous progression of sight and sound here forwards a feeling of lightness and calm content.

To understand fully Cather's craft here means switching from these initial "what" and "why" questions to "how": How is *this* feeling, this dignified rhythm created? Having now seen that there is more here than meets the eye at first glance, we notice first how grammar and syntax work, how the passage opens with a measured pace as simple sentences in the subject-verb-object pattern are repeated, and how the opening sentence's closing participial phrase propels us smoothly forward into the paragraph. The group responsible for charting the passage's rhythm suggests that at sentence four the inversion "There was" masses the first four sentences together prior to the swelling rhythm of its main clause and of the lengthy compound-complex sentence five. Then we notice how the cumulative rhythm of the opening sentences is displaced into a lengthier, more complex sentence just as Jim's vision stretches out across the stream and captures the play of light on the sandbars and willow thickets—and how in the next sentence this crescendo of sight and sound falls away into a laconic statement just as in parallel fashion his description records the breeze sinking to stillness. Although the moment briefly regains its intensity as Jim's description connects the sounds of owl and dove in the passage's only other compound sentence, it returns in the last two sentences to the graded pace and soft sounds of the opening sentences.

With this groundwork accomplished, the connection we make concerns the relations among syntax, rhythm, and content. Thus we discuss how the paragraph's abstract formal shape encloses the compound sentences with simple sentences having similar patterns and length. With this lead, students readily point to how the insistent alliteration, assonance (*e, i*), consonance (*l, g, s*), and repetitive sounds (*t*) and sentence openers function to stay the passage's forward movement. The group tracking verb forms and tenses is asked to consider the significance of the numerous intransitive verbs (e.g., "the owl hooted"), and they note that such a strategy also contends against the prose's forward momentum since subjects have no direct objects to receive action. The major point emerges: the passage's style matches the stasis felt by the girls listlessly leaning against each other in the grass. Moreover, as we broaden the scope of the discussion, we understand how the simple majesty that results entirely accords with the respectful quietness following Ántonia's linking the fates of Coronado and Nebraska pioneers and creates a tranquil interlude prior to the sudden appearance of the plow in the group's line of vision.

I use the verb *enclose* above purposefully, for it should be recalled now that Jim is attracted visually to open yet bounded spaces. Here we move outward to note other descriptive passages revealing Jim's preference for this kind of topography: the nest of grass (26) or "flowery pagoda" (238) Jim and Ántonia enter together; the sunflower-bordered roads (29); the nest Ántonia makes in her hair for a green insect (39); the Indian ring outlined by the fallen snow (62); Mr. Shimerda's gravesite (118); Jim's tree-lined swimming hole nicknamed "No Man's Land" (233); the hayloft, orchard, and fruit cellar on Cuzak's farm in book 5. I ask at this point what the significance of this kind of space is and, by looking briefly at the description of the orchard in book 5, the appropriate conclusion surfaces: that such magical spaces stimulate Jim's memory and imagination and provide for him a safe refuge from time and history and the onset of old age. To clinch this point about Jim's character, I ask the class to recall the numerous lines in the novel's last two books where Jim wishes he could be a little boy again or admits that he desires to keep his memories of the past from being destroyed by the realities of the present. In the end, then, I stress how this paragraph's shape, sounds, and syntax empower what the novel is forwarding in its surface content.

By proceeding in this fashion, we are brought closer to the essence of Jim's romanticism and also see more clearly the rightness of the novel's epigraph concerning the fleeing first of one's best days. When we turn to the next paragraph and the "curious sight," according to Jim, which concludes the episode, I ask the students to take Jim at his word: that is, not to dwell on what we've already seen of Cather's dominant stylistic strategies (repetition, sounds, monosyllabic words, intransitive verb forms) but to think about what is "curious"—surprising, different, novel—about the prose style here as compared to the previous paragraph. This topic inevitably leads to a discussion of three other important features of Cather's style: the use of ellipsis, imagery, and verb tenses to provoke in our minds "the verbal mood, the emotional aura of the fact or the thing or the deed" ("The Novel Démeublé" 41–42).

> Presently we saw a curious thing: There were no clouds, the sun was going down in a limpid, gold-washed sky. Just as the lower edge of the red disk rested on the high fields against the horizon, a great black figure suddenly appeared on the face of the sun. We sprang to our feet, straining our eyes toward it. In a moment we realized what it was. On some upland farm, a plough had been left standing in the field. The sun was sinking just behind it. Magnified across the distance by the horizontal light, it stood out against the sun, was exactly contained within the circle of the disk; the handles, the tongue, the share—black against the molten red. There it was, heroic in size, a picture writing on the sun.   (245)

We quickly notice how this paragraph, unlike the previous one, moves. Though the scene is organized by the play of light and color imagery, it moves steadily forward as Jim traces the moment-by-moment process of perception (we note the prepositional-phrase temporal markers). After the deflation caused by the brief moment of recognition, the prose regains intensity as Jim clarifies the dimensions of the vision, as he compresses the meaning of the experience into the complicated grammar of the last two sentences. By noting that Jim presents the moment by offering an enigma, solving it, and then redescribing its impact and import, we see that what really happens here is that things change into or are replaced by other things: stillness and listlessness are transposed into springing and straining; the sound of doves and owls is replaced by visual images; parts of the plow become dissolved into a play of colors; the play of black against red becomes "heroic in size"; seeing becomes a "vision" of a "picture." And from here it is rewarding to chart the parallel transformations in the passage's grammar and sounds—and to recognize the particular effectiveness of the punctuation in the penultimate sentence in promoting the undeniable sense of transfiguration released here as Jim transposes Spanish stirrup fragments into a metal plow, which stands as his synecdoche for the immigrant pioneer's experience.

To discover further the functional power of Cather's style we shift, paradoxical as this might sound, to the passage's anomalies and paradoxes. While the grammar and syntax of the last two sentences invite attention, I first ask the students to examine the paragraph's final phrase. We are so used to stressing the visual sense that it is easy here to miss the strangeness of this phrase "a picture writing on the sun." How can a picture write? Why indeed stress the word *picture* and the act of writing? And why writing on the sun? With these questions we move outward from the passage to examine the presence and import of "pictures" and photographs in the novel, and with the previous discussion of temporality in our minds (as well as our personal experience with photographs), we understand how such visual images—like the womblike topography in the novel—also serve as a bulwark against time's passage. I now ask whether Jim's thematic effort to defeat time is complemented by the passage's other prominent stylistic features. The students following Cather's use of imagery indicate how the sunset image traditionally connotes temporal decay and death; yet the simultaneous use of the plow's black image causes some difficulty in grasping the overall interpretation of the imagery. Here we need to remember that Jim later associates the plow and furrow with the pen and the page (264). Thus, to write pictures on or against the sun is figuratively to try to stave off the passage of time. The class notes also how the passage moves from past through progressive tenses and ends in a present participial, "writing." Finally, the climactic last sentence gets extensive attention since the "it was" clause ("There it was, [it was] heroic in size, [it was] a picture writing on the sun") necessary for parallelism is lopped off. And by considering the significance of resting in the present tense and of refusing to present completed thoughts, we realize how the effort to defer through writing the closure symbolized by the sunset image is also made emphatic through the paragraph's shift in tenses and its elisions of subjects and verbs.

Like the painted glass in Black Hawk's Methodist church, then, the passage's style tries to "hold" us "there" on the page (174), to "contain" us within its boundaries just as at one moment the plow is exactly contained within the outline of the setting sun. The discussion at this point can move in several different directions. Connecting the passage's stylistic features to the novel's thematic concern with time helps explain the particular relevance of the inset stories in the novel, for they too serve as pictures writing on the sun by stretching the boundaries of the present moment so as to contain the past. Or we can discuss how this moment signifies the apotheosis of Jim's adolescence, for as the sun sets and the black plow fades into insignificance the narrative shifts to Jim's "dark" introduction to the force of sexual desire during the Wick Cutter episode. Influences on the development of Cather's style can be introduced (Stouck, "Impressionist Novel") and, if time allows, comparisons made to pivotal moments in her other novels. Finally, to indicate not just the functional beauty but also the power of Cather's style, I find it beneficial to discuss the aural qualities of Cather's style and how the acoustical space of sound generates a sense of the sacred (Ong). Whatever the route taken, by closely reading for the narrative's sounds, rhythms, and structures we can better appreciate how Ántonia and her world are brought to as much life on the page as they are, so the introduction says, brought to life during the railway conversations between the editor "Cather" and the narrator Jim Burden, better see how words and their forms in *My Ántonia* work to transport us, like the infirm old actress in *Camille*, "across [the] long years . . ." (278).

PARTICIPANTS IN SURVEY OF MY ÁNTONIA INSTRUCTORS

The following scholars and teachers of My Ántonia generously agreed to participate in the survey of approaches to teaching My Ántonia that preceded preparation of this volume. Without their valuable assistance and support, the volume simply would not have been possible.

Nancy P. Arbuthnot, U. S. Naval Acad.; Barbara Bair, Univ. of California, Los Angeles; Jennifer Bradley, Univ. of California, Los Angeles; Patricia M. Brandow, Minneapolis, MN; Robert W. Cherny, San Francisco State Univ.; Josephine Donovan, Portsmouth, NH; Richard W. Etulain, Univ. of New Mexico; James L. Evans, Pan American Univ.; Mary Anne Ferguson, Univ. of Massachusetts, Amherst; Robert L. Gale, Univ. of Pittsburgh; Blanche H. Gelfant, Dartmouth Coll.; Phil Gerber, State Univ. of New York, Brockport; Charlotte Goodman, Skidmore Coll.; Melody Graulich, Univ. of New Hampshire; Elizabeth L. Hacking, Houghton Mifflin Co.; Robert D. Harper, Estes Park, CO; Sally Hartshorne, Dedham, MA; Robert Harwick, Hastings Coll.; Jim Healey, Eastern Montana Coll.; Evelyn J. Hinz, Univ. of Manitoba; Arthur Huseboe, Augustana Coll.; Starr Jenkins, California Polytechnic State Univ.; Fran Kaye, Univ. of Nebraska, Lincoln; William F. Kimes, Orange Coast Coll.; W. C. Kvasnicka, Spark, NV; Deborah J. Leonard, Union Coll.; Glen A. Love, Univ. of Oregon; Joseph P. Lovering, Canisius Coll.; Francie Malpezzi, Arkansas State Univ.; Julian Mason, Univ. of North Carolina, Charlotte; Charlotte S. McClure, Georgia State Univ.; Sally A. McNall, Univ. of Kansas; Barbara H. Meldrum, Univ. of Idaho; Constance Mierendorf, Minneapolis Community Coll.; Pat Morrow, Auburn Univ.; John J. Murphy, Brigham Young Univ.; Hal Nagel, Kearney State Coll.; Robert J. Nelson, Univ. of Illinois; Ferner Nuhn, Claremont, CA; Paul A. Olson, Univ. of Nebraska, Lincoln; Linda Pannill, Transylvania Univ.; Tom Quirk, Univ. of Missouri; Barbara Rippey, Univ. of Nebraska, Lincoln; Darlene Ritter, Midland Lutheran Coll.; Ann Ronald, Univ. of Nevada; Larry Rubin, Georgia Inst. of Technology; Jean Schwind, Earlham Coll.; Hal Shiffler, Hastings, NE; Anneliese H. Smith, State Univ. of New York; C. L. Sonnichsen, Arizona Heritage Center; David Stouck, Simon Fraser Univ.; Robert Thacker, St. Lawrence Univ.; Clara Thomas, York Univ.; Jane S. Vogel, Pennington, NJ; Loretta Wasserman, Grand Valley State Coll.; Floyd C. Watkins, Emory Univ.; Gerald Weales, Univ. of Pennsylvania; James Woodress, Univ. of California, Davis.

WORKS CONSULTED

Abrams, M. H. *Natural Supernaturalism: Tradition and Revolution in Romantic Literature.* New York: Norton, 1971.

Adams, Henry. *The Education of Henry Adams.* Ed. Ernest Samuels. 1918. Boston: Houghton, 1973.

Alcott, Louisa May. *Little Women.* 1869. New York: Crowell, 1955.

Amack, W. Rex. *Historic Webster County: Then and Now.* N.p.: n.p., n.d. (Available through Willa Cather Pioneer Memorial and Educational Foundation, 326 N. Webster St., Red Cloud, NE 68970.)

Ammons, Elizabeth. "Jewett's Witches." *Critical Essays on Sarah Orne Jewett.* Ed. Gwen L. Nagel. Boston: Hall, 1984. 165–84.

Arnheim, Rudolf. *Visual Thinking.* Berkeley: U of California P, 1969.

Arnold, Marilyn. *Willa Cather: A Reference Guide.* Boston: Hall, 1986.

Bailey, Jennifer. "The Dangers of Femininity in Willa Cather's Fiction." *Journal of American Studies* 16 (1982): 391–406.

Baltensperger, Bradley H. *Nebraska: A Geography.* Boulder: Westview, 1985.

Bennett, James D. *Frederick Jackson Turner.* Boston: Twayne, 1975.

Bennett, Mildred R. Personal interviews. Red Cloud, NE. Summers of 1980, 1982, 1983.

———. *The Red Cloud Chief.* N.p.: n.p., 1971. (Available through Willa Cather Pioneer Memorial and Educational Foundation, 326 N. Webster St., Red Cloud, NE 68970.)

———. "Willa Cather of Red Cloud." Virginia Faulkner 124–30.

———. *The World of Willa Cather.* 1951. Lincoln: U of Nebraska P, 1961.

Bergson, Henri. *Creative Evolution.* Trans. Arthur Mitchell. 1911. Norwood: Telegraph, 1981.

Bettelheim, Bruno. *The Uses of Enchantment: The Meaning and Importance of Fairy Tales.* New York: Random, 1976.

Billington, Ray Allen. *America's Frontier Heritage.* 1966. Albuquerque: U of New Mexico P, 1974.

———, ed. *The Frontier Thesis: Valid Interpretation of American History?* 1966. Melbourne: Krieger, 1977.

Blassingame, John W. *The Slave Community: Plantation Life in the Antebellum South.* New York: Oxford UP, 1972.

Bloom, Edward, and Lillian Bloom. *Willa Cather's Gift of Sympathy.* Crosscurrents: Modern Critiques. Gen. ed. Harry T. Moore. Carbondale: Southern Illinois UP, 1962.

Bloom, Harold, ed. *Willa Cather.* Modern Critical Views. New York: Chelsea, 1985.

Bloom, Lillian, with Edward A. Bloom. "The Poetics of Willa Cather." Murphy, *Five Essays* 97–119.

Bohling, Beth. "The Husband of *My Ántonia*." *Western American Literature* 19 (1984): 29–39.

Bohlke, L. Brent, ed. *Willa Cather in Person: Interviews, Speeches, and Letters*. Lincoln: U of Nebraska P, 1986.

Bolton, Herbert E. *Coronado: Knight of Pueblos and Plains*. 1949. Albuquerque: U of New Mexico P, 1964.

Bourne, Randolph. Rev. of *My Ántonia*. *Dial* 14 Dec. 1918: 557.

Brink, Pamela J., ed. *Transcultural Nursing*. Englewood Cliffs: Prentice, 1976.

Britton, James. *Language and Learning*. Miami: U of Miami P, 1971.

Brown, E. K., completed by Leon Edel. *Willa Cather: A Critical Biography*. New York: Knopf, 1953. Lincoln: U of Nebraska P, 1987.

Butcher, Solomon D. *Pioneer History of Custer County*. Ed. Harry E. Chrisman. 1901. Rev. ed. Broken Bow: Purcells, 1976.

Carter, John E. *Solomon D. Butcher: Photographing the American Dream*. Lincoln: U of Nebraska P, 1985.

Castañeda de Nágera, Pedro de. *The Narrative of the Expedition of Coronado by Castañeda*. Trans. George Parker Winship. 1896. Rpt. in *Spanish Explorers in the Southern United States*. Ed. Frederick W. Hodge and Theodore H. Lewis. 1907. New York: Barnes, 1946. Austin: Texas State Historical Assn., 1984.

Cather, Willa. *Alexander's Bridge*. 1912. Introd. Bernice Slote. Lincoln: Bison–U of Nebraska P, 1977.

———. *Alexander's Bridge*. 1912. Pref. Cather. Boston: Houghton, 1922.

———. "Before Breakfast." *"The Old Beauty" and Others*. New York: Knopf, 1948. 141–56.

———. *Death Comes for the Archbishop*. 1927. New York: Vintage-Random, 1971.

———. *Early Novels and Stories*. Ed. Sharon O'Brien. New York: Library of America, 1987.

———. *The Kingdom of Art: Willa Cather's First Principles and Critical Statements, 1893–1896*. Ed. Bernice Slote. Lincoln: U of Nebraska P, 1986.

———. Letter to Miss Bishop. [Feb. 1918]. Houghton Mifflin Art Dept., Houghton Library, Harvard Univ.

———. Letter to Elizabeth Shepley Sergeant. 12 Sept. 1912. Pierpont Morgan Library.

———. Letters to Ferris Greenslet. Houghton Library, Harvard Univ.

———. Letters to Sarah Orne Jewett. Houghton Library, Harvard Univ.

———. Letters to Carrie Miner Sherwood. Willa Cather Historical Center, Red Cloud, NE.

———. *A Lost Lady*. 1923. New York: Vintage-Random, 1972.

———. *Lucy Gayheart*. 1935. New York: Vintage-Random, 1976.

————. *My Ántonia*. Boston: Houghton, 1918.

————. *My Ántonia*. 1918. Boston: Houghton, 1977.

————. *My Ántonia*. 1918. Boston: Houghton, 1988.

————. "My First Novels [There Were Two]." *On Writing* 89–98.

————. "Nebraska: The End of the First Cycle." *Nation* 5 Sept. 1923: 236–38. Rpt. in Virginia Faulkner 1–8.

————. "Neighbour Rosicky." *Obscure Destinies*. 1932. New York: Vintage-Random, 1974. 3–74.

————. *Not under Forty*. 1936. New York: Knopf, 1953.

————. "The Novel Démeublé." *Not under Forty* 43–51. Rpt. in *On Writing* 35–43.

————. "Old Mrs. Harris." *Obscure Destinies*. 1932. New York: Vintage-Random, 1974. 75–192.

————. *One of Ours*. New York: Knopf, 1922.

————. *On Writing: Critical Studies on Writing as an Art*. 1949. New York: Knopf, 1968.

————. *O Pioneers!* 1913. Boston: Sentry-Houghton, 1962.

————. *The Professor's House*. New York: Knopf, 1925.

————. *Shadows on the Rock*. 1931. New York: Vintage-Random, 1971.

————. *The Song of the Lark*. Boston: Houghton, 1915.

————. *The Song of the Lark*. 1915. Boston: Houghton, 1943.

————. *Willa Cather's Collected Short Fiction: 1892–1912*. 1965. Ed. Virginia Faulkner. Introd. Mildred R. Bennett. Lincoln: U of Nebraska P, 1970.

————. *The World and the Parish: Willa Cather's Articles and Reviews, 1893–1902*. 2 vols. Ed. William M. Curtin. Lincoln: U of Nebraska P, 1970.

"Catherland through the Artist's Eyes." *Nebraskaland* Feb. 1982: 24–31.

Chaffee, John. *Thinking Critically*. Boston: Houghton, 1985.

Chauncey, George, Jr. "From Sexual Inversion to Homosexuality: Medicine and the Changing Conceptualization of Female Deviance." *Salmagundi* 58–59 (1982–83): 115–46.

Cherny, Robert W. *Populism, Progressivism, and the Transformation of Nebraska Politics: 1885–1915*. Lincoln: U of Nebraska P, 1981.

————. "Willa Cather and the Populists." *Great Plains Quarterly* 3 (1983): 206–18.

Chodorow, Nancy. *The Reproduction of Mothering: Psychoanalysis and the Sociology of Gender*. Berkeley: U of California P, 1978.

Coles, William E., Jr. *The Plural I: The Teaching of Writing*. New York: Holt, 1978.

Commager, Henry Steele. "The Study of Immigration." *Immigration and American History*. Ed. Commager. Minneapolis: U of Minnesota P, 1961. 3–7.

Cooper, James Fenimore. *The Prairie: A Tale*. 1827. Ed. and introd. James P. Elliott. New York: NAL, 1964. Albany: State UP of New York, 1985.

Cooper-Skjelver, Mabel R. *Webster County: Visions of the Past*. N.p.: n.p., [1981?]. (Available from Webster County Historical Museum, Red Cloud, NE 68970.)

Cott, Nancy F., and Elizabeth H. Pleck, eds. *A Heritage of Her Own: Toward a New Social History of American Women.* New York: Simon, 1979.

Crane, Joan. *Willa Cather: A Bibliography.* Lincoln: U of Nebraska P, 1982.

Crane, Stephen. *"Maggie" and Other Stories.* Ed. Austin McC. Fox. New York: Washington Square, 1960.

Crèvecoeur, Michel-Guillaume-Dean de. *Letters from an American Farmer.* 1782. New York: Everyman, 1982.

Curran, Thomas J. *Xenophobia and Immigration, 1820–1930.* Boston: Twayne, 1975.

Curtin, William M. "Willa Cather and *The Varieties of Religious Experience.*" *Renascence* 27 (Spring 1975): 115–23.

~ Daiches, David. *Willa Cather: A Critical Introduction.* New York: Collier, 1962.

Dante Alighieri. *The Paradiso.* Trans. John Ciardi. New York: Mentor-NAL, 1970.

Day, Bess Eileen. "A Famous Nebraska Friendship: Anna Pavelka Lives On in Cather's *My Ántonia.*" *Omaha World Herald Magazine of the Midlands* 28 July 1957: 4G.

Dick, Everett. *The Sod-House Frontier, 1854–1890: A Social History of the Northern Plains from the Creation of Kansas and Nebraska to the Admission of the Dakotas.* 1937. Lincoln: Bison–U of Nebraska P, 1979.

Donovan, Josephine. "Nan Prince and the Golden Apples." *Colby Library Quarterly* 22 (Mar. 1986): 17–27.

———. *New England Local Color Literature: A Women's Tradition.* New York: Ungar, 1983.

———. *Sarah Orne Jewett.* New York: Ungar, 1980.

———. "Silence or Capitulation: Prepatriarchal 'Mothers' Gardens' in Jewett and Freeman." *Studies in Short Fiction* 23 (1986): 43–48.

Douglas, Ann. *The Feminization of American Culture.* New York: Knopf, 1977. New York: Avon, 1978.

Dreiser, Theodore. *Sister Carrie.* Ed. Donald Pizer. New York: Norton, 1970.

Edwards, Betty. *Drawing on the Right Side of the Brain.* Los Angeles: Tarcher, 1979.

Elbow, Peter. "Freewriting." *Writing without Teachers.* New York: Oxford UP, 1973. 3–11.

Emerson, Ralph Waldo. *The Selected Writings of Ralph Waldo Emerson.* Ed. Brooks Atkinson. New York: Modern Library, 1950.

Etulain, Richard W. *Owen Wister.* Boise: Boise State Coll. P, 1973.

Faderman, Lillian. *Surpassing the Love of Men: Romantic Friendship and Love between Women, from the Renaissance to the Present.* New York: Morrow, 1981.

Faulkner, Virginia, ed. *Roundup: A Nebraska Reader.* 1957. Lincoln: Bison–U of Nebraska P, 1974.

Faulkner, William. *Go Down, Moses.* 1942. New York: Vintage-Random, 1973.

Fite, Gilbert C. *The Farmers' Frontier: 1865–1900.* 1966. Albuquerque: U of New Mexico P, 1977.

Freedman, Estelle. "Separatism as Strategy: Female Institution Building and American Feminism, 1870–1931." *Feminist Studies* 5 (1979): 513–29.

Fritz, Eunice. Personal interview. July 1982.

Fryer, Judith. *Felicitous Space: The Imaginative Structures of Edith Wharton and Willa Cather.* Chapel Hill: U of North Carolina P, 1986.

Fussell, Edwin. *Frontier: American Literature and the American West.* Princeton: Princeton UP, 1965.

Gale, Robert L. "Willa Cather and the Usable Past." *Nebraska History* 42 (1961): 181–90.

Gelfant, Blanche H. "The Forgotten Reaping-Hook: Sex in *My Ántonia.*" *American Literature* 43 (1971): 60–82. Rpt. with a new introd. in *Women Writing in America: Voices in Collage.* Hanover: UP of New England, 1984. 94–116.

Gerber, Philip. *Willa Cather.* Twayne's United States Authors Series. Boston: Hall, 1975.

Giannone, Richard. "Willa Cather and the Human Voice." Murphy, *Five Essays* 21–49.

Gilbert, Sandra M., and Susan Gubar. *The Madwoman in the Attic: The Woman Writer and the Nineteenth-Century Literary Imagination.* New Haven: Yale UP, 1979.

Gilligan, Carol. *In a Different Voice: Psychological Theory and Women's Development.* Cambridge: Harvard UP, 1982.

Gilman, Charlotte Perkins. *Herland.* 1915. New York: Pantheon, 1979.

Glasgow, Ellen. *Barren Ground.* 1933. New York: Sagamore, 1957.

Goetzmann, William H., and Joseph C. Porter. *The West as Romantic Horizon.* Omaha: Center for Western Studies, Joslyn Art Museum, 1981.

Gold, Michael. *Jews without Money.* 1930. New York: Avon, 1965.

Goodman, Charlotte. "The Lost Brother, the Twin: Women Novelists and the Male-Female Double *Bildungsroman.*" *Novel: A Forum on Fiction* 17 (1983): 28–43.

Greenslet, Ferris. Letter to Willa Cather. 5 May 1943. Houghton Library, Harvard Univ.

———. *Under the Bridge.* Boston: Houghton, 1943.

Grove, Frederick Philip. *Fruits of the Earth.* 1933. Introd. M. G. Parks. Toronto: McClelland, 1965.

———. *In Search of Myself.* 1946. Introd. D. O. Spettigue. Toronto: McClelland, 1965.

Gusfield, Joseph R. *Symbolic Crusade: Status Politics and the American Temperance Movement.* 1963. Westport: Greenwood, 1980.

Gutman, Herbert G. *The Black Family in Slavery and Freedom: 1750–1925*. New York: Vintage-Random, 1977.

———. *Work, Culture, and Society in Industrializing America: Essays in America's Working Class and Social History*. New York: Vintage-Random, 1977.

Hampsten, Elizabeth. *Read This Only to Yourself: The Private Writings of Midwestern Women, 1880–1910*. Bloomington: Indiana UP, 1982.

Handlin, Oscar. *Immigration as a Factor in American History*. Englewood Cliffs: Prentice, 1959.

———. *The Uprooted*. Boston: Little, 1951.

Hardon, John. A. *Modern Catholic Dictionary*. Garden City: Doubleday, 1980.

Harris, Richard C. "Renaissance Pastoral Conventions and the Ending of *My Ántonia*." *Markham Review* 8 (Fall 1978): 8–11.

Hawthorne, Nathaniel. *The Scarlet Letter*. 2nd ed. 1850. New York: Washington Square, 1961.

Helmick, Evelyn. "The Mysteries of Ántonia." *Midwest Quarterly* 17 (1976): 173–85.

Hicks, John D. *The Populist Revolt: A History of the Farmers' Alliance and the People's Party*. 1931. Westport: Greenwood, 1981.

Higham, John. *Send These to Me: Immigrants in Urban America*. Rev. ed. Baltimore: Johns Hopkins UP, 1984.

———. *Strangers in the Land: Patterns of American Nativism 1860–1925*. 1955, 1963. Westport: Greenwood, 1981.

Howarth, William. "The Country of Willa Cather." Photographs by Farrell Grehan. *National Geographic* July 1982: 70–93.

Irving, Washington. "A Tour of the Prairies." *The Crayon Miscellany*. 1835. Ed. Dahlia Kirby Terrell. New York: Twayne, 1979. Vol. 22 of *The Complete Works of Washington Irving*. Gen. ed. Richard Dilworth Rust. 1969–81. 5–122.

James, Henry. *The Portrait of a Lady*. Ed. Robert D. Bamberg. New York: Norton, 1975.

James, William. *The Principles of Psychology*. 2 vols. 1890. Cambridge: Harvard UP, 1981.

———. *Psychology: Briefer Course*. 1892. Cambridge: Harvard UP, 1984.

Jensen, Joan M., ed. *With These Hands: Women Working on the Land*. Old Westbury: Feminist, 1981.

Jewett, Sarah Orne. *The Country of the Pointed Firs*. 1896. Pref. Willa Cather, 1925. Garden City: Doubleday, 1956.

———. *The Letters of Sarah Orne Jewett*. Ed. Annie Fields. Boston: Houghton, 1911.

Jones, Alexander, ed. *The Jerusalem Bible*. Reader's ed. Garden City: Doubleday, 1974.

Jung, C. G. "Psychological Aspects of the Mother Archetype." *The Archetypes and the Collective Unconscious.* Vol. 9, pt. 1, of *Collected Works of C. G. Jung.* Trans. R. F. C. Hull. Bollingen Series 20. Princeton: Princeton UP, 1968. 73–110.

Kennan, George F. *The Fateful Alliance: France, Russia, and the Coming of the First World War.* New York: Pantheon, 1984.

Kiniry, Malcolm, and Ellen Strenski. "Sequencing Expository Writing: A Recursive Approach." *College Composition and Communication* 36 (1985): 191–202.

Kolodny, Annette. *The Land before Her: Fantasy and Experience of the American Frontiers, 1630–1860.* Chapel Hill: U of North Carolina P, 1984.

———.*The Lay of the Land: Metaphor as Experience and History in American Life and Letters.* Chapel Hill: U of North Carolina P, 1975.

Kraut, Alan M. *The Huddled Masses: The Immigrant in American Society, 1880–1921.* Arlington Heights: Davidson, 1982.

Kroetsch, Robert. "The Fear of Women in Prairie Fiction: An Erotics of Space." *Crossing Frontiers: Papers in American and Canadian Western Literature.* Ed. Dick Harrison. Edmonton: U of Alberta P, 1979. 73–83.

———. *The Studhorse Man.* 1970. New York: Beaufort, 1984.

Kučera, Vladimír. *Czech Dramas in Nebraska.* Lincoln, NE: n.p., 1979.

———. *Czech Music in Nebraska.* Lincoln, NE: n.p., 1980.

Kučera, Vladimír, and Alfréd Nováček, eds. *Czechs and Nebraska.* Ord, NE: n.p., [c. 1967].

Kutak, Robert I. *The Story of a Bohemian-American Village: A Study of Social Persistence and Change.* 1933. Salem: Ayer, 1970.

Lanham, Richard A. *Style: An Anti-Textbook.* New Haven: Yale UP, 1974.

Laska, Vera. *The Czechs in America, 1633–1977.* Dobbs Ferry: Oceana, 1978.

Lawrence, D. H. *Studies in Classic American Literature.* 1923. New York: Viking, 1970.

Lessing, Doris. *The Grass Is Singing.* 1950. New York: NAL, 1976.

Le Sueur, Meridel. *Salute to Spring.* 1940. New York: International, 1983.

Lewis, Edith. *Willa Cather Living: A Personal Record.* New York: Knopf, 1953.

Lewis, R. W. B. *The American Adam: Innocence, Tragedy, and Tradition in the Nineteenth Century.* 1955. Chicago: U of Chicago P, 1968.

Lewis, Sinclair. *Babbitt.* 1922. New York: NAL, 1961.

Love, Glen A. "The Cowboy in the Laboratory: Willa Cather's Hesitant Moderns." *New Americans: The Westerner and the Modern Experience in the American Novel.* Lewisburg: Bucknell UP, 1982. 107–169.

Luebke, Frederick C., ed. *Ethnicity on the Great Plains.* Lincoln: U of Nebraska P, 1980.

———. "Ethnic Minority Groups in the American West." *Historians and the American West.* Ed. Michael P. Malone. Lincoln: U of Nebraska P, 1983. 387–413.

———. *Immigrants and Politics: The Germans of Nebraska, 1880–1900.* Lincoln: U of Nebraska P, 1969.

———. "Regionalism and the Great Plains: Problems of Concept and Method." *Western Historical Quarterly* 15 (1984): 19–38.

Manley, Robert N. *Centennial History of the University of Nebraska: 1. Frontier University (1869–1919).* Lincoln: U of Nebraska P, 1969.

Martin, Terence. "The Drama of Memory in *My Ántonia*." *PMLA* 84 (1969): 304–11.

Marx, Leo. *The Machine in the Garden: Technology and the Pastoral Ideal in America.* New York: Oxford UP, 1964.

McFarland, Dorothy Tuck. *Willa Cather.* New York: Ungar, 1972.

Mead, Margaret. "One Vote for This Age of Anxiety." *New York Times Magazine* 20 May 1956. Rpt. in *Invention and Design: A Rhetorical Reader.* Ed. Forrest D. Burt and E. Cleve Want. 4th ed. New York: Random, 1985. 286–90.

Melville, Herman. *Great Short Works.* Ed. Warner Berthoff. New York: Harper, 1969.

Mencken, H. L. "Mainly Fiction." *Smart Set* Mar. 1919: 140–41.

———. "Sunrise on the Prairie." *Smart Set* Feb. 1919: 143–44.

Menuhin, Yehudi, and Phyllis C. Robinson. "Historic Houses: Willa Cather." *Architectural Digest* Nov. 1985: 228–33.

Meyer, Roy W. *The Middle Western Farm Novel in the Twentieth Century.* Lincoln: Bison–U of Nebraska P, 1974.

———. "The Scandinavian Immigrant in American Farm Fiction." *American Scandinavian Review* 47 (1959): 243–49.

Miller, James E., Jr. "*My Ántonia*: A Frontier Drama of Time." *American Quarterly* 10 (1958): 476–84.

———. "*My Ántonia* and the American Dream." *Prairie Schooner* 48 (1974): 112–23.

———. "Willa Cather and the Art of Fiction." Slote and Faulkner 121–48.

Mitchell, W. O. *Who Has Seen the Wind.* 1947. Toronto: Macmillan, 1972.

Moers, Ellen. *Literary Women.* Garden City: Doubleday, 1976.

Momaday, N. Scott. *House Made of Dawn.* 1968. New York: Harper, 1977.

———. *The Way to Rainy Mountain.* 1969. Albuquerque: U of New Mexico P, 1976.

Morris, Wright. *Ceremony in Lone Tree.* 1960. Lincoln: Bison–U of Nebraska P, 1973.

———. *The Home Place.* 1948. Lincoln: U of Nebraska P, 1968.

Mountford, Miriam, ed. *One Hundred Years of Red Cloud.* Red Cloud, NE: n.p., 1971.

Murphy, John J., ed. *Critical Essays on Willa Cather.* Critical Essays on American Literature. Gen. ed. James Nagel. Boston: Hall, 1984.

———, ed. *Five Essays on Willa Cather: The Merrimack Symposium.* North Andover: Merrimack Coll., 1974.

———. *A Teacher's Guide to Willa Cather's* O Pioneers! *and* My Ántonia. Boston: Houghton, 1980.

————. "The Virginian and Ántonia Shimerda: Different Sides of the Western Coin." Stauffer and Rosowski 162–178.

Myres, Sandra L. *Westering Women and the Frontier Experience, 1800–1915.* Albuquerque: U of New Mexico P, 1982.

O'Brien, Sharon. "Mothers, Daughters, and the 'Art Necessity': Willa Cather and the Creative Process." *American Novelists Revisited: Essays in Feminist Criticism.* Ed. Fritz Fleischmann. Boston: Hall, 1982. 265–98.

————. " 'The Thing Not Named': Willa Cather as a Lesbian Writer." *Signs: Journal of Women in Culture and Society* 9 (1984): 576–99.

————. *Willa Cather: The Emerging Voice.* New York: Oxford UP, 1987.

O'Gara, W. H., comp. *In All Its Fury: A History of the Blizzard of January 12, 1988, with Stories and Reminiscences.* Ed. Ora A. Clement. 1947. Lincoln: Jenkins, 1975.

O'Kieffe, Charley. *Western Story: The Recollections of Charley O'Kieffe, 1884–1898.* Lincoln: U of Nebraska P, 1960.

Olsen, Tillie. *Yonnondio: From the Thirties.* New York: Delacorte, 1974.

Olson, James C. *A History of Nebraska.* 2nd ed. Lincoln: Bison–U of Nebraska P, 1966.

Olson, Paul A. *Broken Hoops and Plains People.* Lincoln: Nebraska Center for Curriculum Development, U of Nebraska, 1976.

————. "The Epic and Great Plains Literature: Rölvaag, Cather, and Neihardt." *Prairie Schooner* 55 (1981): 263–85.

Ong, Walter J. *The Presence of the Word: Some Prolegomena for Cultural and Religious History.* 1979. Minneapolis: U of Minnesota P, 1981.

Parkman, Francis. *The Oregon Trail.* Ed. E. N. Feltskog. 1849. Madison: U of Wisconsin P, 1969.

Pavelka, Anna Sadilek. Letter to Frances Samland. 24 Feb. 1955. Photocopy at Willa Cather Pioneer Memorial and Educational Foundation, Red Cloud, NE.

————. Letter to Carrie Miner Sherwood. 26 Dec. 1933. Willa Cather Pioneer Memorial and Educational Foundation, Red Cloud, NE.

Peck, Stanley Z. *The Czech Revolution of 1848.* Chapel Hill: U of North Carolina P, 1969.

Peterman, Michael. " 'The Good Game': The Charm of Willa Cather's *My Ántonia* and W. O. Mitchell's *Who Has Seen the Wind.*" *Mosaic* 14 (1981): 93–106.

The Pioneers. Ed. editors of Time-Life Books. Text by Huston Horn. New York: Time-Life, 1974.

Poggioli, Renato. *The Oaten Flute: Essays on Pastoral Poetry and the Pastoral Ideal.* Cambridge: Harvard UP, 1974.

Pollack, Norman. *The Populist Response to Industrial America.* Cambridge: Harvard UP, 1976.

Porter, Katherine Anne. Afterword. *The Troll Garden.* By Willa Cather. 1961. Rpt. in Murphy, *Critical Essays* 31–39.

Pratt, Annis. *Archetypal Patterns in Women's Fiction*. Bloomington: Indiana UP, 1981.

Propp, V. I. *Morphology of the Folktale*. 2nd ed. Trans. Laurence Scott. Austin: U of Texas P, 1968.

Rabinowitz, Howard N. "Race, Ethnicity and Cultural Pluralism in American History." *Ordinary People and Everyday Life: Perspectives on the New Social History*. Ed. James B. Gardner and George Rollie Adams. Nashville: American Assn. for State and Local History, 1983. 23–49.

Rabinowitz, Peter J. "The Turn of the Glass Key: Popular Fiction as Reading Strategy." *Critical Inquiry* 11 (1985): 418–31.

Randall, John H., III. *The Landscape and the Looking Glass: Willa Cather's Search for Value*. 1960. Westport: Greenwood, 1973.

———. "Willa Cather and the Pastoral Tradition." Murphy, *Five Essays* 75–96.

Redfield, Robert. *The Little Community: Viewpoints for the Study of a Human Whole*. Chicago: U of Chicago P, 1971.

Reinhold, Meyer. *Classica Americana: The Greek and Roman Heritage in the United States*. Detroit: Wayne State UP, 1984.

Rev. of *My Ántonia*. *Sun* [New York] 6 Oct. 1918, sec. 5: 1.

Riley, Glenda. *Frontierswomen: The Iowa Experience*. Ames: Iowa State UP, 1981.

Robinson, Phyllis C. *Willa: The Life of Willa Cather*. Garden City: Doubleday, 1983.

Rölvaag, O. E. *Giants in the Earth: A Saga of the Prairie*. Trans. Lincoln Colcord and O. E. Rölvaag. 1937. New York: Harper, 1965.

Rose, Phyllis. "Modernism: The Case of Willa Cather." *Modernism Reconsidered*. Ed. Robert Kiely. Cambridge: Harvard UP, 1983. 123–45.

Rosický, Rose. "Bohemians in Nebraska." Address. Nebraska State Historical Soc. Omaha, 30 Apr. 1926.

———. *A History of Czechs (Bohemians) in Nebraska*. Omaha: National Printing, 1929.

Rosowski, Susan J. "Discovering Symbolic Meaning: Teaching with Willa Cather." *English Journal* 71 (1982): 14–17.

———. *The Voyage Perilous: Willa Cather's Romanticism*. Lincoln: U of Nebraska P, 1986.

———. "Willa Cather and the Fatality of Place: *O Pioneers!*, *My Ántonia*, and *A Lost Lady*." *Geography and Literature: A Meeting of the Disciplines*. Ed. William E. Mallory and Paul Simpson-Housley. Syracuse: U of Syracuse P, 1987.

———. "Willa Cather's Women." *Studies in American Fiction* 9 (1981): 261–75.

Ross, E. A. *The Old World in the New: The Significance of Past and Present Immigration to the American People*. 1914. Englewood: Ozer, 1971.

Ross, Sinclair. *As for Me and My House*. 1941. Lincoln: U of Nebraska P, 1971.

Roucek, Joseph. "Czechoslovak Americans." *One America*. 3rd ed. Ed. Francis J. Brown and Joseph Roucek. Englewood Cliffs: Prentice, 1952. 157–68.

————. *The Czechs and Slovaks in America*. Minneapolis: Lerner, 1967.

Sahli, Nancy. "Smashing: Women's Relationships before the Fall." *Chrysalis* 8 (1979): 17–27.

Sandoz, Mari. *Love Song to the Plains*. 1961. Lincoln: U of Nebraska P, 1966.

————. *Old Jules*. 1935. Lincoln: U of Nebraska P, 1985.

Schaars, Mary Jo. "Teaching *My Ántonia*, with Guidance from Rosenblatt." *English Journal* 77 (1988): 54–58.

Schach, Paul. "Russian Wolves in Folktales and Literature of the Plains: A Question of Origins." *Great Plains Quarterly* 3 (1983): 67–78.

Schissel, Lillian. *Women's Diaries of the Westward Journey*. New York: Schocken, 1982.

Scholes, Robert E. *Textual Power: Literary Theory and the Teaching of English*. New Haven: Yale UP, 1985.

Schwind, Jean. "The Benda Illustrations to *My Ántonia*: Cather's 'Silent' Supplement to Jim Burden's Narrative." *PMLA* 100 (1985): 51–67.

Seibel, George. "Miss Cather from Nebraska." *New Colophon* 2 (1949): 195–208.

Sergeant, Elizabeth Shepley. *Willa Cather: A Memoir*. New York: Lippincott, 1953.

Seymour, Gabriel North. *Willa Cather's Red Cloud*. Text by Willa Cather. Salisbury: Lime Rock, 1980.

Sherman, Sarah W. "Victorians and the Matriarchal Mythology: A Source for Mrs. Todd." *Colby Library Quarterly* 22 (Mar. 1986): 63–74.

Shklovsky, Victor. "Art as Technique." *Russian Formalist Criticism: Four Essays*. Trans. and ed. Lee T. Lemon and Marion J. Reis. Lincoln: U of Nebraska P, 1965. 3–24.

Showalter, Elaine, ed. *The New Feminist Criticism: Essays on Women, Literature, and Theory*. New York: Pantheon, 1985.

Slote, Bernice. Introduction. *Alexander's Bridge*. By Willa Cather. 1977. Rpt. in Murphy, *Critical Essays* 97–111.

————. "Willa Cather." *Sixteen Modern American Authors: A Survey of Research and Criticism*. Ed. Jackson R. Bryer. (Pub. 1970 as *Fifteen American Authors: A Survey of Research and Criticism*.) Rev. ed. Durham: Duke UP, 1974. 29–73.

————. *Willa Cather: A Pictorial Memoir*. Photographs by Lucia Woods et al. 1973. Lincoln: U of Nebraska P, 1986.

Slote, Bernice, and Virginia Faulkner, eds. *The Art of Willa Cather*. Lincoln: U of Nebraska P, 1974.

Slotkin, Richard. *Regeneration through Violence: The Mythology of the American Frontier, 1600–1860*. Middletown: Wesleyan UP, 1973.

Smith, Henry Nash. *Virgin Land: The American West as Symbol and Myth*. Cambridge: Harvard UP, 1978.

Smith-Rosenberg, Carroll. "The Female World of Love and Ritual: Relations between Women in Nineteenth-Century America." *Signs: Journal of Women in Culture and Society* 1 (1975): 1–29.

Solomon, Barbara H., ed. *Short Fiction of Mary Wilkins Freeman and Sarah Orne Jewett*. New York: NAL, 1979.

Stauffer, Helen W., and Susan J. Rosowski, eds. *Women and Western American Literature*. Troy: Whitston, 1982.

Stegner, Wallace, ed. *The American Novel from James Fenimore Cooper to William Faulkner*. New York: Basic, 1965.

———. *Wolf Willow: A History, a Story, and a Memory of the Last Plains Frontier*. 1962. Lincoln: Bison–U of Nebraska P, 1980.

Stouck, David. "Marriage and Friendship in *My Ántonia*." *Great Plains Quarterly* 2 (1982): 224–31.

———. "Willa Cather and the Impressionist Novel." Murphy, *Critical Essays* 48–65.

———. *Willa Cather's Imagination*. Lincoln: U of Nebraska P, 1975.

Stratton, Joanna. *Pioneer Women: Voices from the Kansas Frontier*. New York: Touchstone-Simon, 1982.

Sutherland, Donald. "Willa Cather: The Classic Voice." Slote and Faulkner 156–79.

Swehla, Francis J. "Bohemians in Central Kansas." *Kansas State Historical Collection* 13 (1913–14): 469–512.

Thacker, Robert. "The Plains Landscape and Descriptive Technique." *Great Plains Quarterly* 2 (1982): 145–56.

Tocqueville, Alexis de. *Democracy in America*. Ed. J. P. Mayer. Trans. George Lawrence. 13th ed., 1850. Garden City: Anchor-Doubleday, 1969.

Turner, Frederick Jackson. "The Significance of the Frontier in American History." *Annual Report of the American Historical Association for the Year 1893*. Washington: GPO, 1894. 199–227.

Twain, Mark. *A Connecticut Yankee in King Arthur's Court*. 1889. New York: Bantam, 1981.

U. S. Dept. of Commerce. Bureau of the Census. *Population: 1920: Composition and Characteristics of the Population by States*. Vol. 3 of *Fourteenth Census of the United States Taken in the Year 1920*. Washington: GPO,1922.

Van Ghent, Dorothy. *Willa Cather*. Pamphlets on American Writers 46. 1964. Rpt. in *Seven American Women Writers of the Twentieth Century*. Ed. Maureen Howard. Minneapolis: U of Minnesota P, 1977. 79–121.

Virgil. *Aeneid*. Trans. L. P. Wilkinson. New York: Penguin, 1983.

———. *Georgics*. Trans. Robert Fitzgerald. New York: Vintage-Random, 1984.

Warne, Frank Julian. *The Immigrant Invasion*. 1913. Englewood: Ozer, 1971.

Wasserman, Loretta. "The Music of Time: Henri Bergson and Willa Cather." *American Literature* 57 (1985): 226–39.

Webb, Walter Prescott. *The Great Plains*. 1931. Lincoln: U of Nebraska P, 1981.

Welsch, Roger L. *Sod Walls: The Story of the Nebraska Sod House*. Broken Bow: Purcells, 1968.

Welsch, Roger R., and Linda K. Welsch. *Cather's Kitchens: Foodways in Literature and Life*. Lincoln: U of Nebrsaka P, 1987.

Wharton, Edith. *A Backward Glance*. 1933. New York: Scribner's, 1985.

Whitman, Walt. *Complete Poetry and Selected Prose*. Ed. James E. Miller, Jr. Boston: Houghton, 1959.

———. *Leaves of Grass*. Ed. Sculley Bradley and Harold W. Blodgett. New York: Norton, 1973.

"Willa Cather Country." Text and pictures by David E. Scherman. *Life* 19 Mar. 1951: 112–23.

Willa Cather Pioneer Memorial Newsletter. Quarterly. Willa Cather Pioneer Memorial and Educational Foundation, 326 N. Webster St., Red Cloud, NE 68970.

Willa Cather's America. Written, prod., and dir. Richard Schickel. Films for the Humanities [PO Box 2053, Princeton, NJ], 1978.

Williams, J. Allen, Jr., David R. Johnson, and Miguel A. Carranza. "Ethnic Assimilation and Pluralism in Nebraska." Luebke, *Ethnicity* 210–29.

Wister, Owen. *The Virginian*. 1925. New York: Vintage-Random, 1983.

Woodress, James. *Willa Cather: Her Life and Art*. 1970. Lincoln: U of Nebraska P, 1982.

———. *Willa Cather: A Literary Life*. Lincoln: U of Nebraska P, 1987.

INDEX